The Catholic
Theological Union
LIBRARY
Chicago, Ill.

THE LIVING TEXT

Essays in Honor of Ernest W. Saunders

Edited by
Dennis E. Groh and Robert Jewett

The Catholic
Theological Union
LIBRARY
Chicago, Ill.

UNIVERSITY
PRESS OF
AMERICA

LANHAM • NEW YORK • LONDON

Copyright © 1985 by

University Press of America,™ Inc.

4720 Boston Way
Lanham, MD 20706

3 Henrietta Street
London WC2E 8LU England

All rights reserved

Printed in the United States of America

ISBN (Perfect): 0-8191-4585-8
ISBN   (Cloth): 0-8191-4584-X

All University Press of America books are produced on acid-free
paper which exceeds the minimum standards set by the National
Historical Publications and Records Commission.

Table of Contents

iii

TABLE OF CONTENTS, CONTINUED

WITHDRAWN

PHOTOGRAPH OF ERNEST W. SAUNDERS

WITHDRAWN

FOREWORD

Professor Saunders joined the faculty of Garrett Theological Seminary in 1950 as Professor of New Testament and became Academic Dean in 1966. In 1974 he was awarded the Harry R. Kendall Chair of New Testament Interpretation, which he held until his retirement in 1978. He is currently Professor Emeritus of New Testament of Garrett-Evangelical Theological Seminary.

Dr. Saunders received a B. S. degree from the School of Religious and Social Work, Boston University (1938) and that university's Distinguished Alumnus Award in 1969. Boston University School of Theology conferred the S.T.B. degree on him (1940) and Duke University the Ph.D. degree (1943). He has done post-doctoral work in the Greek Orthodox monasteries of Mount Athos, Greece (1952-53), as a Fulbright Research Scholar, and again was in Athens (1971-72) related to the University of Athens and the American School of Classical Studies; he engaged in further research on mediaeval Greek biblical manuscripts and late Byzantine exegesis. He was a member of the Patmos (Greece) Monastery Library Project sponsored by the Institute for Antiquity and Christianity and the Greek Center for Byzantine Studies. He also carried on post-doctoral research at the University of Basel (1958) and in Rome (1966) as a Faculty Fellow of the Association of Theological Schools. Dr. Saunders is a member of numerous professional societies.

His colleagues honor Ernest W. Saunders not only for his learning, but also for his generosity to associates and beginning scholars. In his classes as a teacher, in his role as an academic dean, and in his position as a biblical colleague, he exuded a style of empowerment, mutuality and critical discussion. His presence even in informal gatherings encouraged ventures like the weekly luncheons of biblical faculty colleagues in which papers were read and ideas shared. He was never too busy, too burdened with his own work, or too important to turn someone away from his door who needed his help. There is an air of hospitality and grace about Ernest Saunders that from his door who needed his help. There is an air of hospitality and grace about Ernest Saunders that allows great creativity to develop in others around him.

Master Hellenist, text-critic, Byzantinist, chronicler of the history of the Society of Biblical Literature and its honorary past president, Ernest W. Saunders has left his signature on a wide range of biblical research. Mowery's bibliography attests to Professor Saunders' impact on scholarship. At the heart of his scholarly work and teaching stands the insistance that the Bible is a living text, continually seeking and being sought in new vehicles of transmission, context and interpretation. These essays are offered to him in appreciation for that insistance and in respect for the way he has contributed to those who work in the history of interpretation by his scholarship, collegiality, teaching, administration and friendship.

The essays by Roth, Stegner, Ringgren, Sundberg, Agourides, Grant and Groh concentrate on aspects of the perdurance of biblical textual models in early Christianity. The contributions of Jewett, Mather, Sanders, Kysar, Fuller, Koester and Pervo explore aspects of the processes involved in the actual creation and transmission of biblical texts.

The editors owe special thanks to President Neal F. Fisher and Dean Wolfgang M. W. Roth for their support of this venture as a project of Garrett-Evangelical Theological Seminary and to Registrar Vera Watts for her stimulus and counsel. Thanks are also due to Robert L. Mowery who provided assistance in proofreading. A heartfelt word of appreciation is extended to Helen Hauldren, Linda Koops, Lisa Krell and Frank Witt Hughes for shouldering so many of the mechanical aspects of producing this manuscript. Frank Hughes is also to be thanked for participating in the creation of the indices. For assistance in word processing, we thank our colleagues Walter J. Cason and Donald F. Chatfield, the latter in particular for help in verifying and printing the indices. The technical production of the final manuscript would not have been possible without the services of Marie Cornelison and Brenda May.
                    D. E. G. and R. J.

CONTRIBUTORS

Savas Agourides
University of Athens
University Town
Anno Ilissia
Athens, Greece

Reginald H. Fuller
The Protestant Episcopal
Theological Seminary
in Virginia
Alexandria, VA 22304

Robert M. Grant
The Divinity School
The University of Chicago
Swift Hall 304
Chicago, IL 60637

Dennis E. Groh
Garrett-Evangelical
Theological Seminary
2121 Sheridan Road
Evanston, IL 60201

Robert Jewett
Garrett-Evangelical
Theological Seminary
2121 Sheridan Road
Evanston, IL 60201

Helmut Koester
The Divinity School
Harvard University
45 Francis Avenue
Cambridge, MA 02138

Robert Kysar
The Lutheran Theological
Seminary
Gettysburg, PA 17325

P. Boyd Mather
The Schools of Theology
in Dubuque
2050 University Avenue
Dubuque, IA 52001

Robert L. Mowery
University Library
Illinois Wesleyan
University
Bloomington, IL 61701

Richard I. Pervo
Seabury-Western
Theological Seminary
2122 Sheridan Road
Evanston, IL 60201

Helmer Ringgren
Uppsala Universitet
Box 1604
Uppsala, Sweden

Wolfgang Roth
Garrett-Evangelical
Theological Seminary
2121 Sheridan Road
Evanston, IL 60201

Jack T. Sanders
Department of Religious
Studies, College of
Arts and Sciences
University of Oregon
Eugene, OR 97403

Ernest W. Saunders
R.F.D. 1, Box 300
Mount Vernon, ME 14352

W. Richard Stegner
Garrett-Evangelical
Theological Seminary
2121 Sheridan Road
Evanston, IL 60201

Albert C. Sundberg, Jr.
3407 Calle La Vita
San Clemente, CA 92672

BIBLIOGRAPHY OF THE WORKS OF
ERNEST W. SAUNDERS

Compiled by Robert L. Mowery

1943

"The Textual Criticism of a Medieval Manuscript of
    the Four Gospels (Duke Ms. Gr. 7)," Ph.D. diss.,
    Duke University. 1943.

1947

Review of The Corinthian Letters of Paul, by G. Camp-
    bell Morgan (New York: Fleming Revell, 1946)
    in The Pastor 10 (April 1947) 41.

1951

Review of The Meaning of the Sermon on the Mount,
    by Hans Windisch, tr. S. MacLean Gilmour (Phila-
    delphia: Westminster, 1951) in Journal of Bibli-
    cal Literature 70 (1951) 246-249.

1952

"Studies in Doctrinal Influences on the Byzantine
    Text of the Gospels," Journal of Biblical Litera-
    ture 71 (1952) 85-92.

Review of What is the Best New Testament?, by Ernest
    C. Colwell (Chicago: University of Chicago,
    1952) in Church History 21 (1952) 273-274.

1953

"Manuscript Research and Biblical Studies," Garrett
    Tower 28 (Sept. 1953) 11-13.

1954

"Hunting Manuscripts at Athos," The Near East 7 (Oct.
    1954) 9-12.

1

MOWERY

Review of <u>Bible Key Words from Gerhard Kittel's Theologisches Wörterbuch zum Neuen Testament</u>, tr. and
ed. J. R. Coates (New York: Harper, 1951) in
<u>Journal of Biblical Literature</u> 73 (1954) 172-174.

1955

"Operation Microfilm at Mt. Athos," <u>Biblical Archaeolo-
gist</u> 18 (May 1955) 22-41.

"What Is the Gospel?" <u>Presbyterian Survey</u> (June 1955)
24-25.

1956

Review of <u>Introduction to New Testament Study</u>, by
Donald T. Rowlingson (New York: Macmillan, 1956)
in <u>Religion in Life</u> 26 (Summer 1957) 461-462.

Review of <u>The Mission and Achievement of Jesus</u>, by
Reginald H. Fuller (Chicago: Allenson, 1954)
in <u>Journal of Biblical Literature</u> 75 (1956) 71-73.

1957

<u>A Descriptive Checklist of Selected Manuscripts in
the Monasteries of Mount Athos</u>, compiled under
the general direction of Ernest W. Saunders,
representative of the Library of Congress for
the selection and microfilming of the manuscripts
at Mt. Athos. Washington: Library of Congress
Photoduplication Service, 1957.

<u>Reader's Guide for the Letter to the Hebrews</u> (Nash-
ville: Board of Education of The Methodist
Church, 1957).

"Theophylact of Bulgaria as Writer and Biblical Interpreter," <u>Biblical Research</u> 2 (1957) 31-44.

1958

Review of <u>Jesus and His Coming</u>, by J. A. T. Robinson
(New York: Abingdon, 1958) in <u>Religion in Life</u>
28 (Winter 1958-59) 140-141.

2

1959

"A Challenge to Theological Maturity," Christian Advocate 3 (Nov. 1959) 5-6.

Review of Biblical Interpretation, by Edwin C. Blackman (Philadelphia: Westminster, 1957) in The Christian Century 76 (June 10, 1959) 703.

1960

The Message of Jesus, by Harvie Branscomb, revised by Ernest W. Saunders (Nashville: Abingdon, 1960).

"The Authority of the Bible," Papers on the Theology of Mission (New York: Division of World Missions of the Board of Missions of The Methodist Church, 1960) 13-17.

1961

Review of Athos, the Mountain of Silence, by Philip Sherrard (London: Oxford, 1960) in The Journal of Religion 41 (April 1961) 145-146.

Review of Images of the Church in the New Testament, by Paul S. Minear (Philadelphia: Westminster, 1960) in Religion in Life 31 (Winter 1961-62) 137-138.

1962

"Abraham's bosom," "Adasa," "Beautiful Gate," "Beroea," "Consul," "Eleutherus," "Harp," "Ituraea," "Paphos," "Perea," "Province," "Sparta," "Theater," and thirty-seven other articles in The Interpreter's Dictionary of the Bible (4 vols. Nashville: Abingdon, 1962).

"Gemeinde," "Gemeindeleitung," "Hippos," "Kirche," "Magdala," "Nain," "Nazareth," and "Tempelreinigung," in Biblisch-historisches Handwörterbuch, hrsg. von Bo Reicke und Leonhard Rost (4 vols., Göttingen: Vandenhoeck & Ruprecht, 1962-1979).

Review of Paul: The Theology of the Apostle in the Light of Jewish Religious History, by H. J.

3

Schoeps (Philadelphia: Westminster, 1961) in
Religion in Life 32 (1962-63) 139-141.

1963

"A Trio of Thomas Logia." Biblical Research 8 (1963)
43-59.

"Baptism," The Westminster Dictionary of Christian
Education, ed. Kendig B. Cully (Philadelphia:
Westminster, 1963).

1964

Review of Salvation History: A Biblical Interpretation, by Eric C. Rust (Richmond: John Knox,
1963) in Interpretation 18 (1964) 213-215.

1965

"The New Concern with the Historical Jesus," The Garrett Tower 40 (1965) 3-8.

Review of Commentary on the Epistle to the Hebrews,
by F. F. Bruce (Grand Rapids: Eerdmans, 1964)
in Journal of Biblical Literature 84 (1965) 448-
449.

1966

Reader's Guide for the Letter to the Hebrews (rev. ed.;
Nashville: Board of Education of The Methodist
Church, 1966).

1967

Jesus in the Gospels (Englewood Cliffs, N.J.: Pren-
tice-Hall, 1967).

"The Colossian Heresy and Qumran Theology," Studies
in the History and Text of the New Testament
in Honor of Kenneth Willis Clark, ed. Boyd L.
Daniels and M. Jack Suggs (Salt Lake City: University of Utah, 1967) 133-145.

"Reflections on the Mithraic Liturgy," with Jerry
Stewardson, in Mithraism in Ostia, ed. Samuel
Laeuchli (Garrett Theological Studies 1; Evans-
ton: Northwestern University Press, 1967) 67-84.

1968

Coming to Life: A Study of the Gospel of John (New York: Joint Commission on Education and Cultivation of the Board of Missions of The United Methodist Church, 1968).

John Celebrates the Gospel (New York: Abingdon, 1970 [1968]).

1970

Review of Jesus and the Christian, by William Manson (Grand Rapids: Eerdmans, 1967) in Interpretation 24 (1970) 412.

1973

Review of The Use of the Old Testament in the New and Other Essays: Studies in Honor of William Franklin Stinespring, ed. James M. Efrid (Durham, NC: Duke, 1972) in Review of Books and Religion 2 (June 1973) 4.

1975

Review of Ho Prophetes apo Nazaret: Historike kai theologike melete tes peri Iesou Christou eikonos ton Euangelion, by John Panagopoulos (Athens: Privately published, 1973) in Journal of Biblical Literature 94 (1975) 458-460.

1976

"Resurrection in the New Testament," The Interpreter's Dictionary of the Bible (Supplementary Volume; Nashville: Abingdon, 1976) 739-741.

Review of Encountering New Testament Manuscripts, by Jack Finegan (Grand Rapids: Eerdmans, 1974) in Anglican Theological Review 58 (1976) 232-234.

1977

"Christian Synagogues and Jewish Christianity in Galilee," explor 3 (1977) 70-77.

Review of The Resurrection According to Matthew, Mark,

and Luke, by Norman Perrin (Philadelphia: Fortress, 1977) in Religion and Life 46 (1977) 517-
518.

1978

"The Bible and Human Rights," Church and Society 69
(Nov.-Dec. 1978) 48-53.

"Ministry in the New Testament." Thesis Theological
Cassettes 8. No. 12 (Jan 1978).

Review of The New Testament Environment, by Eduard
Lohse (Nashville: Abingdon, 1976) in Biblical
Archeologist 41 (1978) 38.

Review of The Parables of the Triple Tradition, by
Charles E. Carlston (Philadelphia: Fortress,
1975) in Anglican Theological Review 60 (1978)
96-97.

1979

Review of The Early Versions of the New Testament,
by Bruce M. Metzger (Oxford: Clarendon, 1977)
The New Review of Books and Religion 3 (Mar.
1979) 23-24.

1980

"A Century of Service to American Biblical Scholarship," Council on the Study of Religion Bulletin
11 (June 1980) 69-72.

1981

Epiphany, with Fred B. Craddock ("Proclamation 2: Aids
for Interpreting the Lessons of the Church Year,"
Series B, Vol. 2. Philadelphia: Fortress Press,
1981).

1 Thessalonians, 2 Thessalonians, Philippians, Philemon
("Knox Preaching Guides." Atlanta: John Knox,
1981).

"The Patmos Monastery Library Project," in The Institute for Antiquity and Christianity Report, 1972-
80, ed. Marvin W. Meyer (Claremont: The Institute, 1981) 47-50.

1982

<u>Searching the Scriptures: A History of the Society of Biblical Literature, 1880-1980</u> ("Centennial Publications of the Society of Biblical Literature." Chico, CA: Scholars Press, 1982).

1983

"Jewish Christianity and Palestinian Archeology," <u>Religious Studies Review</u> 9 (July 1983) 201-205.

Review of <u>He Ekklesia ton propheton: To prophetikon charisma en te Ekklesia ton duo proton aionon</u>, by John Panagopoulos (Athens: Historical Publications, Stephanos Basilopoulos, 1979) in <u>Journal of Biblical Literature</u> 102 (1983) 511-513.

Forthcoming

Review of <u>Manuscripts of the Greek Bible</u>, by Bruce M. Metzger (New York: Oxford, 1981) to be published in <u>Journal of Biblical Literature</u>.

Review of <u>The Making of the English Bible</u>, by Gerald Hammond (New York: Philosophical Library, 1983) to be published in <u>Interpretation</u>.

PART ONE

SCRIPTURAL TEXT AS LIVING MODEL

CHAPTER ONE

JESUS AS THE SON OF MAN:
THE SCRIPTURAL IDENTITY OF A JOHANNINE IMAGE

Wolfgang Roth

Introduction

Even after Passover pilgrims had welcomed Jesus
to Jerusalem with shouts of praise (John 12: 12-13),
they remained uncertain about his identity. Jesus
responded to their welcome with a discourse on the
imminent exaltation of the Son of Man (John 12: 20-
30). They countered with the observation that they
had heard that the Anointed One will live forever
and hence were puzzled by Jesus' words. They concluded
their response with the question, "Who is this Son
of Man?" (John 12:34).

In the Gospel of John that question remains without answer--or so it seems. The repeated and different
references to the Son of Man do supply items of information. Do the various aspects which describe the
Johannine Jesus as the Son of Man coalesce into a
coherent image, encouraging the readers in their
search? In what manner is the reference of Jesus
to the "search of the Scriptures" because they "bear
witness to me" (John 5:39), a directive?

The paper seeks to show that these questions
must be answered in the affirmative. The evidence
of the gospel--and, for purposes of this enquiry,
of that gospel alone--suggests that its portrayal
of Jesus as the Son of Man is shaped by a traditional
model, that is, one encountered in the Hebrew Scriptures.

The enquiry begins with (1) the compilation of
a composite portrait of Jesus as the Son of Man, based
on the occurrences of that term in the gospel. On
its basis, (2) the Hebrew Scriptures are scanned and

11

ROTH

that section identified, to which the Johannine portrayal of Jesus seems to point. (3) The review of
that section leads to the identification of one of
its figures as the model of the Johannine image.
(4) The tentative identification is then tested against
the composite portrait of Jesus with which the enquiry
began. Finally, (5) the proposed identification of
the scriptural model is set into the context of Johannine theology.

I
The Portrayal of Jesus as the Son of Man

Thirteen occurrences of the phrase "(the) Son
of Man" are scattered through the first thirteen chapters of John. These passages deal with different
subject matters and so highlight different aspects
of that role of Jesus. They deal with:
(1) his heavenly existence in past, present and future
(John 3:13, 6:62, 1:51, 5:27),
(2) his gift of heavenly food to his own in the earthly
sphere (John 6:27, 6:53),
(3) the recognition of his heavenly identity by human
beings in present and future (John 9:35, 8:28),
(4) the necessity of his being "lifted up" or "exalted"
when "his hour" has come (John 12:34, 3:14) and
(5) his exclusive knowledge of the point in time when
this hour is present, the hour in which he leaves
the earthly sphere (John 12:23, 13:31).

At this point, a fuller description of each of
the five aspects is indicated.

(1) Jesus' heavenly role in past, present and
future is the subject of John 6:62, 3:13, 1:51 and
5:27. According to John 6:62, the climax of Jesus'
work will be the moment when his disciples see him
ascending to the place "where he was before." According to John 3:13, Jesus said to Nicodemus, who had
come to him by night to debate the Galilean teacher's
mission, that "no one has ascended to heaven except
the one who has come down from heaven, namely, the
Son of Man." Jesus' statement refers to an ascension
of the Son of Man into heaven and his subsequent descent to earth, both of which are events which took
place at unspecified times in the past. According
to John 1:51, Jesus said to Nathanael, the last of
the first five disciples whom he called, that his
disciples will at some unspecified time in the future

12

see messengers ascending from the Son of Man into
the open heavens, and descending from there upon him.
Finally, according to John 5:27, the son of the divine
father, who brings to life both now and in the future
those whom he chooses, has been given authority to
carry out judgment, "because he is (the) Son of Man."
These four texts describe the first aspect of the
Johannine Son of Man: Jesus' heavenly role in past,
present, future.

(2) The second aspect is the gift of heavenly
food by the Son of Man to those who are his own.
According to John 6:27, the 5,000 people whom Jesus
had miraculously fed and who had come to Capernaum
in search of him, were exhorted by Jesus not to concern
themselves with perishable food but with "the food
which lasts so as to provide to them the life into
the age," and it is that food which "the Son of Man
will give you." According to John 6:53, that food
is the flesh and the blood of the Son of Man. These
two texts describe the second aspect of Jesus' role
as the Son of Man, that of the supplier of spiritual
sustenance.

(3) The third aspect is the recognition by human
beings that Jesus is the Son of Man, both now and
in the future. According to John 9:35, Jesus asked
the congenitally blind man whose eyes he had opened,
whether he "believes in the Son of Man." Upon the
man's question who that Son of Man is, Jesus declared
that it is the person whom the blind man has seen
and who now speaks with him. To this the man responded
with belief in and adoration of the Son of Man. On
the other hand, according to John 8:28, Jesus responded
to the Judeans who had countered his claim with the
question, "Who then are you?" with the affirmation
that at a certain time in the future, "when you will
lift up the Son of Man, you will come to know that
it is I who is the Son of Man." These two texts are
concerned with the third aspect, the recognition of
the heavenly identity of the Son of Man.

(4) The fourth aspect is the claim that it is
necessary for the Son of Man to "be lifted up" or
"exalted." Thus, according to John 12:34, the people
in Jerusalem who are with Jesus could not understand
why the Son of Man must be lifted up, and they questioned Jesus about this his claim. The answer to
their question in John 3:14 is provided by Jesus'

13

affirmation that "as Moses lifted up the snake in the wilderness, so the Son of Man must be lifted up." The future exaltation of Jesus will provide to the Judeans the insight that he is indeed the Son of Man (John 8:28). Hence these two texts highlight the fourth aspect, Jesus' exaltation.

(5) The fifth and last aspect is evident in two sayings of Jesus in which he identifies "his hour" as having arrived at a certain time in his life. According to John 12:23, Jesus reacts to the desire of some Greek-speaking Passover pilgrims "to see him" with the words, "The hour has come that the Son of Man be glorified." On the other hand, a short period afterwards, when Jesus was at meal with his disciples and when Judas Iscariot had gone out into the night to betray him (John 13:31), Jesus states that "now the Son of Man has been glorified," that is, his violent death is sealed. These last two texts deal with the fifth aspect, "the hour" of Jesus.

This review of the scriptural evidence makes possible the compilation of a chronologically arranged sequence of the mentioned events of his life, 'a biography of the Son of Man,' as it were:

(a) The Son of Man ascended to heaven at an unspecified time in the past (John 3:13, 6:62).
(b) The Son of Man has been given authority to carry out judgment in the present and future (John 5:27).
(c) The Son of Man descended from heaven after his earlier ascension.
(d) While he is on earth after his second descent (i) he is recognizable as the Son of Man by those whose eyes he opens (John 9:35), (ii) he gives to his own the heavenly bread which, unlike the manna which the Israelites ate in the wilderness from Moses' hands, conveys life which lasts "into the age" (John 6:27); in fact, his flesh is that heavenly bread (John 6:53), and (iii) he stands in communication with the heavenly sphere which is evident when some of his disciples see heavenly messengers ascend from him to heaven and descend from there upon him (John 1:51).
(e) At a predetermined time known only to the Son of Man, he ends his second sojourn on earth, that is, "when his hour has come." (i) This point in time is reached when Greek-speaking pilgrims, who had come to Jerusalem, wish to see Jesus while he spends the third and last Passover of which the Gospel tells,

in the city (John 12:23). (ii) This point in time marks the glorification of the Son of Man which occurs when Judas Iscariot, one of the Twelve, has left the supper which Jesus and his disciples held, and has gone out into the night in order to betray him.
(f) The manner of the second ascension of the Son of Man is and must be that of "exaltation" (John 8:28, 3:14), and it is this exaltation which puzzles the people who enquire of him about the future existence of the Anointed One (John 12:34).

II
The Search of the Scriptures

After the review of these features of the biography of the Johannine Jesus portrayed as the Son of Man, the question: "Who is this Son of Man?" (John 12:34) remains the challenge even more clearly. Does John's work supply an answer? Yes. But it does so in its own way. It refers the questioners to the Scriptures and asks them to search there.

Thus in the discourse of the Johannine Jesus on the unity of his work with that of his divine father (John 5:29-47), he discusses in one section (John 5:31-40) the four witnesses who attest him: (1) John the Baptist, (2) Jesus' own works, (3) the one who sent him, and (4) the Scriptures. The series of four witnesses is climactic: the second is greater than the first, the third greater than the second, and the fourth greater than the third. The most decisive witness is thus that offered by Sacred Writ. Hence Jesus says: "You search the Scriptures! . . . They are the ones who bear witness to me" (John 5:39).

Yet the manner of that search is not suggested. How is it discovered? How carried out? How tested? The inductive method adopted in the next two sections uses especially the first of the already identified aspects of the portrayal of the Son of Man as a heuristic base for a fuller description of that figure through related biblical texts. This leads to the recognition of a scriptural role model, or rather, identity, of John's Jesus as the Son of Man. The method itself may be judged valid to the extent to

15

which its results are deemed persuasive.[1]

The first item of the 'biography' of the Son of Man is his ascent to heaven at an unspecified time in the past. Also other passages in the Gospel refer to what is usually called "the pre-existence of Jesus." Thus, according to John 8:21-59, Jesus engaged in a debate with Judeans while he was on his second pilgrimage to Jerusalem, celebrating the Festival of Booths. The Judeans at first were favorably disposed to Jesus' teaching (John 8:21-30). But when he laid out for them its implication for their own claim that as children of Abraham they had the highest religious legitimacy, they had second thoughts and eventually came to consider Jesus' words as blasphemy (John 8:31-59).

The reason was simple: Jesus claimed nothing less than to have existed before Abraham lived! Abraham was seen as the guarantor of the supreme status of the Judeans who were Jesus' partners in the debate. They challenged Jesus "Are you greater than our father Abraham who died? Whom do you make yourself?" (John 8:53). But he responded that, "Abraham, your father, looked in joyful anticipation forward to the day of my appearance, then witnessed it and rejoiced" (John 8:56). This drew the rejoinder of the opponents: "You are not even 50 years old and yet have already seen Abraham?" (John 8:57). It is at this point that the Johannine Jesus ended the polemical exchange with the forbidding, but also puzzling assertion: "Before Abraham was, I am." (John 8:58). The narrator ends the section with the comment that Jesus left when his opponents got ready to stone him. Clearly, they considered his claim blasphemy. Offense apart, John's Jesus claims to have existed before Abraham, the patri-

---

[1]Recent research is illustrated by the five articles on the Johannine Son of Man, published by Rudolf Pesch and Rudolf Schnackenburg in <u>Jesus und der Menschensohn</u> (Anton Vögtle Festschrift; Freiburg: Herder, 1975) 300-386. The method adopted in this study differs fundamentally from historical- and literary-critical approaches. For this reason its argumentation proceeds without reference to literature related to them. The writer's method of enquiry is illustrated by his essay "The Secret of the Kingdom," <u>The Christian Century</u> (March 2, 1983) 179-181.

arch of whom the Bible speaks in Genesis 12-25. Does this claim not direct the search of the Scriptures to what precedes the Abraham story, that is, to Gen 1-11? Indeed, it is that section to which the search is now drawn.

Other passages supply more precise information. Thus Jesus prays that his disciples may come to behold his glory with which his divine father loved him "before the founding of the earthly realm" (John 17:24, similarly 17:5). Moreover, the evangelist speaks of Jesus as God's only-begotten son, who is exclusively the one who ever saw God; so he is also the one who can tell his disciples what he has seen and heard in the heavenly sphere (John 1:18, 3:32). Already then and there his divine father loved him and held him close to his heart (John 1:18, 17:24). Again it is evident that the audience is referred broadly to the writings of Moses, that is, to the Pentateuch (John 5:46-47), and there specifically to the creation narratives, that is, to the first chapters of Genesis!

Thus a review of these texts in greater detail is in order. In the first two chapters of Genesis two stories of creation are presented. While the central theme of both is "creation" and hence the same, the stories also differ. The one given first (Gen 1:1-2:4a) describes in an orderly and systematic fashion the creation of "heaven and earth" and all that is between them. In six days eight works of creation were accomplished, concluded by a seventh day of rest.

The other creation story (Gen 2:4b-25) begins with the words, "On the day when God created the heaven and the earth," and then relates in lively fashion the story of the Garden of Eden which was planted by God, of the placing of Adam in it, of the creation of the animals, and finally of Adam's wife. But it does not end there: it continues by telling of Eve's and Adam's disobedience, of their eviction and resettlement to the east of the Garden, the entry to which was from then on guarded by a flaming sword (Gen 3:1-24). This narrative passes into its sequel story (Gen 4:1-26), in which the birth of Adam's and Eve's two sons, Cain and Abel, is told, but also the murder of Abel by Cain, of Cain's and his descendants' banishment, and of the birth of a substitute for the murdered Abel, who is given the name Seth. Seth and his de-

17

scendants populate the earth through several generations; he was begotten by Adam in the image of the
first human being (Gen 5:1-32).

This is the sequence of biblical stories at the
beginning of the Hebrew Scriptures to which the Johannine Gospel directs the search. But how do they relate
to the Johannine Jesus as the Son of Man?

Excursus: The Two Spheres of Creation

Before an answer is given, an observation in
relation to these two creation stories is necessary.
There are two, and since the two cannot be told, or
read or heard, at the same time, one must be put first,
the other second. However, such sequencing effects
that the second story is heard and interpreted in
the light of the first. In this case the second creation story may be understood to be relating in detail
what the first narrative tells summarily and generally. In other words, both seem to speak not only of
one and the same act of creation, but also of one
and the same object of creation.

But the text, as it stands, may also be understood
differently, to be speaking of two creations, more
exactly, of two separate and different spheres of
creation. The one told first is that of the creation
of the terrestrial sphere naturally known to human
beings. It is marked by the rhythm of day and night,
confined by the firmament above and the earth beneath,
contains bodies of water, the land and its vegetation,
has sun, moon and stars for the regulation of the
seasons, is supplied with water, air and land animals,
and is the home of human beings. All of these come
into being in the course of six days; each of them
is identified by the day on which it was created.

The other creation story, that of the garden
in Eden, and that of Adam and his wife as its keepers,
is placed into a different time frame. Its story
begins with the words: "On the day when God created
the heaven and the earth . . ." (Gen 2:4b, so both
the Septuagint and the Masoretic Text). When these
words are heard in the light of the preceding story
of six creation days, the question suggests itself
to hearers: to which of the six days mentioned in
the first narrative does the second story relate?
On the second day the firmament was established and

called by God "heaven" or "sky," while on the third
day the dry land appeared and was called "earth."
Thus "the heaven and the earth" were according to
Gen 1:6-10 not created on one day, but on two, while
the Eden story speaks of "the day on which God made
the heaven and the earth" (Gen 2:4b).

One may take the phrase as a loose reference
to the preceding story and thus interpret the one
so introduced as an elaboration of the one told first.
But one may also perceive a logical discrepancy and
search for an explanation. The inconsistency is overcome by the assumption that "the day on which God
made the heaven and earth" (2:4b) is a day different
from the seven days mentioned in Gen 1:3-2:4a. In
that case, did that day follow or precede the 7-day
sequence? The answer then may be gathered from the
unusual way in which the first day of the 7-day sequence is counted: as "Day One," not as "the first
day." In other words, while the second through the
seventh day are identified by ordinal numbers, the
first in the 7-day sequence is counted with the cardinal number "one." In other words, it is identified
only as the first day of that 7-day sequence but not
as the first day within the whole initial period of
divine creativity. This accords with the "prevalent
view in the rabbinic sources . . . that paradise was
created before the world."[2]

In short, Gen 1:3-2:4a and 2:4b-25 can and have
been read as the creation stories of two realms:
(1) the earthly sphere, limited in time and space,
and (2) the pre- and extra-earthly realm--Eden and
its paradise. Small wonder that popular piety in
synagogue, church and mosque has insisted on the belief
that two spheres exist, both made by the creator:
an earthly one and a heavenly one; the sphere in which
human beings live, and Paradise, the sphere in which
heavenly beings reside. Moreover, the celestial realm
exists not only beyond the earthly one in space, it
also antedates it in time.

[2]Louis Ginzberg, The Legends of the Jews V (Philadelphia:
Jewish Publication Society, 1968) 29 n. 76.

III
The Scriptural Identity of the Son of Man

In the light of the excursus, the search for the scriptural "witness" to Jesus (John 5:39) can be pursued further. According to John 17:24-25, the Johannine Jesus claims to have been with the divine creator even _before_ the founding of the terrestrial sphere. In other words, the identity-model of "The Son of Man" must be sought in the stories in Gen 2:4b-4:26 which tell of the first-created, celestial sphere: Eden and its paradise. This limits our search to the male figures who appear there: Adam, Cain, Abel and Seth. Of these, Seth is an unlikely candidate because he was only Abel's substitute and became as such the progenitor of the firstborn line of Adam's descendants; he remained on earth in life and in death (Gen 4:25, 26a; 5:3, 6-8). Cain is not a candidate at all because he, the murderer of his brother, was banished from the divine presence (Gen 4:1-16). On the other hand, the title "the Son of Man" excludes Adam because he was not the son of any man!

There is only one possibility left: Abel. Is he the identity model of the Johannine Jesus? The answer is yes. Not only do the characteristic features of the Johannine Jesus as the Son of Man lead to this conclusion, but also the title itself points to it. "The Son of Man" is a literal translation of the corresponding Septuagintal phrase, which is in turn a rendering of the Hebrew term _ben 'adam_. The Hebrew word _adam_ is used both as a generic noun as well as a proper name. As a generic noun it refers to humankind; as a proper name it serves to designate the male human being created to guard and care for the Paradise-Garden in Eden (see also Gen 5:2). Hence the Johannine term must properly be rendered not "the Son of Man," but "the Son of Adam."

IV
The Test of the Hypothesis

Do the events in the "biography" of the Son of Man, identified above, confirm the hypothesis that the Johannine Jesus is portrayed as Abel-Re-Incarnate? The following review of each in the light of the scriptural "witness" shows that this is indeed the case.

(a) There is the claim that the Son of Man at an unspecified time in the past ascended to the heavenly realm (John 3:13). If the Johannine Son of Man/Son of Adam is Abel Re-Incarnate, then he must have ascended to the divine creator after he had been slain by his brother. To be sure, Scripture does not say that; it does, however, state that Abel's blood continued to cry from the ground to God for vengeance (Gen 4: 10). Then Abel did not ascend? Scripture does not mention his burial and so leaves open that possibility. Later, the notion of Abel's ascension was indeed developed haggadically in Hellenistic-Jewish stories circulating already in Jesus' time; they tell of the presence of Abel, the righteous one, in heaven; he as the first martyr was assumed (back) into the pre- and extra-terrestrial sphere.

Thus both recensions of the first or second century C.E. Jewish-Christian apocryphal "The Testament of Abraham"[3] have Abraham traverse the heavenly realm under the guidance of the archangel Michael. When the two reach the double entrances to Paradise and Hell, Abraham, according to the one recension, sees there placed a fearful, fiery throne. On it is seated "a wondrous man, shining like the sun, similar to a son of God" (Test Abr A XII). He is faced by a table on which the heavenly book recording all transgressions and good deeds of human beings has been placed, and flanked by two angelic secretaries. The wondrous man acts as judge of all the souls of the deceased who are brought to the entrances of Heaven and Hell. But Abraham, not knowing who that judge is, asks Michael about his identity. He is told: "This one is the son of Adam, the first created one, who is called Abel, whom the evil Cain killed. Now he is seated here to judge all creation and to bring to light who is righteous and who a sinner. This is why God has said: 'I do not judge you, but every human being is judged by a human being.' (Test Abr A XII-XIII).

---

[3]Quoted according to the (re-edition and) translation by Michael E. Stone, The Testament of Abraham -- The Great Recensions (Texts and Translations 2, Pseudepigrapha Series 2; Missoula: Society of Biblical Literature, 1972).

It is evident that this Jewish-Christian writing,
roughly contemporary with the Johannine literature,
shows Abel, the son of Adam, seated in heavenly glory
at the gates of Paradise and Hell, and acting as the
judge of all human beings. This portrayal of Abel
in the Testament of Abraham is evidently also based
on the kind of interpretation of Gen 2:4b-4:26 which
has been identified in this paper as the matrix of
the Johannine notion of Jesus as the Son of Man/the
Son of Adam!

Furthermore, the Testament of Abraham is not
the only Jewish-Christian writing of the first two
centuries of our era, which portrays Abel as assumed
into the heavenly realm. Two Christian apocryphal
writings also attest to the notion that Abel, being
the first and hence the chief martyr, is present in
the celestial sphere. According to the Ascension
of Isaiah,[4] the prophet sees in the seventh heaven
"all the righteous from Adam. And I saw there the
holy Abel and all the righteous. And there I saw
Enoch and all who were with him, stripped of the gar-
ment of the flesh, and I saw them in their higher
garments, and they were like the angels who stand
there in great glory" (9:7-9). On the other hand,
the Apocalypse of Paul[5] recounts the apostle in heavenly encounters with many biblical figures, notably
Abel. He introduces himself as the one "whom Cain
killed when I was presenting a sacrifice to God" (51).

These ancient references to Abel's heavenly existence are born of the same interpretation of Gen 2:4b-
4:26 as the Johannine portrayal of Jesus as Abel-Re-
Incarnate.

(b) Not only the first but also the second item
in the composite description of Jesus as the Son of
Man/of Adam can now be confirmed: The Testament of
Abraham attests him as the heavenly judge and so offers
independent evidence for the second feature. In its
light the word of Jesus can be understood: "As the

[4]Quoted according to the translation by R. McL. Wilson
in Edgar Hennecke/Wilhelm Schneemelcher, New Testament
Apocrypha II (Philadelphia: Westminster, 1965) 642-663.
[5]Quoted according to the translation by R. McL. Wilson
in Hennecke/Schneemelcher, Apocrypha, II, 755-798.

father has life in himself, so he has given life to
the son to have within himself. Moreover, he has
given him the authority to carry out the judgment
because he is the Son of man" (John 5:26-27). Thus
Jewish legends portray Abel as the type of the pious
man who died a martyr's death, unmarried and childless;
in fact, he is of celestial origin and, after his
exaltation to heavenly glory, is the judge of the
heavenly court.[6]

(c) The third feature of the Johannine Jesus
as the Son of Man is the claim that he descended from
heaven after an ascension which had taken place prior
to his descent (John 3:14). This affirmation identifies Jesus of Nazareth with Abel who, as the Testament
of Abraham (A XI-XIII), the Ascension of Isaiah (9:7-
9), and the Apocalypse of Paul (51) illustrate, was
by certain authors believed to be alive in the celestial sphere. These writers also believed that such
heavenly figures appear in the terrestrial sphere
in order to accomplish tasks set for them by the powers
in heaven. Thus Jewish legend alive in the traditions
of the Kabbalah saw in Jacob and Moses the soul of
Abel returning to the terrestrial sphere.[7] The Jerusalem Talmud, on the other hand, opposes anyone who
claims for himself to be Abel Re-Incarnate and to
ascend to heaven. Thus Rabbi Abbahu (approximately
300 C.E.) said: "If a man says . . . 'I am the Son
of Man (ben 'adam),' he will regret it, 'I ascend
to heaven' - he will not carry it out" (jTaan 2, 1).[8]
It is precisely the claim of the Johannine Jesus
that he is the Son of Man/of Adam, that is, Abel Re-
Incarnate, which is both the characteristic feature
of the Johannine literature and the cause of the opposition which that claim evoked.

(d) The fourth feature of the Johannine Son of
Man relates to his existence while present among his
own in the terrestrial sphere: the recognition of
him as the Son of Man by those whose eyes he opens
(John 9:35); his gift of heavenly manna in the form

[6]Ginzberg, Legends, I (1909) 108; II (1920) 203; V,
54, 129, 133, 138, 142.
[7]Ginzberg, Legends V, 142.
[8]Quoted according to Hermann L. Strack and Paul Biller-
beck, Kommentar zum Neuen Testament aus Talmud und
Midrasch, I (München: Beck, 1922) 486.

of his own flesh (John 6:27, 53); and his communication with the celestial sphere (John 1:51). These features are as such not found in the scriptural picture of Abel (Gen 4:1-16) but are haggadic motifs broadly consistent with the evolving portrait of Abel, the first martyr.[9]

(e) The fifth feature of the Johannine Son of Man/of Adam relates to the identification of the point in time when he meets his fate: the death of the martyr. "His hour" has come when Greek-speaking pilgrims at his last Passover in Jerusalem wish to see him (John 12:23). His "glorification" (that is, his martyr's death) is sealed when Judas Iscariot has, in the last night, left the supper circle of the disciples, morsel in hand, in order to reveal to the authorities where Jesus was staying overnight and could be easily arrested without stirring up turmoil among the pilgrim crowd (John 13:31).

(f) Finally, the sixth feature of the Johannine Jesus as the Son of Man is the manner of his death (John 12:34, cf. 3:14, 8:28). Unlike Abel, who died in the open field after he had been struck by his brother (Gen 4:8), Jesus was crucified by the Roman authorities. His manner of death is different from that of his scriptural-role paradigm--hence the pointed affirmation that Jesus chose to die this manner of death (John 12:33, 18:32, cf. 10:17-18, 13:27, 18:3-9)! This feature--and only this feature--called for explanation.

In sum, the review of the six aspects of the 'biography' of the Son of Man/of Adam in the light of its scriptural identity supports the hypothesis fully. Moreover, it is able to elucidate at least two features which have remained unexplained so far: (1) the prior ascent of the Son of Man/of Adam (John 3:14) and (2) his role as celestial judge (John 5:27).

---

[9]For an annotated compilation of post-Biblical storytelling on Cain and Abel in Judaism, Christianity and Islam, see V. Aptowitzer, Kain und Abel in der Agada (Veröffentlichungen der Alexander Kohut Memorial Foundation; Bd. I; Wien/Leipzig: R. Löwit, 1922).

V
A New View of John's Gospel

The scriptural identity of the Johannine Jesus as the Son of Man/of Adam calls for the exploration of other distinctive features: "his hour," as well as his abode when he came; and whither he returns; his glorification through martyrdom and that in exaltation on a cross; his many "I am" sayings as well as the judgment he renders. However, their investigation goes beyond the scope of this paper.

Suffice it to say that like Abel, Jesus was betrayed by one who as his disciple was his brother. Like Abel, Jesus ended his life through the violence of others, and, like Abel, he died an innocent victim, a martyr. So the Johannine literature presents Jesus' death as re-enactment of the death of the first martyr of the Scriptures. But while Abel died not of his own accord, Jesus did end his life of his free will (John 10:17-18, cf. 13:27, 18:3-9). In this manner he became the one who restored what through Cain's fratricide was broken; and thus through Jesus' death God's creation is enabled to return to its original wholeness and oneness.

Here the wide horizon of John's theology appears: the universal knowledge of the one, true God, the divine creator, which abounds in the celestial realm and is brought to the terrestrial sphere through Jesus, the Son of Man/the Son of Adam/Abel Re-Incarnate, and is sealed by his freely chosen martyr's death (John 17:3, 10:17-18). So "the Book of Signs" (John 20:30) is basically a narrative re-enactment of Gen 1:1-4:26--but in reverse: while Gen 1:1-4:26 portrays the progressive deterioration of God's creation, the Johannine writings portray its progressive restoration.

In this comprehensive vision the Johannine Jesus, as Abel Re-Incarnate, assumes the crucial role and informs the verbal imagery. For instance, the Johannine work portrays Jesus as the good shepherd. Was not Abel, in contrast to Cain, a shepherd (Gen 4:2; John 10:1-19)? The old, yet new commandment, the only commandment which John's Jesus gives to his own, is that they love each other with brotherly love--was not the hate of Abel's brother what brought fratricide

25

and evil (Gen 4:4-8; John 13:34-35, cf. 1 John 2:7-11)? The Johannine Jesus is the only-begotten son of his divine father (John 1:14, 18, 3:16-18)--is that not the unique role of Abel, who was without any doubt conceived from Adam (unlike Cain)? Most of all, the well-known notion of Jesus' "pre-existence" appears in a new and plausible light. Finally, the insight which informs this paper also speaks out of 1 John: "This is the message which you have heard from the beginning, that we should love one another. We should not be like Cain out of evil, and (so) slaughtered his brother. And why did he do it? Because his works were evil, but those of his brother were righteous" (3:11-12).[10]

---

[10]The paper is a revised form of the lecture presented on the occasion of the writer's installation into the Frederick Carl Eiselen Professorship of Old Testament Interpretation at Garrett-Evangelical Theological Seminary on March 18, 1981.

CHAPTER TWO

THE PARABLE OF THE GOOD SAMARITAN AND LEVITICUS 18:5

William Richard Stegner

In dealing with Luke 10:25-37 the critical question is whether this pericope is a genuine unit or whether Mark 12:28-34 has been conflated with the formerly independent parable of the Good Samaritan. Let us briefly examine two sides of the dispute.

Rudolf Bultmann believes that verses 30-36 (the parable itself) circulated for a time as an independent piece of tradition and then was "artificially blended into its context by Luke."[1] Accordingly, the original intent of the parable had nothing to do with the question: "And who is my neighbor?" Rather, "the point of the story lies in the contrast of the unloving Jews and the loving Samaritan."[2] Thus Luke has sufficiently altered Mark 12:28-34 to introduce the parable and thereby made a controversy dialogue out of both pieces.

On the other side of the dispute stand such scholars as J. Jeremias and I. Howard Marshall who believe that the pericope is a genuine unity. For example, Marshall says, "The two sections in fact fit perfectly together, and it is difficult to imagine the parable without its present setting to provide a context for it."[3] Consequently, both Marshall and Jeremias conclude that Luke is telling a story different from the scholastic dialogue found in Mark 12:28-34. Jeremias emphatically contests the view that Mark 12:28-34 and Luke 10:25-28 are simply parallel accounts of

---

[1] Rudolf Bultmann, The History of the Synoptic Tradition (New York: Harper and Row, 1963) 178.
[2] Bultmann, History, 178.
[3] I. H. Marshall, The Gospel of Luke (Grand Rapids: William B. Eerdmans, 1978) 440.

the same incident:
> In fact, the only connection is the doubled com-
> mand to love; all the rest is completely differ-
> ent, and it is quite likely that Jesus often
> expressed so central a thought as that contained
> in the double command.[4]

Nevertheless, the incidents are similar enough that
Luke does not repeat the double commandment later
in the Gospel when he is apparently following Mark.

While neither side has been able to convince
the other, the purpose of this paper is not to restate
the arguments for the unity of the passage. Rather
the purpose of this paper is to examine the relationship of Leviticus 18:5 to both parts of the pericope
in order to bring new data to bear on the argument.
Then, we hope to show the significance of Leviticus
18:5 for establishing the unity of the passage.

A number of scholars such as Alfred Plummer and
S. MacLean Gilmour[5] have suggested that Jesus was
quoting Leviticus 18:5 in verse 28 in his response
to the lawyer's coupling of the Shema with Leviticus
19:18 in verse 27. Certainly, the two key verbs found
in the Septuagint translation of Leviticus 18:5, "do"
and "live" (ποιήσας and ζήσεται), are the key verbs
in Jesus' reply. In addition, the future tense of
the verb "live" in both passages makes the identification more probable. Whereas Jesus replies to the
lawyer in the second person "do this, and you will
live," the Septuagint uses the third person since
the subject of the clause is "a man" (ἄνθρωπος).
If, as we shall argue below, Jesus and/or the Greek
translator of the passage was (were) consciously employing rabbinic methods of exegesis, the use of other
words and phrases from Leviticus 18:5 makes the case
even stronger. For example, the systematic way in
which words from the main Old Testament quotation

---

[4]J. Jeremias, Rediscovering the Parables (New York:
Charles Scribner's Sons, 1966) 158.
[5]A. Plummer, Gospel According to St. Luke (ICC; New
York: Charles Scribner's Sons, 1900) 285; I. H. Marshall, Gospel of Luke, 444; S. MacLean Gilmour, The
Gospel According to St. Luke, (IB, vol. 8; Nashville:
Abingdon-Cokesbury, 1952) 194; John Drury, Tradition
and Design in Luke's Gospel (London: Darton, Longman
and Todd, 1976) 77,81.

are paraphrased or quoted throughout the passage is a characteristic of a pattern that Peder Borgen[6] has found in Philo, John, and the Palestinian Midrashim. Thus the presence of ποιήσας both in the lawyer's initial question and in his final statement[7] could be a direct quote from the Septuagint since the case and tense are the same in both passages. As we shall see, the rabbinic exegesis makes much of the word "man"; and ἄνθρωπος in the same case and number is found in both passages. Finally, the opening of the lawyer's question, literally "having done what," is very similar to the construction in the Septuagint: where the lawyer's question uses as object of the participle the neuter singular of the interrogative pronoun, the Septuagint employs the neuter plural of the relative pronoun as object of the participle.

However, Earle Ellis, unlike previous interpreters who merely called attention to the presence of Leviticus 18:5, has shown how Leviticus 18:5 establishes the unity of the pericope. The citation of this text in Jesus' response to the lawyer in verse 28 and then the concluding allusions to the same text in verses 37a and 37b (ποιήσας and ποίει) establishes a pattern

---

[6]P. Borgen, Bread from Heaven (NovTSup X; Leiden: Brill, 1965) 28-58 (especially p. 47).

[7]No previous interpreter seems to have noticed that the presence of the nominative singular masculine participle (ποιήσας) in both the opening question of the lawyer and in his closing statement in verse 37 forms an inclusion which is also a characteristic of rabbinic exposition. Note how Raymond Brown defines inclusion: "At the end of a passage the Gospel will often mention a detail or make an allusion which re-calls something recorded in the opening of the pas-sage. This feature, well attested in other biblical books, . . .can serve as a means of packaging a unit or a subunit by tying together the beginning and the end." R. Brown, The Gospel According to John (AB 29; Garden City: Doubleday, 1966) CXXXV. Actually, the presence of the exact term (ποιήσας) from the Septuagint in the lawyer's initial question, as well as the noun form instead of the verb form of "live" (ζάω), could mean that the lawyer was paraphrasing Leviticus 18:5 in asking his initial question!

similar "to the pattern of the rabbinic commentary."[8]
Also, the presence of the catchword "neighbor" in
verses 27, 29, and again in 36 is another example
of the same pattern. Hence, the exegetical pattern
in Luke 10:25-37, whereby catchwords from the main
texts are repeated in the conclusion of a given passage, was "widespread in Judaism" and is "found elsewhere in the Gospels."[9] Significantly, the pattern
is also found in St. Paul. For example, he concludes
his "Midrash" in Romans 9:6-29 with a one word allusion
to the opening text of his argument in verse 7.[10]

However, this article will argue that the significance of Leviticus 18:5 goes beyond Ellis' contribution
in establishing the unity of the passage and in aiding
in its interpretation. First, let us show how Jesus'
reference to Leviticus aids in interpreting the meaning
of the passage.

When the lawyer asks what he must do to inherit
eternal life, he is obviously referring to the future
life after death. However, only a few commentators
have said that Jesus' response to the lawyer in verse
28 is also alluding to the future life. Thus, by
citing Leviticus 18:5 Jesus is probably telling the
lawyer that, if he "does" the summary of the law,
he will attain eternal life. His response would fit
the lawyer's question exactly. However, the Hebrew
of Leviticus 18:5 does not sustain that interpretation. How did Jesus arrive at that meaning? Apparently, Jesus was simply following the conventional exegesis of Leviticus 18:5 of that day, although no commen-
tator I have read recognizes this point.

What evidence is there that the conventional

---

[8]E. Earle Ellis, "New Directions in Form Criticism,"
Jesus Christus in Historie und Theologie, edited by
Georg Strecker (Tübingen: J.C.B. Mohr, 1975) 311ff.
Also see Borgen, Bread From Heaven, 47-49.
[9]Ellis, "New Directions," 314 (esp. see note no. 63).
[10]See my forthcoming article: W. R. Stegner, "Romans
9:6-29 -- A Midrash," Journal for the Study of the
New Testament (21), October, 1984. Ellis did not
note the presence in this Lukan text of another rabbinic pattern which we have noted above whereby words
from the main Old Testament quotations are quoted
throughout the passage.

exegesis of Jesus' day applied the promise of Leviticus 18:5 to the future? First, the Sifra, a tannaitic Midrash to Leviticus, interprets the Hebrew of Leviticus 18:5 to apply to the world to come: <u>le olam habah</u>. The author goes on to say, "And if you will say 'in this world,' is not death its end? This is why I apply the words 'and he will live by them' to the world to come."[11] Secondly, both Targum Onqelos and Targum Pseudo-Jonathan use the Aramaic equivalent of the Hebrew term for the world to come (<u>behave 'lm'</u>). In addition, the Palestinian Targum Pseudo-Jonathan adds the phrase "and his portion shall be with the righteous."[12] Finally, in the Septuagint the promise of life found in Leviticus 18:5 and other places was taken to mean eternal life.[13]

How are we to interpret this evidence? The sources cited above do not prove that Jesus had access to the Sifra or the Targums that we can read today. Rather, the situation is similar to that presented by Bruce Chilton who compared certain sayings of Jesus with passages in the Targum to Isaiah. Chilton concluded that the verbal agreements between the gospels and the Targum "led us to conclude in each case that the Targumic interpretation provided the background of the dominical saying."[14] In the above sources the common agreement concerning the interpretation of Leviticus 18:5 points to a Palestinian tradition

---

[11]<u>Sifra de Vei Rav</u>, edited by A. H. Weiss (Jerusalem, 1959), Aharei Mot, Pereq 12, 10. The translation is mine.
[12]<u>Leviticus, Mikra'oth Gedaloth</u>, vol. 3 (New York: A. I. Priadman, 1971) pp. 234f. However, Targum Neofiti I does not mention the future life. See <u>Leviticus, Neophyti</u> 1, vol. 3, edited by A. D. Macho (Spain: Bilbao, 1971) 123.
[13]G. Bertram, <u>Theological Dictionary of the New Testament</u>, vol. 2 (Grand Rapids: Eerdmans, 1964) 832-875, esp. 854.
[14]B. Chilton, <u>A Galilean Rabbi and His Bible: Jesus' Use of the Interpreted Scripture of His Time</u> (Wilmington: Michael Glazier, 1984) 107. Chilton also found that when Jesus referred to the Targum, he did not quote exactly, but "there is a richly creative element in Jesus' use of Targumic tradition" (p. 110). This is precisely the way in which Jesus referred to the Leviticus text in our pericope.

of interpretation[15] that could have been known by Jesus and the Greek translator of this passage. We are simply saying that Jesus probably followed the conventional exegesis of this passage that was later incorporated into the Sifra and the Targums.

The next section of the paper will attempt to demonstrate the relationship between Leviticus 18:5 and the parable in verses 30-35. Of the eight occurrences of Leviticus 18:5 in the Babylonian Talmud,[16] three, which are practically identical, are associated with the famous Rabbi Meir. Each deals with the study of the Torah and each seeks to define the meaning of the term "man" in the passage. The three passages follow:

> Is it not taught: R. Meir used to say, "Whence do we know that even an idolater who studies the Torah is equal to a High Priest? From the following verse: <u>Ye shall therefore keep My statutes and My ordinances which, if a man do, he shall live by them</u>. It does not say 'If a Priest, Levite, or Israelite do, he shall live by them,' but 'a man'; here, then, you can learn that even a heathen who studies the Torah is equal to a High Priest!"[17]

> Rabbi Meir used to say, "Whence do we know that even a heathen who studies the Torah is as a High Priest? From the verse (<u>Ye shall therefore keep my statutes, and my judgments:</u>) <u>which, if a man do, he shall live in them</u>. Priests, Levites, and Israelites are not mentioned, but <u>men</u>: hence thou mayest learn that even a heathen

---

[15]M. D. Herr, "Sifra," <u>Encyclopedia Judaica</u>, Vol. 14 (Jerusalem: Macmillan, 1970) 1517-1519. The Sifra originated in the school of Akiba and "would seem to have been compiled and arranged in Erez Israel." p. 1518. "The Pentateuch Targum called Pseudo-Jonathan reflects a different, presumably Palestinian form of Aramaic such as is known from the Jerusalem Talmud." Chilton, <u>op.cit.</u>, p. 43.

[16]<u>The Babylonian Talmud. Index Volume</u>, ed. I. Epstein (London: Soncino Press, 1935) 511.

[17]<u>The Babylonian Talmud: Abodah Zarah</u> 3a, ed. I. Epstein (London: Soncino Press, 1935) 5.

who studies the Torah is as a High Priest!"[18]

But it has been taught: R. Meir used to say, "Whence can we learn that even where a gentile occupies himself with the study of the Torah he equals (in status) the High Priest? We find it stated:...which if a man do he shall live in them; it does not say 'priests, Levites and Israelites,' but 'a man,' which shows that even if a gentile occupies himself with the study of the Torah he equals (in status) the High Priest." [19]

In addition, Midrash Rabbah Numbers also quotes Leviticus 18:5 in a passage which seeks to allegorize the animals used in the sacrificial worship of the temple. Significantly, Leviticus 18:5 bears the same interpretation which we have seen in the talmudic passages. According to the allegory, the animals of Numbers 7:15 and 16 stand for the following categories:

one young bull	= the priests
one ram	= the Levites
one male lamb	= the Israelites, and
one male goat	
for a sin offering	= "the proselytes who

would embrace Judaism in the future and to those who were present on that occasion, indicating that they were all worthy (to study) the Torah, as may be inferred from the text, Mine ordinances, which if a man do, he shall live by them. It does not say 'priests' or 'Levites' or 'Israelites,' but 'a man.' This teaches that even an idolater who becomes a proselyte and studies the Torah is like a High Priest." [20]

---

[18]The Babylonian Talmud: Sanhedrin 59a, ed. I. Epstein (London: Soncino Press, 1935) 400. In the above quote the phrase "studies the Torah" includes "observing." See footnote 6.
[19]The Babylonian Talmud: Baba Kamma 38a, ed. I. Epstein (London: Soncino Press, 1935) 214.
[20]The Midrash Rabbah: Numbers (Naso) XIII, 15, 16, (ed. H. Freedman; London: Soncino Press, 1977) 536. Numbers Rabbah I, which includes the above quote, was compiled about the middle of the 12th century. Since it includes a large variety of sources, it is difficult to assign the above quote to a particular source. See M. D. Herr, "Numbers Rabbah," Encyclopaedia

Also, another source must be considered here.
Two of the three talmudic passages are introduced
by a technical term "tanya" which can be translated
"and so it has been taught," and in general means
"to report a tradition." Here, if the attribution
to Rabbi Meir is correct, it is referring to a Baraitha
or a tradition (in this case the interpretation of
Leviticus 18:5 attributed to Meir) that was excluded
from the Mishna of Judah haNasi.[21] Since the famous
Rabbi Meir flourished in the third generation of the
Tannaim around A.D. 130 to 160, and contributed to
the codification of the Mishna,[22] we are talking about
a "source" that preceded the Mishna (usually dated
around A.D. 200).

What can we learn from these four passages?
Note that all four passages distinguish between
priests, Levites, and Israelites on the one hand,
and on the other "a man." Then, the four say that
a "man" who studies (and observes) Torah is equal
(in status) to a high priest! Clearly we seem to
be dealing with an exegetical tradition involving
the interpretation of Leviticus 18:5. An exegetical
tradition means simply that whenever the rabbis thought
of Leviticus 18:5, they also thought of Meir's interpretation of it. By exegetical tradition we mean,
for example, the kind of interpretative tradition
which equated the term "Lebanon" (wherever it occurred
in the text) with the temple or Jerusalem and which
continued unchanged for centuries.[23] In the interpretative tradition associated with Leviticus 18:5 attention was focused on the term "a man" who was explicitly

Judaica, vol. 12 (Jerusalem: Macmillan, 1971) 1261-
1263.
    [21]M. Jastrow, A Dictionary of the Targumim, the Talmud
Babli and Yerushalmi, and the Midrashic Literature,
vol. II (Tel Aviv: 1972) 1681. If the attribution
to Rabbi Meir is correct, this particular baraitah
originated in the land of Israel. See B. DeVries,
"Baraita, Beraitot," Encyclopedia Judaica, vol. 4
(Jerusalem: Macmillan, 1971) 189-193. Some Beraitot
predate the Mishna, and others have been based upon
it.
    [22]H. L. Strack, Introduction to the Talmud and Midrash
(New York: Jewish Publication Society, 1959) 115.
    [23]G. Vermes, Scripture and Tradition in Judaism (Leiden:
Brill, 1973) 36ff.

identified as a "heathen'/"idolater", not a Jew. If
that given "heathen"/"idolater"/"proselyte" studies
and observes Torah, he is equal to a high priest.

Could Jesus have known this interpretative tradition? The tradition first appears in the Babylonian
Talmud which is quite late. However, we have seen
that the Talmud introduces the passage by means of
a technical term tanya which indicates the passage
is found in an earlier source. If the attribution
to Meir is correct, the tradition can be traced to
about a century after Jesus. However, such attribu-
tions are not always reliable, and scholars are no
longer sure what such an attribution means. Traditionally, an attribution to such a well-known rabbi was
assumed to mean the saying originated with him. However, it can mean the saying was attributed to him because (in the case of Meir) of his open attitude to
Gentiles. It can also mean that the saying originated
with someone else but was repeatedly taught by the
rabbi in question. Clearly, the tradition cannot
be traced back to the time of Jesus in view of the
limited data at hand.

Nevertheless, we propose that Jesus could have
known this interpretative tradition. The methodology
employed by Bruce Chilton, whereby verbal agreements
between certain sayings of Jesus and the Targum to
Isaiah were compared, led him to conclude that "the
Targumic interpretation provided the background of
the dominical saying." However, the agreements must
not be "explicable in respect of other ancient versions
of the Old Testament."[24] While we will employ the
same methodology, the cases are not completely analogous. Chilton was comparing isolated sayings of Jesus
with isolated passages from the Targum to Isaiah.
Here, an extended saying or parable is being compared
with an exegetical tradition that occurs in four
places. Since we are dealing with a narrative or
parable, it is much more difficult to control the
data. Our problem does not lie with verbal agreements
from "other ancient versions of the Old Testament,"
but with verbal agreements and motifs drawn from the
biblical material itself. For example, since 1914
many authorities have pointed out the affinities between the parable and the story of the conscience-

---

[24]Chilton, A Galilean Rabbi, 107.

stricken 'Samaritans' in 2 Chronicles 28:8-15.[25] Thus, we are not denying that Jesus drew on Old Testament passages in creating this story. Nevertheless, the striking verbal agreements between the parable and the interpretative tradition furnishes evidence that Jesus could have known this material.

Note the striking verbal agreements between the parable and the "raw material" furnished by Meir's exegesis of Leviticus 18:5. Who does the law and acts as neighbor to the man who was beaten? The neighbor was not the priest, not the Levite, but a man. Note how Duncan Derrett, writing without knowledge of the significance of Leviticus 18:5 or Meir's exegesis of it, focuses on the term "man" in delineating the main thrust of the parable.

> It is from our parable alone that we know that Jesus accepted the ratio behind the famous dictum, and that to him "neighbour" for this purpose means "man." Mark's and Matthew's version of the midrash leaves it open whether 'neighbour' means any Jew, for the implications of πλησίον, ...are not conclusive.[26]

Here, "a man" (we have already noted the presence of this key term from Leviticus 18:5 and Meir's exegesis in the parable) becomes a Samaritan. There is even a verbal agreement between the talmudic term for heathen/idolater (ayobed cocbim) and Samaritan. In Mishnaic times and before, the Jews began to call the Samaritans "Cutheans" (2 Kings 17:30, cf. 17:-24) and the term "Cutheans" was interchangeable with

---

[25]J. D. M. Derrett, "Law in the New Testament: Fresh Light on the Parable of the Good Samaritan," NTS 11 (1964) 22-27. Especially see p. 23, note 9. Also, there are verbal agreements with Hosea 6:9. Also, Derrett has drawn up a section entitled "The raw material" in which verbal agreements and common motifs drawn from OT material is noted. However, the very multiplicity of sources, together with the fact that only one or two verbal agreements may be assigned to any one Old Testament passage, makes the whole section problematical. See Derrett, "Law in the New Testament," 23f.
[26]Derrett, "Law in the New Testament," 34.

the term for "idolater." [27]   But what happened to the
Israelite in Rabbi Meir's exegesis? The audience
would see the man who went down from Jerusalem to
Jericho "as a Jew like themselves." [28] Thus, the Israelite is the man who was robbed. In summary, four
striking verbal agreements with the talmudic saying
are found in the terms "priest," "Levite," "Samaritan,"
and "a man." The term "Israelite" is implied. Thus,
the personnel of Meir's exegesis reappear in a start-
ling manner in this parable.

Some may object that the action in the parable
has not been derived from Meir's saying. Here Jeremias' supposition that "the story . . . has, at least
in its local setting, probably arisen out of an actual
occurrence," [29] points to the truth that a story or
parable and a saying are different literary forms.
Complete coherence cannot be expected: the presence
of a high priest in the parable would be grotesque.
Rather, the argument has been conducted on the basis
of verbal agreements, the main thrust of both passages,
and the continuity of personnel.

What makes the above reconstruction even more
plausible is the thoroughly rabbinic nature of the
Lukan pericope. Recent interpreters, such as Marshall,
Derrett, and Gerhardsson have all made this point.
Perhaps Birger Gerhardsson goes further than the rest
in calling the composition a midrash:

> To find the parable of the Good Samaritan in
> Luke standing as a midrash . . . conforms wholly
> with the use of parables as we find it in the
> old Jewish tradition. We are not forced to assume
> that it is a secondary laboured composition by
> the evangelist himself. [30]

---

[27]J. Jeremias, Jerusalem in the Time of Jesus (Philadelphia: Fortress Press, 1978) 354f. Also see
Kwty, Jastrow, Vol. 1, op.cit., 627. Various rabbinic
comments about the idolatrous nature of the Samaritan
cult may be found in Strack-Billerbeck, Kommentar
zum Neuen Testament aus Talmud und Midrash, vol. 1
(München: C. H. Beck, 1922) 538, 549, 553.
[28]Derrett, "Law in the New Testament," 22.
[29]Jeremias, Rediscovering, 159.
[30]B. Gerhardsson, The Good Samaritan--The Good Shepherd?
(Lund: C. W. K. Gleerup, 1958) 25.

Jesus may very well have been working as a darshan in the creation of the parable and in giving unity to the whole composition through the use of catchwords.

Conclusions

In contrast to R. Bultmann and others who feel that the dialogue with the lawyer and the following parable were originally two separate units "artificial-ly blended" together by Luke, we have posited Jesus' use of Leviticus 18:5 as the source of unity of the whole pericope.

Apparently, even in Jesus' day conventional exege-sis of Leviticus 18:5 focused on the two words "will live" and "a man." Since the word "will live" was interpreted to mean eternal life, Jesus' response to the lawyer's coupling of the Shema with Leviticus 19:18 is a perfect answer to his initial query about inheriting eternal life.

An exegetical tradition attributed to Rabbi Meir interpreted the term "a man" to designate a human being as such, rather than a Jew. This exegetical tradition, and an actual occurrence on the Jerusalem-Jericho road, constitute most of the raw material out of which Jesus fashioned his parable. Verbal agreements between the talmudic material and the para-ble make plausible the thesis that the talmudic materi-al provides the background for the parable.

While the problem of dating presents genuine difficulties for the thesis, striking verbal agreements may be a way around the dilemma of dating.

Apparently, Jesus was following the rabbinic custom of telling a parable to elucidate a verse of scripture. In this case, however, part of the raw material for the parable was found in the very exegeti-cal tradition associated with that verse of scripture. The growing consensus about the thoroughly Jewish/rabbinic nature of the language and dialogue in the pericope strengthens the thesis that Leviticus 18:5 is the focus of unity for the pericope. The thesis draws a picture of a tightly-constructed unit. The very unity of the construction and the simplicity of the explanation for its origin weigh heavily in favor of its plausibility.

CHAPTER THREE

THE USE OF THE PSALMS IN THE GOSPELS

Helmer Ringgren

According to Luke 24:44, Jesus says to his disciples that all that was written in the Law, the Prophets
and the Psalms about him has to be fulfilled. The
Psalms obviously stand for the Writings, or ketubim,
because they were the most important and best known
part of the third part of the Hebrew Bible. A closer
study reveals that the Psalms are quoted or alluded
to in the New Testament more than any other part of
the Writings. We shall confine ourselves here to
the Gospels, but even so, it emerges that the Psalms
were at that time, as they are today, a living word.

The Psalms were sacred Scripture and could thus
be used in theological argumentation. According to
the Gospels, Jesus referred to them several times
in his discussions with opponents. Mark has one example in 12:36 (with parallels in Matthew and Luke),
where Ps 110:1 is quoted in order to show that the
Messiah is more than "the son of David." The quotation
agrees with the LXX with the exception that κύριος
is used without the article and ὑποκάτω stands instead
of ὑποπόδιον (= MT). None of these differences is
theologically significant, the latter being perhaps
caused by a reminiscence from Ps 8:7b. Stendahl,
discussing the same quotation in Matthew, thinks that
it makes better sense in a Greek surrounding using
κύριος for Christ.[1] But it seems obvious that the
subject κύριος is God, not the Christ, and consequently
the discussion is possible also on the basis of the
Hebrew text. The problem is whether the argument
implies that Jesus was not really of Davidic descent;

---

[1]Krister Stendahl, The School of St. Matthew and Its
Use of the Old Testament (Acta Seminarii Neotesta-
mentici Upsaliensis XX; Uppsala: Gleerup, 1954) 79.

but this is not a necessary conclusion, since the point is that the Messiah is more than the mere son of David.

Another example is found in Matt 21:16. Speaking of the children who were crying Hosanna in the temple, Jesus quotes Ps 8:3: "Out of the mouths of babes and sucklings thou hast brought praise." Jesus is thus supposed to quote the verse according to the LXX, which, as is well known, translates oz, "strength," as αἶνος . The translation is hardly defendable, but the quotation would lose its point if it were corrected. The question, then, is: was Jesus so familiar with the LXX that he could quote it verbally; or is the story a creation of the evangelist, who, as we know, felt free to use any translation that he found applicable?[2] The New Testament use of Ps 8 as a whole is interesting in itself. The fact that the psalm contains the expression "son of man" made it easy to apply it to Jesus. It has been argued that ben 'adam was originally a royal epithet,[3] but this can hardly be proved. The psalm speaks very clearly of man or mankind in general. But if we assume that on some cultic occasion in ancient Israel the king appeared as the representative of mankind--and expressions as "crown," "glory" and "honor" seem to strengthen this assumption--the Messianic use of the psalm would also receive some support. [4]

Matthew 16:27 is less clear as a quotation. Jesus says that the Son of Man will come and "he will repay every man for what he has done." The same words appear in Ps 62:13; however, Matthew uses πρᾶξις instead of the ἔργα of the LXX. The same words occur in Proverbs 24:12. The quotation is hardly characteristic; rather, it represents the expression in Biblical language of a general principle.

On the other hand, there is a clear and intentional quotation in the temptation story which Matthew

---

[2]The question is discussed by Stendahl, School of St. Matthew, 134.
[3]I. Engnell, A Rigid Scrutiny (Nashville: Vanderbilt University Press, 1969) 238.
[4]For details see H. Ringgren, Svensk exegetisk arsbok 37-38 (1972-73) 16ff., summarized in Theologisches Wörterbuch zum Alten Testament III, col. 667.

shares with Luke. Here the devil quotes Ps 91:11-12.
Matthew's quotation is shorter than Luke's, but both
follow the LXX word for word. If we consider the
pericope to be a midrash on the desert wandering,
the insertion of a quotation from the Psalms may seem
remarkable, since Ps 91 has nothing to do with Israel
in the desert. However, a midrash is entirely free
to quote any Biblical passage that may seem suitable.

Matthew 13:35 contains an interesting quotation
from a psalm. Matthew explains that Jesus spoke in
parables in order to fulfill what was said by "the
prophet": "I will open my mouth in parables, I will
utter what has been hidden since the foundation of
the world." This is a quotation from Ps 78:3, where,
however, the second line runs: "I will utter dark
sayings (ḥidot) from of old." Matthew makes his own
translation, rendering ḥidot "riddles, dark sayings"
by κεκρυμμένα , thereby changing the meaning of the
sentence: it is not a question of age-old riddles,
but of things hidden from the beginning of the world
but now revealed.[5]

An intentional quotation that is firmly rooted
in the Gospel tradition is the Hosanna greeting from
Ps 118:25-26, which occurs in all the four Gospels
(Mark 11:9, Matt 21:9, Luke 19:38, John 12:13). The
retention of the Hebrew word hosanna gives some credi-
bility to the assumption that Jesus was really greeted
with that old cultic formula. It is noteworthy, however, that another quotation from the same psalm is
found only a little later in all the Synoptics (Mark
12:10-11 and parallels), namely, v 21 f.: "The stone
which the builders rejected, etc." Jesus quotes the
psalm text at the end of a parable. The quotation
is verbally from the LXX, which in this case is very
close to MT.[6] On this ground it is impossible to
decide whether it belongs to the original tradition
or has been added by the Greek author.

In the description of Jesus' suffering on the
cross, Mark uses the expressions "they divided his
garments among them, casting lots for them" (15:29)
and "wagging their heads" (v 29), which are clear
allusions to Ps 22, vv 19 and 8, respectively. The

[5]Stendahl, School of St. Matthew, 116f.
[6]Stendahl, School of St. Matthew, 67-68.

Gospel uses the same verbs as the LXX, but the grammatical forms are different. A somewhat vague allusion to the Ps 69:22 may be found in v 36. It thus seems that the language of Pss 22 and 69 has contributed to the shaping of the Gospel tradition, which probably also means that the psalms were regarded as prophecies fulfilled. The combination may have been prompted by the unanimous synoptic tradition that Jesus quoted Ps 22:1 on the cross -- in Aramaic! The question is whether this means that he prayed the whole psalm[7] or just quoted the first verse as an adequate expression of his anguish.

The allusions to Ps 22, already present in Mark, are expanded by Matthew, as he reports the bystanders as saying: "He has put his trust in God, let God deliver him now, if he desires him," which is a quotation from Ps 22:9. The quotation differs from the LXX on two points: it uses πέποιθεν instead of ἔλπισεν (both Matt and LXX however agree in reading the perf. gal for MT gol), and 'ρυσάσθω instead of σωσάτω . Thus Matthew presents his own translation of the Hebrew text, possibly under influence from Wis 2:18, where ῥύσεται is used in connexion with a reference to Ps 22.[8]

Luke has added still another allusion to Ps 22. Luke 23:35 alludes to Ps 22:8 in the wording of the LXX: "And the people stood by, watching, but the rulers scoffed at him" (cf. "All who watch me scoff at me"). Thus it emerges clearly how important Ps 22 was in the shaping of the passion tradition.

It should be mentioned here that John's use of Ps 22:19 (John 19:24) takes us one step further, since we have here an example of misunderstanding Hebrew parallelism: dividing the garments and casting lots in the psalm refers to one set of actions, while John understands them as two separate events (a similar example in Matt 21:1-7). Luke has two more psalm allusions in the passion story. According to Luke 23:46 Jesus uses Ps 31:6 on the cross: "Father, in thy hands I commit my spirit." Luke here uses the present tense instead of the future of the LXX. Fur-

---

[7]E. Stauffer, <u>Jesus, Gestalt und Geschichte</u> (Bern: Francke Verlag, 1957) 106.
[8]Stendahl, <u>School of St. Matthew</u>, 140f.

thermore, in 23:49 Luke says that "all his acquaint-
ances ... stood at a distance," which seems to be
a combination of Pss 88:9 and 38:12 according to the
LXX.

Another allusion may be found in Mark 14:18,
where the words "who eats with me" could allude to
Ps 41:10. Matthew changes the wording, and Luke is
entirely different. John actually expands the sentence
to a real quotation: "he who ate my bread has lifted
his heel against me." In other parts of the Gospels,
the allusions are less numerous. In the parable of
the mustard seed (Mark 4:32 and parallels) there might
be an allusion to Ps 104:12 ("the birds of heaven
built their nests in its shadow"). But there is an
even more similar expression in Dan 4:9,18 and another
one is Ezek 17:13; hence, it is a common saying rather
than an intentional allusion.

Luke alludes to Ps 91:13 in 10:19: "I have given
you authority to tread upon serpents and scorpions,"
although the species of the animals differs from the
LXX ἀσπίδα καὶ βασιλίσκον . In Luke 13:27 Jesus says
that he will say to those who are not worthy: "Depart
from me, all you workers of iniquity" which is a quotation from Ps 6:9, though not according to the LXX
(ἐργάται ἀδικίας instead of ἐργαζόμενοι τὴν ἀνομίαν).

According to John 2:17, the disciples remember
that it is written: "Zeal for thy house has consumed
me," which refers to a somewhat obscure passage in
Ps 69:10. As usual, it is used without regard to
its original context. The quotation from Ps 78:24
in John 6:31, "he gave them bread from heaven to eat,"
on the other hand, is entirely in accordance with
the original context.

John 15:25 says: "It is written in their law:
they hated me without a cause." The quotation is
not from the Law but from Ps 35:9 or 69:5, where we
find the expression οἱ μισοῦντές με δωρεάν ; John,
however, uses the finite verb ἐμίσησαν .

Finally, it should be mentioned that the Magnificat of Luke 1:46-55 and the Benedictus of Luke 1:68-79
sound like an echo of Qumran psalmody, containing
numerous allusions both to Psalms and other Old Testament texts.

PAUL: A CHRISTIAN JONAH?

Albert C. Sundberg, Jr.

I am glad through this small study to extend my congratulations on this happy occasion to Professor Ernest W. Saunders who, for a decade and a half, was my friend and senior colleague in New Testament at Garrett-Evangelical Theological Seminary. It was a rich experience!

I

In his recent commentary on Galatians, H. D. Betz has struck off in a few sentences the critical issues in dealing with the questions of Paul's becoming a Christian and the timing of his subsequent preaching the gospel to the gentiles. Betz' remarks are related to Paul's autobiographical statement in Gal 1:11-2:10, in which Paul cryptically relates his activities from his becoming a Christian to the so-called "conference in Jerusalem." Betz says,

> . . . it is by no means clear that he (Paul) began by preaching his gospel as including freedom from Torah and circumcision. All he says is that he always preached the law-free gospel to the Gentiles. How he had preached it to the Jews we do not know. Clearly, the concept of a gospel free from Torah and circumcision must have been a secondary development. Only when this concept was developing could the opposition to it have developed. It is also clear that for this law-free gospel Paul was not depending upon the authorities in Jerusalem.[1]

The usual answer to the complementary questions, when and how did Paul come to preach to gentiles, and when and how did Paul come to preach a gospel apart from the law, are usually answered by asserting

---

[1]H. D. Betz, _Galatians_ (Philadelphia: Fortress, 1979) 85.

that Paul received both by revelation when he became a Christian as indicated in Gal 1-2.[2] These sentences by Betz, however, re-open the issue, though Betz has not pursued that re-opening in his commentary.

Close examination of Gal 1:11-2:10, however, shows that Paul does not state what this answer presupposes. 1) Paul's remark about preaching to the gentiles in Gal 1:15-16 is not a declarative statement; it is a statement of purpose. Though, like Jeremiah (1:5),[3] Paul was set apart by God before he was born, Paul certainly did not have pre-natal knowledge of his future gentile mission. Neither does Paul's having been called through God's grace, nor the revelation of his son to Paul carry any connotation of gentile mission. The clause, "in order that I might preach him among the gentiles" (ἵνα εὐαγγελίζωμαι αὐτὸν ἐν τοῖς ἔθνεσιν , 1:16b), is a purpose clause[4] that, as it is stated by Paul, is without date-line. Paul is saying that it was in order for God to fulfill his ultimate purpose for Paul--that of preaching among the gentiles--that God set him apart before he was born, called him through his grace, revealed his son to him. But here Paul gives no hint as to when that "preaching among the gentiles" began.[5]

---

[2]A. D. Nock, St. Paul (New York: Harper and Brothers, 1938) 66-68; A. C. Purdy, "Paul the Apostle," IDB (New York: Abingdon Press, 1962) 3.685; Betz, Galatians 85-90; etc.

[3]Cf. Isa 49:1.

[4]Betz' "redemptive" ἵνα (Galatians 71 n. 153) is a theological and not a grammatical term.

[5]Cf., E. de W. Burton, The Epistle to the Galatians (ICC; Edinburgh: T. & T. Clark, 1921) 48-54; E. P. Blair, "Paul's Call to the Gentile Mission," BR 10 (1965) 23-25. Even if ἵνα is taken as result (not the simpler, more obvious reading), the construction does not constitute a "commission 'to preach the gospel among the Gentiles,'" as Betz suggests (Galatians, 71). In any event ἵνα cannot sustain the burden Betz puts on it of "the gospel message which he was ordered by Christ to proclaim;" "while the order to proclaim the gospel among the Gentiles implies a verbal revelation" (Galatians, 64)' "The purpose and result (ἵνα ['so that'] of Paul's vision of Christ was his commission 'to preach the gospel among the Gentiles'" (Galatians, 71).

2) Actually, Paul does not tell us when he began to preach. In this autobiographical statement Paul's first mention of his preaching activity is not until v 23 where he says, ". . . they (the Judean churches) only heard it said, 'He who once persecuted us is now preaching the faith he once tried to destroy.'" That preaching, I take it, was in the regions of Syria and Cilicia (v 21). However, even that preaching probably did not consciously include preaching to gentiles. Paul's report of what was heard in Judea about his preaching lacks the critical phrase "to the gentiles" (ἐν τοῖς ἔθνεσιν). Since this is Paul's own report about his own activities, it must be given precedence as the only primary material in this matter.

3) Moreover, Paul makes no mention of having discussed preaching to gentiles during his "after three years" visit with Cephas and James in Jerusalem (vv 18-20). If Paul had been preaching to gentiles prior to that visit and did not discuss it with Cephas and James, we then would have to regard him either as reticent (which seems not to have been the case) or devious (which I prefer not to believe about him). On the other hand, if Paul had discussed preaching to gentiles with Cephas and James and had gained their approval at that time, he certainly would have said so here. This is an instance in which the argument from silence carries weight, since Paul is at pains to point out the approval of Cephas, James, and the Jerusalem church at the later so-called "Jerusalem conference." Indeed, on that occasion, the "after fourteen years" visit (Gal 2:1-10), Paul raises the question of preaching to gentiles de novo; the issue is not mentioned previously in this autobiographical statement.

Thus Paul does not give us a clear statement as to when or under what circumstance he began preaching to the gentiles. Neither does he tell us when or how he came to preach a gospel apart from law. From this autobiographical statement in Galatians we may deduce that his preaching to gentiles commenced sometime between his preaching "in the regions of Syria and Cilicia" (1:21) and the "after fourteen years" visit to Jerusalem (2:1-10).

4) Alternative suggestions as to the origin of Paul's gentile mission are derived primarily from

Acts.[6] However, Acts proves to be a disappointing secondary source due to the variety of information it provides. In Acts 9:1-22, Ananias is told that it is revealed that Paul is to preach to the gentiles, but there is no indication that Ananias communicated this information to Paul. In Acts 9:26-29, the Hellenists with whom Paul disputed were probably Jewish.[7] In Acts 13, where Barnabas and Paul, chosen from among the prophets and teachers, are sent off "to the work to which I [the Holy Spirit] have called them," there is no mention of preaching to gentiles.[8] It was not until Antioch of Pisidia (Acts 13:14b) that gentiles are first depicted as responding to the gospel, and that was associated with Paul's synagogal preaching. However, in Acts 22:1-21, Paul's defense before the people of Jerusalem, Ananias is depicted as telling Paul that he will be a witness to all men; in Acts 22:17-21, on his return from Damascus, Paul, in a trance in the temple was told by the risen Jesus, "I will send you far away to the Gentiles." In Acts 26:1-12, Paul's defense before King Agrippa, Paul's commission to the gentiles is pushed all the way back to his road-to-Damascus revelation; there the risen Jesus says to him, ". . . I have appeared to you for this purpose, to appoint you to serve and bear witness to the things in which you have seen me and those in which I will appear to you, delivering you from the people and from the Gentiles -- to whom I send you to open their eyes. . . ." [9] It is evident that solutions to the problem of the origin of Paul's gentile preaching cannot be convincing, since the accounts in Acts are too many and too varied to provide

---

[6]H. Conzelmann, Die Apostelgeschichte (HNT 7, Tübingen: Mohr, Siebeck, 1963) 6 and loc. cit.; Blair, "Paul's Call," 19-33.

[7]Cf. E. Haenchen, The Acts of the Apostles (Philadelphia: Westminster Press, 1971) 333 and n. 1; M. Hengel, "Zwischen Jesus and Paulus. Die 'Hellenisten' die 'Sieben' und Stephanus (Apg 6,1-15; 7,54-8,3)," ZTK 72 (1975) 151-206.

[8]But cf. Haenchen, Acts, 396, "--it is indeed fundamentally the mission to the Gentiles (14.26!)."

[9]Cf., Haenchen's slip on Acts 22:21: "Jesus himself commands the Gentile mission as Paul's task; this is so expressed neither in Chapter 9 nor in Chapter 26" (where it is expressed).

dependable historical information.[10]

II

It is the purpose of this paper to suggest an alternative solution to the questions concerning the origins of Paul's mission to the gentiles and his gospel apart from law. The argument will be built upon Paul's autobiographical statements in his letters, especially upon Gal 1:11-2:10 and an additional datum: Paul insisted that he always preached one gospel (Gal 1: 6-9, cf. 2 Cor 11:4).

1) As has been intimated above, Paul's earliest preaching, in all probablility, was to Diaspora Jews. It is apparent from Gal 1:21-23 that Paul was preaching in the regions of Syria and Cilicia when the Judean churches heard that he was preaching the gospel; but Paul makes no claim of having preached to gentiles there. It may be possible to extrapolate backwards from Paul's known gospel to gentiles to his probable gospel to Jews, since he insists that he only preached one gospel. When preaching the gospel to Jews, there was no thought or concern about what would have been appropriate preaching if a gentile might be present and should happen to believe. Hence, Paul preached to Jews a gospel that was appropriate for Jews. This gospel would have had as its central content what Paul learned about the gospel in his conversion experience. Since he had been a persecutor of the church,[11] Paul must have had some information about Christianity that brought him to that position.[12] He probably knew that a Jew, Jesus, even though he had been crucified, was believed and proclaimed by Christians to have been raised to heaven by God and was expected to return to earth as God's promised messiah. I know of no Jewish proscription against claiming to be messiah or having such claims made in one's behalf. Josephus reflects no Jewish hostility against the several pseudo-messiahs he reports. The death of such claimants simply ended the episode; but only

---

[10]J. C. Hurd, "Paul the Apostle," IDBSup (Nashville: Abingdon, 1976) 649.
[11]Gal 1:13,23; 1 Cor 15:9; Phil 3:12.
[12]Purdy, "Paul," 65; W. D. Davies, "Paul and Jewish Christianity according to Cardinal Danielou: A Suggestion," RSR 60 (1972) 69-79.

enthusiasm by Jews is reported to the claim itself.[13] Gal 3:13 may give the hint as to what Paul and other Jews found objectionable in the Christian message. Jesus had been crucified; and Paul and other Jews knew the law's decree, "a hanged man is accursed by God."[14] For Christians to claim that one who had been hanged upon a tree (crucified), rather than being accursed, was God's blessed one, the coming messiah, was probably regarded by Paul and other Jews as blasphemy.[15] Paul tells us nothing about a verbal revelation made to him at his conversion. What he does tell us is that God "was pleased to reveal his Son to (ἐν) me" (Gal 1:16a).[16] Paul learned by this revelation that the Christian proclamation was true, that the crucified Jesus was alive, a heavenly being, God's son, the messiah who was coming. That probably was the content of God's revelation to Paul on the road to Damascus; it was all that Paul needed to know. For Paul, knowing that was knowing everything; Judaism supplied the rest.[17] This revelation changed Paul from being a persecutor into becoming a proclaimer of the gospel.[18]

I have said that Paul's earliest preaching was probably to Jews.[19] Its content was probably the glad announcement that God had indeed raised Jesus and made him Lord Messiah. This he had opposed as persecutor; as a believer in Jesus, he now affirmed this as God's revelation to him, i.e., the truth of the Christian gospel that he had opposed as persecutor. It was probably of this that he wrote, "for

---

[13]Cf., J.W. 2.55-65, Ant. 17.269-85; J.W. 2.117, Ant. 17.4; J.W. 2.258-63, Ant. 20.167-72; J.W. 2.433-46; etc.

[14]Deut 21:23b.

[15]Cf. Mark 14:61b-64 written in the light of early Christian experience.

[16]Burton, Galatians, 49-51, 433-35; W. G. Kümmel, The Theology of the New Testament (Nashville: Abingdon Press, 1973) 150-151.

[17]J. A. Fitzmyer, "The Gospel in the Theology of Paul," Int 33 (1979) 339-50.

[18]Cf. Kümmel, Theology of NT, 150-151.

[19]M. Hengel, "Die Ursprünge der christlichen Mission," NTS 18 (1971) 15-38; against E. P. Sanders, "Paul's Attitude Toward the Jewish People," USQR 33 (1978) 175-87.

I did not receive it from man, nor was I taught it, but it came through a revelation of Jesus Christ" (ἀλλὰ δι᾽ ἀποκαλύψεως Ἰησοῦ Χριστοῦ , Gal 1:12).

2) It was probably preaching this gospel to Jews that provided Paul with his first experience with gentile hearers and then believers. Both Luke and Josephus know of gentile adherents to Judaism who, nevertheless, were not fully proselytes. These were gentiles who appreciated Judaism for its monotheism and its high morality. They apparently attended synagogue.[20] Luke tells of a centurion, of whom elders of the Jews said that "he loves our nation and built us our synagogue" (Luke 7:2-5). In Acts, Luke tells of an Ethiopian eunuch (therefore, not a Jew) who had come to Jerusalem to worship and who had and read the Jewish Prophets (Isaiah, 8:26-38), and of another (Roman) centurion, Cornelius, who was "an upright and God-fearing man, who is well spoken of by the whole Jewish nation," "a devout man who feared God with all his household," and "who gave alms liberally to the people, and prayed constantly to God" (10:1-48; 11:11-17).[21] Such Gentile adherents to Judaism in some synagogue very probably were the first gentiles to hear Paul preach the gospel. The gospel they heard was the gospel Paul preached to Jews, containing no preaching about keeping the law and containing no requirement of proselytizing to Judaism. Under Paul's preaching some gentile(s) came to believe in Jesus as God's Christ, with accompanying signs of their espousal of this new faith. They converted to Christianity, without their first becoming proselytes to Judaism. Thus, the gospel Paul preached to them was the same gospel he had preached from the first, initially to Jews, a gospel without a Jewish proselytizing component. In their enthusiasm, these new gentile converts to Christianity, without a Jewish proselytizing component, provided Paul with other opportunities

---

[20]In Acts 13:16, "you that fear God," and 13:26, "those among you that fear God," are references to such. Cf. Haenchen, Acts, 346 and n. 3 for bibliography.
[21]Cf. Gal 3:2. T. Holtz, "Die Bedeutung des Apostelkonzel für Paulus," NovT 16 (1974) 110-48; Hengel, "Die Ursprünge," 15-38.

to preach to gentiles.[22]

Within such a configuration it becomes possible
to understand how Paul could claim, on the one hand,
that he only preached one gospel, and that that gospel
was not received from or taught him by man, but that
he received it by revelation and, on the other hand,
find it unnecessary to force upon Paul the preaching
to Gentiles from the very inception of his preaching
ministry. Similarly, his gospel need not have included
a gentile mission as a part of the road-to-Damascus
vision. Thus, Paul's preaching to gentiles, probably
in the earliest instances, arose out of the circumstances of the attendance of gentile "God-fearers"
at synagogue services. As Betz says, ". . . it is
by no means clear that he (Paul) began by preaching
his gospel as including freedom from Torah and circumcision."[23]

3) As to the time when this first occurred,
I would suggest that Paul's first gentile converts
date from not too long before Paul's "after fourteen
years" visit to Jerusalem. I make this suggestion
from the following considerations. a) In the primary
document, Gal, there is not the slightest hint of
an inter-church struggle concerning the acceptability
of gentile converts prior to that visit. The idea
of inter-church conflict is found only in Acts 15:1-5,
which has strong similarities to the Cornelius-Peter
story and its aftermath in Acts 10-11. This suggests
a certain stylization of the Acts accounts. Suggestions of an inter-church struggle over gentile converts
as the background to Gal 2:1-10 all arise from harmonization of this passage with Acts 15:1-5.[24] b) Although
Paul went up to Jerusalem with Barnabas, taking Titus
along as an exhibitable gentile Christian, Paul writes

----

[22]It is evident, therefore, that the primitive gospel
preached to Jews by Jewish Christians, of whom Paul
was one, was without a law-component and was antecedent
to the discussion of whether gentile believers should
or should not proselytize to Judaism and keep the
law; against Betz, Galatians, 85, "Clearly, the concept
of a gospel free from Torah and circumcision must
have been a secondary development. Only when this
concept was developing could the opposition to it
have developed."
[23]Idem.
[24]Against Betz, Galatians, 85-90.

of his going to Jerusalem for this visit in highly personal terms. Even though Barnabas was his companion, Paul's description is accented with first person singular verbs: "I went up to Jerusalem;" "taking Titus along with me;" "I went up by revelation;" "I laid before them." "I laid before them the gospel which I preach;" "lest somehow I should be running or had run in vain;" "Titus who was with me." Not until v 4 does Paul write in terms of "we" and "us," which one would expect to have followed v 1 throughout. In view of Barnabas' later disassociation from Paul, it could be argued that it would have been to Paul's advantage, bettering his case, to have associated Barnabas with himself at every step of this Jerusalem visit. But Paul writes in insistent first person singualar verbs; these repeated first person singular verbs leave no doubt in the Galatians text but that the "after fourteen years" visit to Jerusalem was, as Paul understood it, an intensely personal matter.[25] To harmonize this intensely personal account with the inter-church struggle account of Acts is, as I see it, to do violence to the text of Paul.[26] If this harmonization of Acts with Paul is allowed, what basis remains for complaint against other harmonizations of Paul with Acts?

Paul's "after fourteen years" visit to Jerusalem

---

[25]Betz' contention that "Paul speaks here only about himself because his collaboration with Barnabas had ended after the Antioch episode (cf. 2:13), so that Barnabas is not included in the present defence" (Galatians, 85 n. 254), is not quite accurate. Barnabas is included in the text of 2:1, "Then after fourteen years I went up again to Jerusalem with Barnabas . . . ." On Betz' supposition, Paul would simply have written, "Then after fourteen years I went up to Jerusalem, taking Titus along . . . ." Moreover, Barnabas is again included in vv 14-16 when Paul returns to "we" and "us" in his writing. Betz does not explain nor escape that Paul, on the one hand, names Barnabas as his companion and, on the other hand, still writes about the Jerusalem visit in such a personalized way. Paul also writes of the revelation to go to Jerusalem as his revelation; he also writes of the issue in Jerusalem as his struggle.

[26]Irenaeus apparently was the first to do so. Cf. Adv. haer. 3.13.3.

occurred before Paul had become accustomed to gentile believers. The longer the time-lapse after Paul experienced the first gentile believer(s) and the greater the increase in their number with the passage of time, the less likely it would have been that Paul would inquire about the matter in Jerusalem. Time and habit would have tended to inure Paul to the problem. Paul's going up to Jerusalem "by revelation" suggests an urgency that belies extended practice.

Paul says that he went up to Jerusalem "by revelation." It is to be noticed that his revelation did not contain the answer to Paul's problem; it only pointed to the place where and the persons who could solve it.

Probably in all of Paul's letters there is a no more untoward phrase for Protestant exegetes than Paul's phrase, "lest somehow I should be running or have run in vain" (μή πως εἰς κενὸν τρέχω ἤ ἔδραμον , 2:2c. The context reads, "I laid before them (but privately before those who were of repute) the gospel which I preach among the gentiles, lest somehow I should be running or had run in vain" (2:2b-c). Roman Catholic scholars have emphasized Paul's deference and submission to church authority; Protestants have sought somehow to escape this implication by suggesting that Paul was interested in church unity or that Paul was negotiating a shrewd power play to force the Jerusalem church into acquiesence to his gospel and the increasingly powerful gentile church.[27] Finding the "plain meaning of the text" that Luther called for[28] has not been easy, and that partly because of Luther's view of Paul. One major hurdle, the assumption that Paul was called to preach to the gentiles at the same time that he became a Christian, we have seen, is a hurdle that need no longer stand in the way. Preaching a gospel free of Jewish proselytizing is not the equivalent of preaching to the gentiles. What we need are pre-Luther readings of the text; such readings from the early Fathers are available.

---

[27]For discussion and bibliography cf., J. Bligh, Galatians (London: St. Paul Publications, 1969) 157-73; Betz, Galatians, 83-103.
[28]Cf., Tertullian, Adv. Marc. 5.3, "Let us attend to the clear (ipsi) sense and the reason of the thing."

Pol. **Phil.** 9, reflects this text. It reads:

I exhort you all, therefore, to yield obedience
to the word of righteousness, and to exercise
all patience, such as ye have seen (set) before
your eyes, not only in the case of the blessed
Ignatius and Zosimus, and Rufus, but also in
others among yourselves, and Paul himself, and
in the rest of the apostles. (This do) in the
assurance that all these have not run in vain
(οὗτοι πάντες οὐκ εἰς κενὸν ἔδραμον), but in
faith and righteousness.

Here Polycarp is seen to regard Paul's visit to Jerusalem as an example of yielding "obedience to the word
of righteousness." Tertullian quotes this phrase
in two places in his **Against Marcion**. In 4.2, counter-
ing the Marcionite claim that Marcion's abbreviated
form of Luke was the true gospel, Tertullian writes:

There would still be wanted that Gospel which
St. Paul found in existence to which ye yielded
and with which he so earnestly wished his own
to agree, that he actually on that account went
up to Jerusalem to know and consult the apostles,
'lest he should run or had been running in vain.'
. . . the enlightener of St. Luke himself desired
the authority of his predecessors for both his
own faith and preaching . . . .

Again in 5.3 he writes:

But with regard to the countenance of Peter and
the rest of the apostles, he tells us that 'fourteen years after he went up to Jerusalem' in
order to confer with them about the rule which
he followed in his gospel, lest perchance he
shoiuld all those years have been running, and
be still running in vain. . . . So great had
been his desire to be approved and supported
by those whom you wish on all occasions to be
understood as in alliance with Judaism! . . .
They therefore gave way (in partial concession),
because there were persons whose weak faith required consideration. For their rudimentary
belief, which was still in suspense about the
observance of the law, deserved this concessive
treatment, when even the apostle himself had
some suspicion that he might have run, and be
still running, in vain.

Here we have three of the earliest readings of
Gal 2:2 in the church, more than a millenium before
Paul became Protestants' patron apostle, two from

Tertullian in the early third century and one from Polycarp from the mid-second. In them the words of the text are taken at their simple straightforward meaning. From them it is evident that Polycarp and Tertullian understood Paul as seeking agreement and approval from those who were apostles before him, not for his preaching of a different gospel, but for his preaching the same gospel as theirs, and for preaching it to gentiles. I find it difficult to understand this phrase, "lest I should be running or had run in vain" otherwise than Paul's bold statement to the Galatian churches that if Peter and the Jerusalem church had disapproved his preaching to the gentiles without requiring circumcision and fealty to the law, Paul would have ceased the practice. For Paul, the decision of the apostles and the Jerusalem church must have had equivalent authority to revelation, since Paul by revelation was sent to Jerusalem to seek it.

Actually, such an understanding of the phrase strengthens Paul's case with the Galatian churches. Paul depicts himself not as a person in stubborn opposition to the Jerusalem church, in the event that that church should disapprove his gentile activity. Rather, his case is that when Paul wondered about the legitimacy of gentile believers who were not proselytized to Judaism, even Jerusalem agreed with him and commissioned him as the preacher to the gentiles-- this Jerusalem church from which some now have claimed to come opposing gentile salvation by faith alone in the gospel. Paul's strength is in his weakness; the power of Paul's case is that he submitted it to Jerusalem and there gained approval, the right hand of fellowship, and the commissioning that he should preach to the gentiles.[29]

Finally we must ask into Paul's probable self-understanding in this new turn of events--gentile acceptance of the gospel, gentiles, the wild olive tree--whereas Paul encountered a substantial rejection of the gospel on the part of Jews. First I would note that however satisfactory Titus seemed to have been as a gentile Christian, Paul's experience of

---

[29]J. D. G. Dunn, "The Relationship between Paul and Jerusalem according to Galatians 1 and 2," NTS 28 (1982) 461-78.

gentile conversion and their receiving Holy Spirit
(Gal 3:2-5) was not an all-sufficient answer for Paul.
Paul, for himself, did not read the will of God directly out of those events, as Peter in Acts (10-11) is
said to have done. Whereas Peter in Acts stoutly
defends the baptism of Cornelius, ". . . the Holy
Spirit fell on them just as on us at the beginning
. . . who was I that I could withstand God?" (11:15b,
17b), Paul went up to Jerusalem as an inquirer, as
a suppliant, however much he may have believed in
his case and however well he may have presented it.
By revelation Paul understood that the answer about
the legitimacy of gentiles becoming Christians by
faith alone was to be found in Jerusalem. This reflects uncertainty, hesitation, on Paul's part.

To this observation we should add what can be
gleaned from Paul's letters regarding his attitude
toward gentiles when he was not thinking of them as
candidates for conversion. There is the extended
description of what I take to be the gentiles in
Rom 1:18-32; it is a derogatory passage. In Gal 2:15
Paul cryptically remarks, "we ourselves, who are Jews
by birth and not Gentile sinners . . . ." There is
the debauched state of pagans implied in 1 Cor 5:1:
"It is reported that there is immorality among you,
and of a kind that is not found even among the pagans;"
to which must be added Paul's lists of gentile sins:
Gal 5:19-21: immorality, impurity, licentiousness,
idolatry, sorcery, enmity, strife, jealousy, anger,
selfishness, dissension, party spirit, envy, drunken-
ness, carousing, etc., and other similar passages.[30]
In the light of these passages Paul appears to have
been a typical first-century Jew with typical first-
century Jewish antipathies to gentiles. There is
no evidence in Paul's letters of Paul's having had
a predisposition favoring gentiles before he became
a Christian. I have argued above that Paul's earliest
preaching was not to gentiles; and, in view of his
typical gentile aversion, he may, in fact, have been
adverse to such a possibility.

In view of the foregoing, the thesis here suggested is that Paul began his preaching as a preacher
to Diaspora Jews. Gentile converts among "God-fearers"
in his synagogue audiences began to appear, somewhat

---

[30]1 Cor 5:9-13; 6:9-11; (Col 3:5-11; Eph 4:25-31).

to Paul's surprise. The status of these gentile converts was not entirely clear to Paul. Troubled about
the situation, it was revealed to Paul that he should
go to Jerusalem to clarify this surprising, if not
somewhat untoward, situation. When Jerusalem approved
what had been occurring, Paul could still claim that
nothing had been added to him, since the events of
gentile salvation had already been occuring (Gal 2:6).

It is evident from the foregoing that Paul's
becoming the apostle to the gentiles was a significant
change of course for the Christian Paul, one for which
he was not initially entirely prepared. It may be
too strong to suggest a close parallel between Paul's
change from preacher to Diaspora Jews to preacher
to the gentiles and Jonah, God's grossly reluctant
prophet to Ninevah. But it does afford a basis for
asking, somewhat whimsically: Paul: a Christian Jonah?

CHAPTER FIVE

IS THERE A VATICINIUM EX EVENTU IN THE APOCALYPSE OF JOHN?

Savas Agourides

Today it is beyond dispute that apocalyptic thought and modes of expression were something normal and common in the primitive church.[1] Well known also is the technique of the apocalyptic writers, pseudonymous as a rule, in using the vaticinium ex eventu. The apocalyptic writer, who usually writes under the guise of a personality of the glorious but distant past, describes as things to happen, events which actually did take place between the times of the alleged and the real writer. He believes that in this way he prompts his readers to reason thus: since the prophet saw in his vision with such accuracy all that happened up to the reader's time, the reader of the apocalypse is justified in expecting the fulfillment of the prophet's visions that have a bearing upon the reader's present and future. The fact that the apocalyptic writer was so successful in prophesying events that happened before the reader's time warrants belief in the fulfillment of his prophecies that regard the future. This is the vaticinium ex eventu.

However, W. Bousset[2] already calls our attention to the fact that we should not understand this intention of the apocalyptic writers too mechanically. In 1 Enoch, for instance, the vision of the beasts which symbolically represent historical realities (chap. 89f.), though originally a figurative conception ends up as a pure farce. Very often, however, this mannerism of vaticinium ex eventu hides a profounder historical experience. This is true for instance

---

[1] M. Kiddle, The Revelation of John (MNTC; New York: Harper and Brothers, 1940) XXII.
[2] W. Bousset, Die Offenbarung Johannis (MeyerK; Göttingen: Vandenhoeck & Ruprecht, 1904) 16.

with the book of Daniel. "Here," as Bousset observes, (in chap. 2 and 7) "the vaticinium ex eventu or the running back to the past becomes a means of understanding and defining the clarity that the present has within the grand plan of God for the world."[3]

But what has all the foregoing to do with the book of the Apocalypse of John, which is of course an apocalpyse, but not pseudonymous or allegedly written by some man of the distant past but by a writer who identifies himself as a contemporary with his readers (1:9-10; 22:8-9)? The reason for relating the vaticinium ex eventu to John's Apocalypse is to be found in the problem of the relationship of the letters to the seven Churches (chap. 2-3) to the rest of the prophetic book. On the subject of this relationship there is great uncertainty in research. For the letters themselves and for their relationship to the rest of the book of the Apocalypse there have been various opinions so far, but no consensus has been reached. The idea I am putting forward is that if we take what is contained in the letters as equivalent to the apocalyptic vaticinium ex eventu, then we have a more concrete and plausible answer to the problem of how chaps. 1-3 of the Apocalypse are related to what follows in the rest of the book.

On the function of the letters in the economy of the book of the Apocalypse one finds in the bibliography a wide spectrum of opinions, which evidently shows our uncertainty. Dibelius, for instance, remarks: "Here we have a familiar literary type for heavenly letters . . . . writings fallen from heaven, or revealed in a vision . . . widespread not only in wars of modern times but also in antiquity. Quite in accordance with this category, the seer writes not to the churches but to their 'angels.' The heavenly Christ deals with heavenly agents of the Christian churches. But what he dictates only refers to a limited extent to the individual addressees . . ."[4]

---

[3]Ibid.
[4]M. Dibelius, A Fresh Approach to the New Testament and Early Christian Literature (New York: Scribner, 1936; reprinted, Westport, CT: Greenwood Press, 1979) 125.

VATICINIUM EX EVENTU IN THE APOCALYPSE

Other scholars, however, supported the view that each letter was written and addressed to some specific Church as an introductory note to the prophecy that followed, before the book had taken its present form. In this sense the letters contain historically reliable information about the Churches in the province of Asia. It was R. H. Charles in his memorable commentary on the Apocalypse who argued that the particular letters were written before the book as a whole, and that John adjusted them and addressed them to all the churches, when he wrote the Apocalypse, of which they are now an integral part.[5] F. B. Clogg, commenting on Charles' opinion, remarked that whatever doubts such an opinion might leave, it is clear that in each letter the writer expressed himself with immediate knowledge of each Church separately, while it is equally clear that his message was addressed to the ecumenical church.[6]

For others, the letters, in a wider sense, belong to a form of Christian exhortation, which, as is commonly accepted, functions as an auxiliary form quite normally alongside the apocalyptic visions about the future. The literary analysis of the letters, particularly of their concluding refrains, carried out by Spitta,[7] substantiated the view that the information given in the letters is both specific and general at the same time. As the content of the letters is concerned, they have no immediate relation to the specific chapters that follow--enigmatic and obscure subjects; only in the last chapters of the Apocalypse there appear subjects corresponding to those we have in the letters. Also, the introductory phrases in the letters correspond to the content of the letter that each time follows, and they are in tune with the general introduction to the book in its present form (1:4-8; 1:10-20). These and many more arguments, such as the reminiscence of Synoptic sayings in the letters, or the identification of Jesus with the Spir-

---

[5]R. H. Charles, The Apocalypse of John (ICC; Edinburgh: T. & T. Clark), vol. I.

[6]F. B. Clogg, note on p. 1372 in The Abingdon Bible Commentary, ed. Frederick Carl Eiselen (New York: Abingdon, 1929).

[7]Friedrich Spitta, Die Offenbarung Johannes (Halle: Waisenhaus, 1889) 32.

it, are put forward by Spitta for promoting the view
that the letters, in their present form, come from
the "redaction" of the book, whose purpose was to
thus make the book as a whole ecclesiastical.

Many scholars have expressed the view that, by
writing to the seven Churches, John addresses the
ecumenical church. Consequently, in the letters he
describes general problems, present in all the churches
of his time: faithful churches, compromising churches,
and those doomed to destruction. These three types
of churches can be found anywhere in the Christian
East at the time of John. The letters are therefore
a composition of John the Prophet, and they were never
meant to be addressed to the concrete addresses, the
seven specific churches of Asia Minor. Bousset, for
instance, among others, believed that the Apocalypse
was from the beginning a vision about the future of
the churches. If there are in the particular communities situations such as those touched upon by the
letters, these are nothing more than typical of the
whole church.[8]

On the other hand scholars like Edgar Goodspeed
have worked out their theories on the Corpus Paulinum
which are of great interest to our argument here.[9]
According to these theories the number of the Pauline
epistles in its first edition as a corpus was seven,
and was headed by the letter to the Ephesians--a post-
pauline writing, but one that did duty as an introduction to the theological and particularly the ecclesio-
logical thinking of the Apostle. This edition of
the Pauline Corpus immediately found imitators, and
among them several scholars mention the Apocalypse
of John.[10] The supporters of such a pauline influence
do not deny the historicity of the information given
by the letters of the Apocalypse, though they admit
they don't know on what grounds the writer of the
Apocalypse chose those particular seven churches and
not others; more so if he even wanted through them
to address the whole church.

---

[8]Cf. Bousset, _Offenbarung_, 236f.
[9]Edgar J. Goodspeed, _New Solutions to New Testament
Problems_ (Chicago: University of Chicago, 1927).
[10]John Knox, _IB_, 9 (1954) 356; Martin Rist, _IB_ 12 (1957)
367-8; Albert Barnett, _Paul Becomes a Literary Influ-
ence_, (Chicago: University of Chicago, 1941) 41-42.

VATICINIUM EX EVENTU IN THE APOCALYPSE

There is no doubt that this problem cannot be answered with certainty; what looks more certain is that the number seven has to do either with the Corpus Paulinum, or with some numerical theology in which the number seven expresses the wholeness, the totality of the Christians (cf. among others, 1:4f) or perhaps something else: the last hebdomad of history after the coming of the Messiah (cf. e.g. the hebdomad in the genealogy of Matthew); or again something wider and more mysterious ("And as I turned I saw seven golden candles and in the midst of them" 1:12; ". . . and having on his right hand seven stars" vs. 16; "the seven stars are angels of the seven churches and the candles are the seven churches" vs. 20b; the seven seals, seven pots, seven bugles.

We come now to the formulation of our proposal: (a) The final form of the book of the Apocalypse, the book as we have it now, clearly and undoubtedly addresses its prophetic words to the "seven churches"; (b) the prophetic part of the book is preceded in the form of exhortation by a description of the state of things in the "seven churches." Even if we accept that the particularities ascribed to each church do not belong exclusively to it but rather express general problems of the whole church, it is absolutely certain that what we have in chaps. 1-3 is revelation of God to the prophet, which enables him to see, when "he became in the spirit" (v 16), what is the real situation within the "seven churches", and in extension within Christianity as a whole. Why did these revelatory statements have to precede the great prophecy which starts with chap. 4? Why should chapters 2-3 offer as revelations things that anybody could have observed personally or have known about through hearsay, just before the mystery-laden prophetic vision of the future following in chap. 4? To me the right answer might be that by doing so, John employs a form of vaticinium ex eventu similar though not identical to the technique which is traditional in apocalyptic literature. The writer of the Apocalypse is eponymous, and identifies himself clearly and unmistakably. If he can induce his readers to give their attention to and their faith in the mysterious prophecy which follows, this can be done by emphasizing: God knows very well what is happening now in the churches; God knows as well what awaits the churches in the future. The revelation about the now which anyone can easily know about either through personal experience or through information, takes in John the place of the argument the <u>vaticinium ex eventu</u> had for the reader of the Jewish apocalypse.

If we accept such a proposal we are in a better position to understand not only the combination of such widely different texts as chaps. 2-3 amd chap 4f., but also why John needed as a starting point for his prophecy, a concrete reality, immediately recognizable by all, wrapped up as revelation. This reality is offered to him by the concrete seven church- es of Asia, whose number gives them an ecumenicity, corresponding to the purpose of the prophecy as a whole. In this way the writer had at his disposal something concrete and general at the same time. This argument is confirmed by the closing section of the book, chap. 22:6, etc., where there is no mention at all of the "seven churches." Whereas the book of the Apocalypse starts so spectacularly with the "seven" churches (chaps. 1-3), the closing section of the book has forgotten them completely, and the "churches" are mentioned in general: "I Jesus have sent my angel to witness these to you throughout the churches" (22:6). The concrete was necessary at the beginning of the book as an encouragement of faith--a function similar to <u>vaticinium ex eventu</u> in the Jewish apocalyptic; but this concrete element, after fulfill- ing its function, is forgotten in the rest of the book; inside the body of the prophecy and at the epi- logue of the book there is no mention whatever of the "seven churches" of Asia.

CHAPTER SIX

"HOLY LAW" IN PAUL AND IGNATIUS

Robert M. Grant

In 1969 Ernst Käsemann reprinted a study he had produced 15 years earlier on "Sentences of Holy Law in the New Testament." This study[1] started from a passage in 1 Corinthians (3:17) where Paul "lays down the law" in regard to God's future action as related to man's present disobedience. The presence of the same verb in protasis and apodosis points to an implicit logical connection. Käsemann then went on to discuss other examples of the same form and, finally, related forms of expression. About half of his examples came from 1 Corinthians, which as it happens was the favorite epistle of Ignatius of Antioch. Though none of the verses cited by Käsemann turns up in the Ignatian letters, the form itself does appear and may point toward an important aspect of the remarkable similarity between Paul and Ignatius.

Käsemann's first example, from 1 Cor 3:17, reads thus: "If anyone destroys the temple of God, God will destroy him."[2] He compares the language with Gen 9:6, "He who pours out human blood will be poured out in place of his blood" (cf. Rev 13:10), as well as with Aeschylus, Choeph. 312f. (actually 309-14). "For word of hate let word of hate be said ... and let murderous blow repay murderous blow. The thrice-aged precept says that 'he who does something must suffer it.'" With the "precept" we may also compare the five gnomic citations on this topic supplied by

---

[1] New Testament Questions of Today (Philadelphia: Fortress Press, 1969) 66-81.
[2] J. Weiss had already noted the "erneute Verschärfung des Tons" at this point (Der erste Korintherbrief, MeyerK, 9th ed.; Göttingen: Vandenhoeck & Ruprecht, 1970 [1910] 86).

Theophilus of Antioch.3   These are as follows: (1)
"He who does something must also suffer" (Aeschylus),4
(2)   "For he who does something should also suffer"
(Pindar),5 (3)   "Suffer patiently, for you were glad
to act.   It is lawful to mistreat an enemy when you
have caught him"   (Euripides),6 (4)   "I think it is
a man's part to treat enemies badly" (Euripides),7
and (5)   "One great thing I know, to repay with dire
evils him who does me harm" (Archilochus).8   The appearance of the first two quotations in Stobaeus shows
that we are on the level of school education in morality.

Käsemann next provides a good example from a
context of Christian prophecy.   "If anyone thinks
he is a prophet or a spiritual, he must recognize
that what I am writing to you is a command of the
Lord; if anyone is ignorant, he will be ignored" (1
Cor 14:37-38).9   Analogously, "if anyone does not
love the Lord, let him be anathema" (16:22).   And
this resembles Gal 1:9, "if anyone preaches a different
gospel to you than the one you received, let him be
anathema."

The whole passage beginning with 1 Cor 5:3 depicts
Paul passing a judgment and delivering sentences of
holy law, while 2 Cor 9:6 and Rom 2:12 show a slightly
different form being used for the same purpose.   The
same kind of expression turns up in Mark 8:38 and
elsewhere; one might add a reference to the Golden
Rule, whether negative or positive.   What is at least
as significant as the "holy law" aspect is the "justice," "equity," or "retribution" aspect.   One good
(or bad) turn deserves another, and will receive it.
The idea recurs in the synoptic savings cited by Poly-

3Ad Autol., ii., 37.
4Augustus Nauck, Tragicorum Graecorum Fragmenta (Lipsiae: Teubner, 1889), Frg. 456, evidently a variant
of Choeph. 313; the anthology of Stobaeus i. 3. 24.
5Nem. iv. 51-52; Stobaeus iv. 5. 8.
6Frg. 1090-91 (Nauck).
7Frg. 1092 (Nauck).
8Theodorus Bergk, ed., Poetae Lyrici Graeci, pars II
(Lipsiae: Teubner, 1915) frg. 65 [75], 400.
9Weiss, Der erste Korintherbrief, 343, spoke of the
expression as "sehr energisch" and noted that "der
Gedanke ist sehr kraftvoll."

carp (Phil. 2:3). "Judge not, so that you be not
judged; forgive and it will be forgiven you; be merci-
ful, and mercy will be shown you; with the measure
you use, it will be measured to you."

J. B. Lightfoot was well aware of this phenomenon
in the letters of Ignatius and elsewhere. In his
commentary on Ignatius, Smyrn. 5, he adduced 2 Timothy
2:12: "if we deny (him) he will deny us," and also
mentioned Gal 4:9, "knowing God, or rather being known
by him." There were also nine passages in the letters
of Ignatius where a similar form turned up. These
were Trall. 5, Rom. 8, Phld. 10-11, Smyrn. 5,10, Pol.
inscr., 3, 6. W. Bauer places his list at Eph. 2:2;
it also includes Trall. 5:2, Rom. 8:1, Phld. 10:1-2,
11:1, Smyrn. 5:1, 10:2, Pol. inscr., 6:1. Bauer leaves
out Lightfoot's Smyrn. 3 and adds 1 Cor 13:12 ("knowing
as I have been known" (by God) and 1 John 4:10 ("not
that we loved God but that he loved us"), 11 ("if
God loved us we ought to love one another"), and 19
("we love because he first loved us"). He refers
to the "Gedankenspiel, dass das Aktivum mit dem Passiv-
um verbindet" (not the case with all his examples)
but does not explain why it is used. In my own commentary (on Pol. 6:1) I omitted Trall. 5:2 because it
is different in intention and added Eph. 21:1, Smyrn.
9:1, 9:2, Pol. 1:2, 6:2. (I should have included
Phld. 7:2.) My list illustrates Ignatius' idea of
"reciprocity," not just a grammatical peculiarity.

I reproduce my examples with additions checked
from the similar study of David Aune.[10] (1) "Crocus
has refreshed me, may the Father refresh him" (Eph.
2:1). (2) "It is appropriate in every way to glorify
Jesus Christ, who has glorified you" (Eph. 2:2, from
Aune). (3) "Remember me as Jesus Christ remembers
you" (Eph. 21:1). (4) "Desire it so that you may
be desired" (Rom. 8:1). (5) "Be imitators of Jesus
Christ as he was of his Father" (Phld. 7:2). (6)
"Glorify his name and you too will be glorified"
(Phld. 10:1-2). (7) "You received them as (may) the
Lord (receive) you" (or, "as the Lord received you")
(Phld. 11:1). (8) "Byrrhus was sent as a mark of
honor, the Lord will honor them" (Phld. 11:2, from
Aune). (9) "He who honors the bishop has been honored

[10]Prophecy in Early Christianity and the Ancient Mediterranean World (Grand Rapids: Eerdmans, 1983) 294-296.

by God" (Smyrn. 9:1). (10) "You refreshed me, may
Jesus Christ refresh you" (Smyrn. 9:2).[11] (11) "You
did not despise my bonds, Jesus Christ will not despise
you" (Smyrn. 10:2). (12) "Help all men as the Lord
helps you" (Pol. 1:2). (11) "We must endure all things
for God so that he may put up with us" (Pol. 3:1).
(12) "Be patient as God is with you" (Pol. 6:2).

Not all of these may immediately suggest the
presence of "holy law." Many remind us of the prover-
bial wisdom Ignatius thought Polycarp was worthy to
receive (Polycarp evidently agreed, Phil. 3:2). Examples from Pol. 1 are these: "Help all men, as the
Lord also helped you. Suffer all in love, as you
indeed do.... Where the toil is greatest the gain
is great." We recall, however, that Ignatius could
make declarations to the churches "with a loud voice,
with God's own voice" and inspired by the Spirit
could demand that Christians pay attention to the
bishop and the presbytery and deacons. One thing
the Spirit said was this: "Be imitators of Jesus
Christ as he was also of his Father" (Phld. 7:1-2)
--a sentence expressing "reciprocity." Indeed the
whole message of the Spirit should be cited, since
at least for Ignatius and his supporters it was indubi-
tably an expression of "holy law."

Ignatius cried out, "Pay attention to the bishop
and the presbytery and deacons." The Spirit preached,
saying this, (1) "Do nothing apart from the bishop,
(2) keep your flesh as a temple of God, (3a) love
unity, (3b) flee from divisions, (4) be imitators
of Jesus Christ, as he was of his Father." Ignatius
himself obeyed the divine call: "I performed my task
as a man created for unity." His "cry" presumably
sums up the central message given by the Spirit, which
we now consider in its four parts. As I pointed out
in my commentary, the ideas are paralleled either
in other Ignatian letters or in 1 Corinthians. (Compare Ignatius' own similar injunctions in Magn. 6:1-2.)
(1) The importance of the bishop is a central concern
of all the Ignatian letters, notably in Magn. 4:1,
7:1, Trall. 2:2, 7:2, Smyrn. 8:1-2. It is ultimately
the subject of divine revelation, according to Eph.

---

[11]Here Aune (Prophecy) adds comparable expressions from
Smyrn. 6:1, 5:1, and 2:1, but they do not seem quite
so "reciprocal" as the others.

20:2. (2) While the idea of keeping the flesh as a temple of God also occurs in 2 Clem. 9:3, it seems to be significantly related to the "holy law" of 1 Corinthians 3:17, as cited above. (3a) Ignatius insists on unity throughout his letters, while (3b) fleeing from divisions can be found in Phld. 2:1, Smyrn. 7:2. (4) To imitate Jesus Christ as he imitated his Father recalls 1 Corinthians 11:1, where Paul asks for imitation of himself as he imitates Christ; but in this context the imitation is to be more specific. Ignatius sets it forth in Magn. 13:2: "Be subject to the bishop and to one another (cf. Eph 5:21, 1 Pet 5:5), as Jesus Christ was subject to the Father and the apostles were subject to Christ and the Father ..." This appears to be the basic content of Ignatius' "holy law." But it is difficult to disengage particular passages from the letters as a whole. There is no reason to assume that sentences beginning "it is fitting" (πρέπον) or "it is profitable" (χρήσιμον) are less authoritative than others; Ignatius says he is writing to the Romans, for example, "in accordance with the mind of God" (8:3).

It is thus difficult to see Käsemann's case confirmed in the case of the Ignatian bishop, who seems to have assumed the role of the Pauline prophet and apostle. (Note that for Ignatius the prophets are those of the Old Testament, and he himself is no apostle, as he says.) Perhaps the difference is due to the difference between an apostle and a bishop. Perhaps, on the other hand, it is due to difficulties in the theory of "holy law" as a literary form.[12]

First, we should consider a few other "reciprocity" passages, beginning with the Pauline epistles and noting that some of the passages cited by various commentators already suggest that the classification "holy law" has little to do with the form but is based primarily on the content. What of the Gal 4:9 passage cited by Lightfoot ("knowing God, or rather being known by him")? This is much the same as 1 Cor 13:12, cited by Bauer ("then I shall know as I have been known"). And this verse leads us back to 1 Cor 8:3: "if anyone loves God, he has been known by him," where the form of expression has been noted to be in the

---

[12]Compare the criticisms of Aune, Prophecy, 237-240.

proximity of Hellenistic mysticism.[13]

And on the other hand, when Paul is making definite decisions about excommunication (1 Cor 5) or remarriage (1 Cor 7) or diet (1 Cor 10), his commands are just as much "holy law" as anything cited by Käsemann, though the formulas, if they are formulas, do not appear. In 1 Cor 5:4-5 he refers to a meeting of his spirit with the Corinthians "to deliver such a man to Satan." In 1 Cor 7:10-12 he differentiates what the Lord commands to those who are married from what he commands to "the others," but gives definite orders in both cases, with much use of imperatives. He has no command of the Lord on the subject of "virgins" but gives his own judgment as a trustworthy follower of the Lord. He also gives his judgment about "widows" and states that he too has the Spirit of God. As for diet, he argues rather discursively in more than two chapters before providing a definite decree (and discussing one special case) in 1 Cor 10:25-29. "Eat everything sold in the meat-market, making no distinctions on account of conscience; for 'the earth is the Lord's and the fulness thereof.'" If some unbeliever invites you and you want to go, eat everything set before you, making no distinctions on account of conscience. But if someone says to you, 'This is meat sacrificed to idols,' do not eat, on account of the informer and conscience, I mean his, not yours." The conclusion, "Imitate me as I imitate Christ" surely makes this as "holy" a law as any other.

As for the Ignatian examples, four involve protases with aorist verbs which state the ground for expecting a future blessing (nos. 1, 6, 8, 9). Four more begin with imperatives that look forward to a similar benefit (nos. 2, 4, 10, 12; in three of these cases there is no verb in the apodosis). Finally, there are three examples -- the closest in form to "holy law"--with imperative verbs, followed by passives in two cases or an active in one instance (nos. 3, 8, 11; see also 7). The last four deserve quotation in this context. "Desire it, so that (ἵνα) you also may be desired" (Rom. 8:1). "... Glorify the name... you yourselves will be glorified" (Phld. 10:1-2, an implicit imperative followed by a future passive indic-

---

[13]Cf. J. Weiss, Der erste Korintherbrief, 217-218.

ative). "We must endure all things ... so that (ἵνα) God may also endure us" (Pol. 3:1). The other example occurs in Smyrn. 9:1: "he who honors" (a participle with the force of an imperative) "has been honored by God" (surely proleptic in force, since he will be honored in the future as well). If there were such a thing as "holy law" determined by form, it seems likely that the last four examples could be so classified. On the whole, however, it seems more likely that the "holy law" form never existed, even though something like holy law (what else is the Didache?) undoubtedly did.

If I were writing an article on "holy law" (though I do not believe in the multiplication of categories or literary forms praeter necessitatem), I should begin with Paul's explicit statement that "the law is holy, and the commandment is holy and just and good" (Rom 7:15). What law? Presumably the decalogue, viewed as perverted by sin but as Christ's law to be observed (Gal 6:2, cf. 1 Cor 9:21), and summed up in "You shall love your neighbor as yourself" (Gal 5:14; cf. Rom 13:8-10). That, if anything is, is identifiably "holy law."

Then I should consider the kinds of laws classified in books of inscriptions as leges sacrae and their parallels in the Pauline epistles. Here the prime example is undoubtedly a liturgical rubric in 1 Cor 14:40, the last word about prophets and prophecy. "Everything is to be done decently and in order (εὐσχημόνως καὶ κατὰ τάξιν). Exactly the same adverbs appear in regulations for the public mysteries at Andania in Messenia in 92 B.C.[14] It is worth noting that Weiss mentioned the inscription in a footnote after stating that "P. scheint hier eine feste Formel zu brauchen;" while Lietzmann refrained from mentioning the parallel at all. W. G. Kümmel, revising the commentary, pointed to Paul's expressions as "merkwürdig profan" and noted the parallel. But why could not a regulation for public worship be "heilig" and "profan" at the same time?

---

[14]Wilhelm Dittenberger, Sylloge inscriptionum Graecarum (3rd ed.; Hildesheim: G. Olms, 1960 [1915]) 736, X.

CHAPTER SEVEN

UTTERANCE AND EXEGESIS:
BIBLICAL INTERPRETATION IN THE MONTANIST CRISIS

Dennis E. Groh

The freedom with which a number of New Testament writers cited the words of the Septuagint text has encouraged more recent scholarship to explore other avenues of explanation for this phenomenon beyond the appeal to citation from memory or from varied text-types.[1] Building on Stendahl's observation that a number of Old Testament quotations in the New Testament show the incorporation of conscious interpretive principles into the wording of the text cited, Ellis suggested that some of these quotations should be considered to be the work of Christian prophets speaking both in an ecstatic mode (e.g., I Cor 12-14) and in a mode explanatory of the Holy Spirit's disclosures (e.g., Acts 21:11).[2] It is these two particular modes of prophetic speaking that I wish to explore in this article--prophetic ecstasy and prophetic disclosure as they affect selected Old Testament citations in the late second-century controversy[3] which we call the Montanist controversy. As we shall see, these two prophetic modes made their impact on citation and exegesis in this early Christian controversy and may be able to contribute, by analogy if not by direct

---

[1]Cf. E. Earle Ellis, Paul's Use of the Old Testament (Edinburgh: Oliver and Boyd, 1957) 18-20 and Prophecy and Hermeneutic in Early Christianity (Eerdmans: Grand Rapids, Michigan, 1978. German original, Tübingen: J. C. B. Mohr, 1978) 147-148.
[2]Ellis, Paul's Use, 111.
[3]Eusebius' approximations on the beginning date of the controversy (C. 170 A.D.) are to be preferred to Epiphanius' earlier dating (Timothy D. Barnes, "The Chronology of Montanism," Journal of Theological Studies, n.s. 21 [1970] 405-406).

filiation, to some recent New Testament debates on "charismatic exegesis."

The term charismatic exegesis was coined by Ginsberg to describe the activity of the Teacher of Righteousness in the Qumran Habakkuk Commentary.[4] The term refers to a specific kind of biblical interpretation which provides the raz or key to the hidden meanings of the sacred text's now contemporary eschatological import as revealed to an inspired interpreter.[5] Ellis had attempted to show the kinship between the pneumatics of I Corinthians and the meskalim at Qumran,[6] as well as the parallel between the Qumran exegetes and Acts 13:16-41.[7] David Hill has raised questions, particularly about the latter parallel, on the grounds that the title "instructors" and their activity at Qumran more closely approximate the role of the teacher in Qumran and, perhaps, the New Testament.[8]

It is precisely our paucity of knowledge about the role and activity of the teacher in early Christianity and the absence of any clear indication that Christian prophets carried out eschatological exegesis that led David Aune to suggest "... that exegesis of the Old Testament, whether simply eschatological or both charismatic and eschatological, was the primary province of the teacher."[9] Aune did allow that there was some evidence of charismatic exegesis of the Old Testament in the New--for example, the exegetical pattern of "mystery/revelation" in Rom 16:25-26 bore a more than "superficial" resemblance to the raz/pesher

---

[4]David E. Aune, Prophecy in Early Christianity and the Ancient Mediterranean World (Grand Rapids, Michigan: Eerdmans, 1983) 339.
[5]Aune, Prophecy 339 and lit. cit.
[6]Prophecy and Hermeneutic, 56.
[7]Prophecy and Hermeneutic, 134.
[8]New Testament Prophecy (New Foundations Theological Library; Atlanta: John Knox, 1979) 105-106. Hill does allow the cautious possibility that Hebrews' striking methodological parallels to some of the 1QpHab might favor a Christian prophetic authorship of Hebrews: New Testament Prophecy, 144.
[9]Aune, Prophecy 345; cf. 344 for his rejection of Ellis' λέγει κύριος formula as indicative of early Christian prophetic activity.

patterns of passages of Daniel and the Qumran Habakkuk Commentary.[10] But he was unable to find a sure Christian example of charismatic exegesis of the Old Testament because of the absence of formal (and formulaic) indications of prophetic activity, noting the inability to establish the link between exegetical patterns and prophetic activity and the assumed (but underinformed) picture of the teacher as the practioner of Old Testament interpretation.[11]

Thus we are at something of a very well-informed impasse in our discussions of the role the Christian prophet played in citation/interpretation/exegesis of the Old Testament. On the one hand there exists a well-researched suspicion, and some small evidence, that Christian prophets played an active part in the interpretation of Old Testament passages.[12] Newer ways of defining and categorizing, and so, of studying, Christian prophecy from functional, situational, and history of religions perspectives have appeared.[13] On the other hand, the evidence for such activity within the New Testament itself is sparse, limited by an absence of easily identifiable prophetic claims[14]; and, of course, the evidence precludes any systematic treatment of the claims of "true" and "false" prophets, such as occur in Hermas' Eleventh Mandate[15] and the Montanist sources.

It is to the latter, the Montanist sources, that

---

[10]Aune, _Prophecy_, 345.

[11]Aune, _Prophecy_, 344-345.

[12]And perhaps in the Jesus tradition: cf. M. Eugene Boring, _Sayings of the Risen Jesus. Christian Prophecy in the Synoptic Tradition_ (Cambridge: University Press, 1982) 180.

[13]Hill, _New Testament Prophecy_, 7-9 (for some functional definitions); Aune, _Prophecy_, for a look at a very thorough history of religions approach. For a situational study, see J. Reiling, _Hermas and Christian Prophecy. A Study of the Eleventh Mandate_ (Leiden: Brill, 1973).

[14]Boring, _Sayings_, 83, also reminds us that in our best example of first-century Christian prophecy (Revelation), there is no clear indication of the psychic state of the prophet; and Boring hesitates to designate the descriptions we do have "ecstasy."

[15]Reiling, _Hermas_, 47, 85, etc.

GROH

I wish to turn. It is precisely at such an impasse
that this controversy may be able to contribute to
phenomenological discussions of the mode of Christian
prophets as they relate to Scriptural interpretation.
I am proposing an examination of the relationship
between utterance and exegesis in this controversy
by the use of soundings in a couple key passages.

While it has been obligatory for scholars studying
Christian prophesy to mention and examine the Montanist
oracles, the sources have not been examined till now
to see if they throw any light on the problem. The
period of Montanism has been characterized as marking
(if not causing) the decline of prophecy,[16] and we
prefer to examine the origins of phenomena. But in
keeping with my training as a patristics scholar and
Professor Saunders' long involvement in the history
of scriptural interpretation, another look is needed.

I

From a scholarly standpoint, Montanism has not
commended itself to students interested in charismatic
exegesis for several reasons.

(1)Lists of authentic oracles have been published
repeatedly without the accompanying exegetical commentary
contained in the preserving sources -- both catholic
and Montanist exegetical polemic.[17] Consequently
most scholars have never seen the exegetical debate
these oracles called forth and, in some cases perhaps,
participated in.

(2)Because the controversy turned theologically
and exegetically on the question of whether or not
a "true" prophet speaks in an ecstatic state or mode,
scholars have tended to view this controversy as the
struggle with a Hellenistic-type religious experience

[16]Hill, New Testament Prophecy, 190, for references.
[17]G. Nathaniel Bonwetsch, Die Geschichte des Montanismus
(Erlangen: Andreas Deichert, 1881) 197-200, though
full texts were published in his later Texte zur Geschichte des Montanismus (Kleine Texte; Bonn: Marcus
und E. Weber, 1914). Kurt Aland, Kirchengeschichtliche
Entwürfe (Gütersloh: Gerd Mohn, 1960), 143-146.
Aland's list of the oracles is reproduced in translation
by Aune, Prophecy, 314-315.

which was trying to make an incursion upon biblical modes of prophecy. Patristics scholars who have more recently examined Phrygian Montanism in its Asia Minor setting have pointed to the influence of biblical books like Revelation and have denied that the pagan cultural experience shaped the Montanist mantic fundamentally.[18] Thus there has been a tendency in recent research to deemphasize the bifurcation of Hellenistic prophetic and biblical (Jewish) prophetic modes of speaking. Both Reiling and Aune have made clear that discussions about prophecy in the A.D. centuries are carried on with some considerable knowledge of wider antique discussions of the psychology and interpretation of oracles, dreams, and visions.[19] Thus when Philo names prophecy the highest form of ecstasy (Heres. 249-258), he knows Hellenistic traditions and may incorporate them; but he also derives this from Genesis 20:7 (LXX) and 15:12.[20] He should not be set aside from (and certainly not over and against) biblical understandings of prophecy.

Moreover, Aune has shown the Hellenistic writers knew a class of naturally inspired (mantic) prophets and a class of wise (skilled) interpreters of signs, dreams, etc. -- a distinction between natural divination and technical divination. When early Christian exegetes like Hippolytus fought for the trained non-ecstatic (but still inspired) exegete's primacy in scriptural interpretation[21] -- what Joseph W. Trigg once called (of Origen) the "charismatic intellectual" -- the great orthodox exegete had not escaped from pagan

---

[18]Aune, Prophecy, 313. Heinz Kraft, "Die altkirchliche Prophetie und die Entstehung des Montanismus," TZ 11 (1955) 271: "Wenn wir an die Rolle denken, die die Johannesapokalypse bei den Montanisten gespielt hat, denn ist ganz unvorstellbar, das der Montanismus ein synkretistisches Gemisch aus Christentum und phrygischen kultur war." Cf. also the excellent discussion by Frederick Charles Klawiter, "The New Prophecy in Early Christianity. The Origin, Nature and Development of Montanism, A.D. 165-220" (Ph.D. dissertation, University of Chicago, 1975) 164-165.
[19]Reiling, Hermas, 26, 41; Aune, Prophecy, 17.
[20]Samuel Sandmel, Philo's Place in Judaism. A Study of Conceptions of Abraham in Jewish Literature (Augmented ed.; New York: Ktav, 1971) 177.
[21]In Daniel IV. 18-20.

categories into biblical ones. He chose a Hellenistic
category more consonant with his understanding of
the biblical. All of this suggests that while we
cannot dismiss Hellenistic situational categories
in discussing questions of the modes of prophecy,
their presence or absence is not automatically an
indication of degree of fidelity to the biblical modes.[22]

(3)Finally, scholars have not looked as rigorously
at the Montanist sources as they might because they
do not expect a charismatic prophet to quote scripture.
Thus Hans von Campenhausen wrote a decade ago concerning
the Montanist prophets:

> Again, their utterances likewise make no appeal
> to Scripture, and contain not one single instance
> of explicit quotation.[23]

His statement is not any truer now than it was then,
and I will be exploring this dimension a bit later
in this article. But this expectation frequently
is carried through the edited sources at every level
-- from that of the critical edition through that
of the abbreviated hand-lists of the oracles. One
example will suffice here. Maximilla has an oracle,
preserved by Eusebius, which reads:

> I am driven like a wolf from the sheep.
> I am not a wolf.
> I am word (ῥῆμα) and spirit and power.[24]

The oracle contains a possible interpretive citation
of the kind that scholars have been searching for
from I Cor.2:4 [25]:

---

[22]Cf. Aune, Prophecy, 17.
[23]The Formation of the Christian Bible (Philadelphia:
Fortress, 1972) 222; cf. 224f. A promise to expand
on this criticism of Campenhausen in my review of
this work ("Hans von Campenhausen on Canon. Positions
and Problems," Interpretation 28 [1974] 340) was not
published. This article attempts to fulfill that
promise.
[24]Eusebius, H.E. V. 16.17 (GCS 9,1,p.466,ed. Schwartz).
[25]J. Stevenson, A New Eusebius (London: S.P.C.K., 1960)
113.

and my speech (logos) and my message were not
in plausible words of wisdom, but in demonstration
of spirit and power.

The oracle is continuously reproduced without so much
as even speculation about the possible scriptural
allusion,[26] thus reinforcing our presuppositions about
the Montanist prophets' distance from scripture.
The oracles therefore need to be reexamined without
bringing such presuppositions to the texts. Before
we do so, we need to turn to a brief examination of
the source which preserves many of our extant authentic
oracles.

II

Our chronolgically earliest sources on Montanism
are preserved by Eusebius of Caesarea in Book V of
his Ecclesiastical History. The second century anti-
Montanist sources he preserves, the most important
of which is an "Anonymous" writing standing closest
in time to the beginnings of the controversy,[27] tell
us the basic facts and immediate consequences of the
outbreak of the "new prophecy" but little about the
substantive matters discussed. We know that assemblies
were held in Asia Minor to evaluate the validity of
the Montanist claims and that these ruled against
the "new prophecy."[28] We learn that a tractarian
literary battle was waged primarily (but not exclusively)
from the "catholic" side, in which refutations flew
back and forth; but we possess only brief notices
from those tracts.[29] We know that both sides exchanged
insults: Montanists called the catholics "murders
of the prophets" (cf. Matt 23:34); the catholic party
launched attacks on the character of the three prophets
(Montanus, Maximilla, and Priscilla) and their followers.[30] We read also that in its Phrygian origins
already some attempt was made to claim a "succession

---

[26]Oracle no. 16 (Aland, Kirchengeschichtliche, 146;
Aune, Prophecy, 315).
[27]Wilhelm Schepelern, Der Montanismus und die phrygischen
Kulte (Tübingen: J.C.B. Mohr, 1929) 4.
[28]Eusebius, H.E. V.16.10.
[29]Catholics: Anonymous (Eusebius, H.E., V.16.1-3);
Miltiades (V.17.5); Apollonius (V.18.1). Montanists
(V.17.1).
[30]Eusebius, H.E. V.16.12 and 18.1-10, respectively.

of prophets" in line with those mentioned in Acts
and that the Montanists may have claimed other prophets
-- in both Old and New (Testaments) -- for their method
of prophesying.[31]   And we know without a doubt that
the controversy turned from the beginning on the cardinal
hinge of the relation of "ecstasy" to true prophecy.
On this point both catholic and Montanist sources
are clear.[32]

The earliest sources leave us in the dark as
to how the Montanist claim to speak ecstatically,
in a tradition which encompassed biblical prophets,
was worked out exegetically and how the catholic exegetes
countered it.   But the very late second- or very early
third-century source (c. A.D. 200) on which Epiphanius
relied for almost his entire account in Panarion haer. 48
preserves exactly these points for us.   Significantly,
this source preserves a number of our most reliable
oracles.[33]   Lipsius had already signaled the antiquity
and integrity of this source, marking its boundaries
off at 48.2-13.[34]   Voigt concurred with the ending
point, but showed the original source began in the
middle of the first paragraph, running through paragraph
13 and thereby excluding 48.14-49.1 from the original
source.[35]   Thus the original source ran from the middle
of 48.1 through 48.13, but excluded 48.14-49.3.[36]
It was an important exclusion; for with Panarion haer.
49.1 Epiphanius begins his shakey and muddled account
of the Quintillians.   Unfortunately, Lipsius could
not quite decide whether a famous and often quoted
Montanist oracle which predicted the New Jerusalem

---

[31]Eusebius, H.E. V.17.3. Cf. H. Kraft, "Die altkirchliche
Prophetie," 263.
[32]Cf. Eusebius, H.E. V.16.7 and 17.1; for the Montanist
position, see the text below.
[33]Aland, Kirchengeschichte, nn. 3-6, 13-15.
[34]D. Richard Adelbert Lipsius, Zur Quellenkritik des
Epiphanios (Wien: Braumüller, 1865) 225.
[35]Heinrich Gisbert Voigt, Eine Verschollene Urkunde
des antimontanistischen Kampfes. Die Berichte des
Epiphanius über die Kataphryger und Quintillianer
(Leipzig: Fr. Richter, 1891) 114. Bonwetsch, Die
Geschichte, 36, followed Lipsius.
[36](GCS, Holl ed.) 48.1.4, line 5 (beginning with the
words δεῖ χάρισμα δέχομαι)-48.13.8 (pp. 220-238). Cf.
Voigt, Urkunde, 129.

would descend at Pepuza (in 49.1.2-3) came from oral
tradition or the early source Epiphanius had employed
in 48.37   The net result was that scholars continued
to publish it as one of the authentic oracles although
Voigt had clearly shown that it belonged to a later
and inferior source.38

The removal of the prediction that the New Jerusalem
would descend in Pepuza to a less credible grade of
source-testimony also removes one of the key disagreements between Tertullian's Montanist community's apocalyptic conviction that the city would descend in Pales-
tine and its projected landing place in original Phyrgian
tradition. A considerable block to Tertullian's information on Montanism is also therefore removed.39
Tertullian's testimony, as we shall see, is exceedingly
important for and relevant to the Panarion haer. 48
source. But first we need to look at the pattern
of citation of the largest unit of this source and
get a general idea of its content.

In Panarion haer. 48, Epiphanius preserves a
source which quotes a Montanist oracle followed by
the catholic repudiation of the truth of the oracle.
Then appears a discussion of the scriptural justification
of the oracle by an unnamed (but inferred) Montanist
source, followed by the catholic counter-interpretation
of the scriptural text. Let us take as an example
the section whose content I intend to discuss in the
next part of this article, Panarion haer. 48.4.1--
48.9.10. The unit quotes the now-famous oracle of
Montanus which says that God plays upon sleeping man
as a plectrum strums a lyre (Pan. haer. 48.4.1), moves
to a catholic denial of the stated words of this oracle
(48.4.2-3), then announces (and denounces) the scriptural
justification for the oracle (48.4.4.; Gen 2:21-24,
in this case), proceeds systematically to counter
Montanist claims to the correct interpretation of
the now-named biblical passage (48.4.5-48.6.6), and
finally moves to include refutation of subsidiary
passages probably brought forward by the Montanists

37Quellenkritik, 230.
38Cf. Bonwetsch, Geschichte, 198, no. 9; Aland, Kirchengeschichtliche, 145, Nr. 12. See Voigt, Urkunde,
130-131.
39Cf. Tert., Adv. Marc. 3.24.4 and Klawiter's negative
remarks ("New Prophecy," 270-271).

for scriptural support (48.7.1-48.9.10). The content of this entire unit turns on the question of whether or not the prophet in Holy Scripture spoke in ecstasy.

Ephphanius has therefore taken over a source which already had made use of the original oracles. He has not collected them himself; nor, in keeping with his principles of handling (or, rather, not handling) heretical sources, has he read the original Montanist tract from which they were taken.[40] He has employed an early source which has already provided a catholic counter-exegesis to the Montanist oracle supported by scriptural proof-text. When the Montanist source was written and by whom cannot be said with certainty; but the catholic counter-exegesis dates from around A.D.200,[41] so a time in the last decade of the second century is not out of line.

Tertullian's evidence reinforces the above dating of the Montanist source (and its catholic redaction) and provides stunning corroboration for the integrity and originality of the source. As scholars have noted since the last century, Tertullian preserves in some of his Montanist-influenced passages, scriptural texts and exegetical postions identical to some of those of the pre-catholic redaction of <u>Panarion haer</u>. 48.[42] The parallel passages date in Tertullian's chronology to between A.D.206 and 208.[43] Thus both the catholic redactor of Epiphanius' source and Tertullian of Carthage independently had read and used an original Montanist treatise which had collected Montanist oracles and provided a scriptural justification of them. The

---

[40]Voigt, <u>Urkunde</u>, 30-31, 135-138.
[41]Pierre de Labriolle, <u>Les Sources de l'histoire du Montanisme. Textes grecs. latins. syriaques</u> (Fribourg [Suisse]: Libraire de l'Universite [Paris: Leroux], 1913) L111.
[42]Especially important to discussions of Gen 2:21-24 in this article are passages from the <u>De Anima</u> (11.4; 21.2; 45.3-6) and <u>Adv. Marc.</u> IV.22. Cf. n. 47 (below) and Voigt, <u>Urkunde</u>, 37-39, 42-47, for disciplinary passage parallels.
[43]That is, between the <u>De Anima</u> and the <u>Adversus Marcionem</u>. My dating follows Timothy D. Barnes, <u>Tertullian. A Historical and Literary Study</u> (Oxford: Clarendon, 1971) 55.

catholic redactor had entirely subsumed these in (as detailed above) a refutation of them. Tertullian (as we shall see) had employed the source in his own writing programme. Modern scholars have in the _Pan. haer._ 48 source and in Tertullian's passages a fine opportunity to assess something of the exegetical stances of Montanist and catholic at the end of the second- and opening decade of the third-century.

Conjectures as to the original author's name have proved to be simply that, but one elaborated thesis which argued a specific theory of authorship needs to be examined. Voigt had explained the commonality between Tertullian's passages and _Panarion haer._ 48 by arguing that Tertullian was the original author of the source used by Epiphanius.[44] Working from Jerome's notice (_De vir. ill._ 40) that Tertullian wrote seven books "_De Ecstasi_," now lost, Voigt argued that Epiphanius' source drew on the Greek original of this work.[45] But as Timothy Barnes has shown, there was no Greek original of _De Ecstasi_ and all attempts to transform Jerome's witness to a Latin title into " Περὶ ἐκστάσεως " are misplaced and misleading.[46] Furthermore, the study of the parallel scriptural passages bearing on disciplinary question in Epiphanius' source and Tertullian argued for the independence of the two sources.[47]

In conclusion, Epiphanius' source and Tertullian both used a common Montanist source dating from the late second or early third centuries. Tertullian preserves small pieces of its scriptural texts and exegetical positions in its Montanist form. Epiphanius preserves it redacted almost entirely with anti-Montanist exegetical polemic. The total source gives us glimpses of some Montanist oracles and the exegetical authentication those oracles called forth by the end of the second century. Epiphanius has this preserved in catholic counter-exegesis of the same stage of the debate, and Tertullian's parallel texts confirm the veracity of the position opposed by the catholic counter-

---

[44]Voigt, _Urkunde_, 35, 41 (pp. 35-57 for texts paralleling Tertullian to Epiphanius; 213-214, 225, 233 for conjectures on possible authorship).
[45]Voigt, _Unkunde_, 35, 95, 321.
[46]Barnes, _Tertullian_, 253-254.
[47]Cf. Labriolle, _Les Sources_, LVIII - LXIV.

GROH

exegesis. It is time now to turn to a consideration
of our sounding on the relationship between utterance
and exegesis as contained in two specific passages
of this source.

III

In the preceding section, I used, as an example
of the fullest unit-pattern of the Epiphanius' source,
the passage which contains a famous oracle of Montanus.
The oracle reads:

> Lo, man (ὁ ἄνθρωπος) is a lyre, and I
> fly across him like a plectrum.
> Man sleeps, and I remain awake.
> Lo, the one who astounds (ὁ ἐξιστάνων)
> the hearts of men and gives them hearts is the
> Lord.[48]

It is the divine voice speaking in the first person,
claiming responsibility and authority for the altered
instrumental state of the human vehicle of revelation.
At the same time its form is that of an "oracle of
self-commendation" (Aune's term), which authenticates
and legitimates the prophet's role as a source of
revelation.[49] Aune's observation that charismatic
exegesis was closer to the interpretation of dreams[50]
is exceedingly apt when we look at this oracle in
its primary exegetical setting (Pan. haer. 48.4.4).
Whether the oracle itself was meant to be a raz on
the prophetic sleep of great figures in scripture,
we cannot say for sure. It is tempting to see the
sleep of ὁ ἄνθρωπος as an interpretive allusion to
Gen 2:21-24; and if it could be so taken, we would
have our first example of a prophet speaking in an
ecstatic mode actually providing the key to a scriptural
text. But lack of verbal coincidence of the oracle
to Gen 2:21-24 restricts any such argument.

What we have instead is an example, in a Christian
mode, which looks like the kind of exegesis which
worked from the original oracle now to unlock the
Scriptures in order to prove that the true prophet

---

[48]Pan. haer. 48.4.1(Holl,235);Aland, Kirchengeschichtliche, Nr. 6, 144.
[49]Aune, Prophecy, 315.
[50]Aune, Prophecy, 340.

84

speaks in the hypnotic sleep of ecstasy. And this
is exactly what the redacted Montanist source preserved
by Epiphanius did with the oracle, bringing forward
as a proof-text, the LXX reading of Genesis 2:21,

> . . . ἐπέβαλεν ὁ θεὸς ἔκστασιν ἐπὶ τὸν Αδαμ καὶ
> ὕπνωσε.

The catholic redactor could not deny Adam's ecstasy;
for the text was absolutely clear (cf. 48.5.1). But
there are a number of types of ecstasy (48.6.1); and
Adam experienced the "ecstasy of sleep" (ἔκστασις
ὕπνου), not the "ecstasy of wits and judgement" (ἔκστασις φρενῶν καὶ διανοημάτων).[51] The Montanist position
on the text is very clear, though it must be seen
entirely through the redactor's reporting. Adam was
one of a string of biblical prophets who prophesied
in ecstasy and to whom the Montanists looked as a
model for the proper mode of true prophecy -- ecstasy.[52]

That Adam was prophesying could not be denied,
since Adam's words to the newly created Eve (Gen. 2:23)
came to revealed fulfillment in the μυστήριον of Christ
and the Church (Eph 5:31-32), a charismatic exegetical
connection already made by the New Testament,[53] whose
import the Montanist Tertullian knew full well:

> For, inasmuch as Adam immediately (**statim**) prophe-
> sied that great mystery (**sacramentum**) of Christ
> and the Church: [quotes Eph 5:31-32], he experi-
> enced the influence (**accidentiam**) of the Spirit:
> for ecstasy fell upon him, the Holy Spirit's
> operative power of prophecy.[54]

Tertullian's use of the term **statim** here is crucial
to recognizing that he is referring to the same exegetical position preserved in Pan. haer 48. While the
Genesis text did not use the term, the Montanists
apparently took the **immediacy** of Adam's (and other

---

[51]Pan. haer. 48.6.4 (Holl, 227); 48.4.6.
[52]Cf. Pan. haer. 48.4.4 (Holl, 225, line 13-226, line
2).
[53]Cf. Aune, Prophecy, 339-340, for the criteria of charismatic exegesis (which this passage seems to meet)
and 341 (for its parallelism to Qumran exegetical
activity).
[54]De Anima 11.4 (CC II, ed. Gerla) 797.

GROH

biblical prophets') speech as further indication of
the ecstatic mode. For Tertullian, Adam himself did
not understand the words of his prophesy; Paul revealed
their true import.[55] And this appears to be the position
of the Montanist writer who is being refuted in Pan.
haer. 48, for the anti-Montanist source contrasts
repeatedly the way Montanus speaks in a pseudo-prophetic
way with the rational understanding the biblical prophets
had of their words -- and here his proof that the
prophets knew what they were saying in that they spoke
immediately.[56] Thus Adam "immediately" upon waking
was able to describe what had happened and to speak
the words of Gen 2:23.[57]

It seems then that Montanus' oracle touched off
a debate on prophetic "sleepers" in Scripture, as
well as on the exact nature of sleep. The anti-Montanist
author explores a psychology of sleep[58] so that he
can oppose an "ecstasy of sleep" to the ecstatic obli-
teration of the senses which the Montanists claimed
for Adam's sleep.[59] In sleep, all the senses rest.
The senses remain (e.g., intact) though their faculties
rest. Thus the sense of hearing remains although
the faculty of hearing rests. When God uses such
a sleep to speak, the author maintains, the part of
the soul that exercises judgement slumbers, but is
not obliterated. And this is his explanation of how
Adam wakes and straightaway remembers what he had
said.[60] It seems highly probable that the redactor's
source contained such a distinction of kinds of sleep.
But, what we can say for sure is that Tertullian's
De Anima contains just such a psychology of sleep
worked out along similar lines.

In the De Anima, Tertullian distinguished between
two kinds of ecstasy. The one is a supernatural kind

---

[55]J.H. Waszink, De Anima. Edited with Introduction and
Commentary (Amsterdam: Meulenhoff, 1947), 198 (further
references cited there).
[56]Pan. haer. 48.4.1 (Montanus); 48.6.4; 48.8.5 (on Acts
11:28f).
[57]Pan. haer. 48.6.4.
[58]Pan. haer. 48.5.
[59]Cf. the text above at n. 51.
[60]Pan. haer. 48.5-6.

such as Adam and Saul experienced.[61]   In this kind
of ecstasy, the soul is moved from the outside by
the Holy Spirit which is added temporarily to the
person as an accidentia or an accidens -- an "attendant
circumstance."[62]   The effect of the Spirit's action
turns the prophet temporarily into another man--
a spiritual man.[63]   Just as the Holy Spirit can temporarily change a person, so can an evil spirit--
behold Saul's fall from grace.[64]   The anthropological
consequence of this temporary force exerted on the
soul is the loss of the human senses or faculties
(what the Panarion discussion of prophecy opposes)
and the attendant passivity of the subject's soul.[65]

But Tertullian also maintains there is another
kind of ecstasy (as the Panarion 48 unit) -- a natural
form of ecstasy. Here, without the gift of the Spirit,
and in distinction from prophecy, the soul can be
moved into a mantic or divining function;[66] or, in
the course of sleep, the soul is moved by a natural
force of its own also called "ecstasy."[67]

Tertullian was fond of using Adam as an example.
As a North African, he loved to argue ex origine --

---

[61]De Anima 11.4-5 (Adam and Saul); cf. De Resurrectione
Mortuorum 55.11. Adv. Marc. 4.22.4 (for Peter).
[62]Waszink, De Anima, 481 (accidens); 198 (accidentia).
[63]De Anima 11.5: "Nam et malus spiritus accidens res
est.   Denique Saulem tam dei spiritus postea uertit
in alium uirum, id est in propheten..."
[64]De Anima 11.5: "...et mali spiritus postea uertit
[Saulem] in alium uirum, in apostatem scilicet."
[65]Waszink, De Anima (on 9.4), 168.
[66]De Anima 6.3; 22.1 "...divinationem interdum, seposita
quae per dei gratiam obuenit ex prophetia."
[67]De Anima 45.3: "Hanc uim ecstasin dicimus, excessum
sensus et amentiae instar...Somnus enim corpori prouenit
in quietum, ecstasis animae accessit aduersus quietem..."
Waszink De Anima, 482, has expressed surprise that
Tert. here calls the natural kind of ecstasy a vis
("of course, in imitation of 11.4"). But at 14.3,
where Tert. opposes Aristotle's division of the soul
into parts, Tert. prefers to speak of "uires et effi-
caciae et operae."   Tert. may then consider this force
ecstasy to be one of these vires.

from the first appearance of a phenomenon.[68] As a
staunch defender of Christian doctrine, Tertullian
used Adam as an example of the first heretic. From
a Montanist standpoint, Adam was considered to be
the proto-Montanist (the first person to experience
spiritual ecstasy), whose breaking of the fast from
the fruit of the tree plunged him back again into
the ranks of the Catholic psychics.[69] In our discussion
at hand, Adam is now seen as the proto-sleeper. Since
Adam's ecstasy, all people experience ecstasy when
they sleep.[70] Thus ordinary dreams and ecstasy are
yoked in his De Anima. Because the soul is divine,
it never sleeps (recall Montanus' oracle); it undergoes
instead a continuous motion which he here designates
as "ecstasy."[71] For Tertullian to espouse an ecstasy
that is natural to the soul itself moves him into
finer and finer distinctions -- not the least of which
is the one he makes to explain how a person can remember
a dream if one has indeed experienced ecstasy.[72]

But rather than trace down the distinctions (already
done brilliantly by J.H. Waszink[73]) we might rather
ask what Tertullian is trying to accomplish here.
First, he is obviously trying to lay an anthropological
basis for an epistemology of "new prophecy." In that
process, Tertullian follows a method he himself has
honed to a fine edge in his pre-Montanist days. For
him there must be some correlation between nature
and nature's God. Reason (especially Christian reason)
must be able to find in nature some bare traces of
its Creator. Hence, while still a Catholic, he could
argue apologetically that the soul is naturally "Christian," and by that he meant "theistic."[74] It is a

[68]W.H.C. Frend, "A Note on Jews and Christians in Third
Century North Africa," Journal of Theological Studies,
n.s. 21 (1970) 93.
[69]Cf. Adv. Marc. 2.2.7 and De Ieiunio 3.2.
[70]De Anima 45.3. Cf. Panarion haer. 48.5 for the anti-
Montanist view. Waszink, De Anima 480.
[71]Note 67 (above). For the sleepless immortality of
the soul, see De Anima 43.5; cf. Epiphanius, Panarion
haer. 48.5 (an anti-Montanist view).
[72]De Anima 45.5. The ecstasy of sleep is only an "image"
of madness, not real madness (Waszink, De Anima, 480).
[73]Waszink, De Anima, 482.
[74]Apol. 17.6. Cf. the argumentation in De Testimonio
Animae 2.6.

large step from that natural knowledge of God to saving knowlege of Christ,[75] but it is a step and not a huge chasm to be leapt. If it were the latter, then Marcion would have made his point, and Creation's God and Christ's father would be discontinuous. Similarly, ecstasy in a prophetic dream must have its distant cousin in an ordinary dream. Thus ordinary human sleep becomes a parable to faith. God daily gives a person "...the outlines of man's state, especially concerning the beginning and the termination thereof; thus stretching out the hand to help our faith more readily by types and parables, not in words only, but also in things."[76]

The Montanism which Tertullian adopts then has been turned to his general systematic. The gift of the Paraclete is a step beyond the revelation granted to an earlier time, but it is not discontinuous with that of the earlier time.[77] The Paraclete teaches nothing contradictory to Scripture or Rule of Faith. He fills the **lacunae** left by Scripture and nature with **disciplinary** proscriptions consistent with both Scripture **and** nature.[78] But He fills those gaps in the church's understanding in a more certain way than could be reached by either exegetical tools or natural reason. Tertullian knew from his theological endeavors the subtlety of exegesis;[79] he knew from his rhetorical

---

[75]**Apol.** 18.4; **De Test. Animae** 1.7. See Ernst Bickel, "Fiunt, non nascuntur Christiani," in **Pisciculi. Studien zur Religion und Kultur des Altertums**, hrsg. Th. Klauser und Adolf Ruecker (Münster in Westf., 1939) 54-61.

[76]**ANF**, vol. 3, 222 (translating **De Anima** 43.11).

[77]**De Virginibus Velandis** 1.5;1.7: "Sic et iustitia (nam idem Deus iustitiae et creaturae) primo fuit in rudimentis, natura Deum metuens; dehinc per legem et prophetas promouit in infantiam, dehinc per euangelium efferbuit in iuuentutum, nunc per Paracletum componitur in maturitatem."

[78]**De Virginibus Velandis** 16.1-2.

[79]Cf. **De Pudicitia** 2.10; for demands for a Scriptural ruling on a problem which the Scriptures did not address directly, see **De Spectaculis** 3 (a Catholic-period treatise) and **De Corona** 4 (a Montanist-period work).

education the problems of customary as opposed to statutory law.[80] Prophetic ecstasy insured a revelation uncorrupted by the frailties of either human transmission or exegetical dilemma. Here Tertullian the rational man and Tertullian the "spiritual" man meet. And like the schema of his own theological system, the two are not discontinuous.

IV

One of the famous oracles of Montanus, contained in the same Panarion source we have been examining, reads: "Neither a messenger (ἄγγελος) nor an ambassador (πρέσβυς) but I the Lord God Father came."[81] The Panarion source which preserves the oracle, has set it in the framework of a discussion which tries to make the oracle a negative self-claim of Montanus. Bypassing Christ, who is the true son and giver of spiritual gifts in the church, Montanus has dared to identify himself with the Father.[82] But this oracle, as others in this section of the Panarion, makes it clear that Montanus claimed only that God the Father himself addresses people in the prophetic word spoken through Montanus.[83]

There is, however, a scandalous immediacy in the revelations claimed by the Montanists which worried their Catholic opponents. Montanus here claims that God himself acts directly without the use of either divine (ἄγγελος) or human (πρέσβυς) intermediary.[84]

---

[80]Cf. De Virginibus Velandis 1.1-2 (on consuetudo) to De Corona 4 (where consuetudo has a positive sense). Cicero, De Inventione II, LIV (162) (Loeb Classical Library, pp. 328-31).
[81]" οὔτε ἄγγελος οὔτε πρέσβυς, ἀλλ κύριος ὁ θεὸς πατὴρ ἦλθον " (Pan. haer. 48.11.9, Holl, 235). Cf. Origen, Contra Celsum VII.9 (and Henry Chadwick, ed. [Cambridge, 1965] note on ἥκω, 402, n.5).
[82]Pan. haer. 48.11.9-10.
[83]Cf. Ignatius of Antioch, Philadelphians, 7.1, where "God's own voice" equals the Spirit's preaching (7.2). Montanus' oracle again represents Aune's "self-commendation" type (n. 49, above).
[84]Pierre de Labriolle, La Crise montaniste (Paris: Leroux, 1913) 39. For the Septuagint's by-passing of a heavenly intermediary between God and the people, see P. Winter, "Isa. LXIII, 9 (Gk) and the Passover

The two terms which underscore the notion of an intermediary -- ἄγγελος and πρέσβυς (especially the latter
term) had been difficult for scholars to identify.[85]
Earlier critical collections of Montanist documents
indicated no Biblical text from which the terminology
might have been drawn.[86] But Karl Holl's edition
of the **Panarion** correctly paralleled the oracle with
the Septuagint text of Isa 63:9.[87]

The Isaiah text reads: "Not an ambassador (πρέσβυς)
nor a messenger (ἄγγελος) but the Lord himself saved
them because he loves them and spares them."[88] In
its context the text refers to God's abiding love
for his people, Israel, which led Him to act directly
on their behalf. The passage read somewhat differently
in the Old Latin versions used by the Fathers. The
Old Latin seems to have taken the Greek aorist tense
("saved") as indicating the Hebrew prophetic perfect
-- that is, as belonging to a divine speech introduced
in the preceding verse.[89] Thus the Fathers took
Isa 63:9 as a prophetic speech by God of what he would
bring to pass, and the Septuagint aorist was rendered
by a future tense in Latin. It was then read as a
prophecy of Christ by Irenaeus, Tertullian, and Cyprian--
God will Himself save His people.[90] Thus Isa 63:9

Haggadah," **VT** 4 (1954) 440.
    [85]Labriolle, **La Crise**, 39 and the discussion in the
text (above) at n.23.
    [86]Migne, **P.G.** 41:871D; Labriolle, **Les Sources**, 133
(no. 88); Bonwetsch, **Geschichte**, 19. Cf. Labriolle,
La Crise, 39 (on πρέσβυς): "Ce mot n'est pas scrip-
taire."
    [87]48.11.9 (Holl, 235).
    [88]" οὐ πρέσβυς οὐδε ἄγγελος, ἀλλ᾽ κύριος ἔσωσεν αὐ-
τοὺς διὰ τὸ ἀγαπᾶν αὐτοὺς καὶ φείδεσθαι αὐτῶν ."
(**Septuaginta**, ed. Rahlfs, vol. 2 [Stuttgart, 1935] 650).
    [89]Isa. 63.8: " καὶ εἶπεν ..." My colleague Dr. Wolf-
gang M.W. Roth is responsible for my understanding
here, but not for my misunderstanding (if any).
    [90]Iren. **Haer.** 3.20.4 (Of God himself taking flesh):
Neque senior neque **angelus** sed **ipse** Dominus saluabit
eos; quoniam diligit eos et parcet eis, ipse liberabit
eos," (in **Contre les heresies**, livre III, edition
critique par F. Sagnard, Sources chretiennes [Paris,
1952], p. 346). Cypr., **Test.** 2.7.1: "Item illic [apud
Esaiam]: 'Non senior neque angelus, sed ipse Dominus
liberabit eos, quia diliget eos et parcet eis, ipse

is set in a prophecy/fulfillment framework in these Christian authors.

But Tertullian's citation of this text in Against Marcion, Book IV, shows us the text was of some importance in the debate on Montanist prophecy. He quotes it as one of a series of Scriptural examples to show the links between Old Testament prophecy and New Covenant fulfillment in Christ. The text reads: "'Not an ambassador, not an angel, but He himself,' says Isaiah, 'shall save them'" [note the future tense]; then comes Tertullian's comment: "for it is He himself who is now declaring and fulfilling the law and the prophets."[91] The Isaiah text thus represented one of the important Old Testament proof-texts for the immediate revelation of "New Prophecy." In this respect the wider context in which Tertullian uses the quote seems important. "New Prophecy" is at the forefront of his argument in this chapter of the Against Marcion. The citation of Isa 63:9 is bracketed by a discussion of the transfiguration in which, Tertullian claimed, Peter prophesied in an ecstasy and said things that he did not understand in the manner of the Montanist prophets.[92] Thus it appears that Tertullian knows the Christological interpretation of Isa 63.9, but associated the text with and uses it in a Montanist exegetical milieu.

The question of whether Tertullian's exegetical

---

redimet eos." (in S. Thasci Caecili Cypriani Opera Omnia, ex recensione G. Harteli, vol. III, pars. I, CSEL [Vindobonae, 1868], p. 72.). Note the wide variation in the text. For the later history of this proof-text, see Rendel Harris, Testimonies, pt. I (Cambridge, 1916), 102. See also 44 (where the Cyprian reference is miscited) and 58 (where the Irenaeus reference is miscited.)

[91]ANF, vol. 3, p. 384. Adv. Marc. 4.22.11: "...non legatus, inquit Esaias, nec nuntius, sed ipse deus saluos eos faciet [Isa. 63.9], ipse iam praedicans et implens legem et prophetas."

[92]Adv. Marc. 4.22.4: The Montanists took Peter's "Sed nesciens, quid diceret" (Luke 9:33) as proof that Peter spoke in ecstasy; the Catholics denied this (22.5). After the citation of the Isaiah (22.11), Tert. returns to a Montanist exegesis of Luke 9:35 (22.12). I have not yet found Isa 63:9 cited elsewhere in Tert.'s writings.

milieu here is drawn from the same source as Pan. haer. 48 is a difficult one. The unit of Pan. haer. 48.11 which preserves this oracle does not follow the neat pattern of the unit we examined earlier. It is considerably shorter and contains two oracles of Montanus (48.11.1 and 48.11.9). Whether the redactor of the source shortened his borrowing (transforming) from the Montanist tract he had read or found it in a very abbreviated manner, we cannot say, but the present source contains no Montanist supporting scriptures.

Peter's ecstasy (in Acts 10:10) was apparently a commonplace of Montanist contention, as we can see from the earlier unit on how Adam and subsequent prophets spoke in Scripture (48.7.3-4). Tertullian associates Isa 63:9 with a discussion of Peter's ecstasy in his treatment of Luke 9:28-36, and does not cite the Acts 10 reference. But here he is constrained by the Lukan text of Marcion and by the thrust of his argument against Marcion -- namely, Peter's testimony to the Christ of the Creator.

What is most important for our purposes is that the appearance of the Isa 63.9 text here shows it is to be associated by Tertullian with prophetic ecstasy, reinforcing the probable authenticity of the Montanus oracle.

We then have at least one clear instance of a Montanist prophet speaking in the state of ecstasy giving an interpretive quotation from the Old Testament. Thus we have our first clear example which can give an affirmative answer to one of the problems of charismatic exegesis raised by Aune:

> Is there any demonstrable connection between charismatic exegesis, whenever and wherever it occurs in early Christian texts, and Christian prophecy?[93]

In the Montanist controversy, as I have demonstrated, we have such an example. Charismatic exegesis did exist in Montanist circles in at least one sense in which the literature discusses it.

In the first sense in which the term is used

---

[93]Aune, Prophecy, 343.

in the scholarly literature, charismatic exegesis
(e.g. the relevant Qumran texts) decodes the meaning
of earlier scriptures with the use of the eschatological
raz revealed to the exegete. Whether Montanus' oracle
on prophetic sleeping and divine activity provided
the actual key for decoding Gen 2:21-24 is difficult
to say. Tertullian did not quote the oracle in his
exegesis of the text, though he has the same understanding of it that the Epiphanius source opposes
and associates with the oracle of Montanus. At the
very least, Gen 2:21-24 provided a premier scriptural
model of prophetic sleep to which supporters of ecstatic
prophecy could point as evidence that their mode of
prophecy was in line with the biblical mode.

In the second sense in which recent literature
employs the term charismatic exegesis, we are on surer
ground in profiling the importance of the Montanist
oracles. Here the Christian prophet, speaking in
an ecstatic mode, utters an interpretive citation
of scripture. Montanus did just that with Isa 63:9;
and it is very probable that Maximilla's oracle made
a less explicit allusion to 1 Cor 2:4-5. Both prophets
quoted their scriptures for purposes, and in the oracular
form, of self-commendation. Historians of interpretation
now need to go to work on the other Montanist oracles
to see if they also will yield scriptural citations.

Whether such evidence has any light to shed on
the presence or absence of prophetic charismatic exegesis
in either sense discussed above within the New Testament
itself remains for scholars of that discipline to
arbitrate. But for Tertullian studies, it is tempting
to suggest that Tertullian's test of the evidence
for Marcion's god should be read as a charismatic
exegete's challenge to that heretic (and, of course,
Tertullian's readers). He says that one should be
able to test it for what he terms "spiritual and prophetic grace and power" -- that is one should be able
to call on the evidence for Marcion's god "...to fortell
the future (praenuntiet futura), to reveal the secrets
of the human heart, and to expound mysteries (sacramenta
edisserat)."[94] The last phrase, "to expound mysteries"
has been taken to refer to prophetic psalms, visions,

---

[94]Adv. Marc. 5.15.5, trans. E.Evans, Tertullian Adversus
Marcionem (Oxford: Clarendon, 1972) 607.

or prayers which required special explication.[95]
It should also refer to the charismatic exegesis of
the Scriptures, examples of which in Scripture, run
all through this same chapter.

---

[95]Sacramenta here corresponds to the "aliquem psalmum,
aliquam visionem, aliquam orationem" of Adv. Marc.
5.8.12: Dimitri Michaelides, Sacramentum chez Tertullien
(Paris: Etudes augustiniennes, 1970) 227.

PART TWO

THE SHAPING OF NEW TESTAMENT TEXTS

CHAPTER EIGHT

THE REDACTION AND USE OF AN EARLY
CHRISTIAN CONFESSION IN ROMANS 1:3-4

Robert Jewett

A widespread consensus has crystallized in the
last generation of New Testament scholarship that
Paul cited an early Christian confession in Romans
1:3-4. The precise extent of the citation has been
debated since the late 1940's, with the result that
every likely option has been carefully examined.
By an experimental approach that weighs the strengths
and weaknesses of these previous hypotheses, the most
likely option can now be made apparent. In addition
to identifying the precise scope of the confession
and the likely causes of its evolution, the relation
of the cited material to Paul's epistolary purpose
needs to be explored. Earlier studies have concen-
trated on identifying the source of this material
and untangling the theological implications, but they
have not addressed the rhetorical issues very sharply.
The citation appears in the exordium of the letter,
a crucial position for defining the goals of the letter
as a whole, so it seems likely that a study of the
recipocal relations between the confession and the
body of the letter will throw light on both.

The thesis of this study is that several levels
of redactional activity are visible in the confession,
revealing the perspective of differing groups in early
Christianity. The confession in Romans 1:3-4 is in
a very real sense a "living text," reflecting the
interests and conflicts between such groups, yet dyna-
mically evolving in the Letter to the Romans itself.
Paul cites and emends this confession in order to
provide a common ground for addressing competitive
groups in Rome. In this sense, the confession of
Rom 1:3-4 is emblematic of the letter as a whole in
seeking to discover common ground between competitive
wings of the early church. It conveys Paul's ambas-

sadorial strategy to unify the branches of Roman Christianity for the sake of a jointly sponsored mission to Spain.

I
The Indications of Confessional Material

The breadth of the current consensus concerning the presence of credal material in the opening verses of Romans is manifest in recent studies.[1] While they differ in detail, a number of features have been cited repeatedly as indications of the non-Pauline origin of this material. The cogency of these observations may be most easily grasped when the structure of the passage is made visible.[2]

3a	περὶ τοῦ υἱοῦ αὐτοῦ	
3b	τοῦ γενομένου	
3c		ἐκ σπέρματος Δαυίδ
3d		κατὰ σάρκα,
4a	τοῦ ὁρισθέντος υἱοῦ θεοῦ	
4b	ἐν δυνάμει	
4c		κατὰ πνεῦμα ἁγιωσύνης
4d		ἐξ ἀναστάσεως νεκρῶν,
4e	Ἰησοῦ Χριστοῦ τοῦ κυρίου ἡμῶν	

The following observations have led researchers to the conclusion that Paul was citing traditional material in these verses.

a. The participial constructions in 3b and 4a are typical for confessional materials elsewhere in the New Testament.[3]

b. The position of the participles at the beginning of the subordinate clauses has been taken as an indication of the citation of traditional confessional material.[4]

c. The parallelism between 3b and 4a; 3c and

---

[1] Cf. Vern S. Poythress, "Is Romans 1:3-4 a Pauline Confession After All?" ExpT 87 (1976) 180-183; Paul Beasley-Murray, "Romans 1:3f: An Early Confession of Faith in the Lordship of Jesus," TynB 31 (1980) 147-154.

[2] This strophic analysis based on grammatical principles is adapted from J. P. Louw, A Semantic Discourse Analysis of Romans (Pretoria, South Africa: University of Pretoria, 1979), Vol. I, 1.

[3] Klaus Wengst, Christologische Formeln und Lieder der Urchristentum (Gütersloh: Mohn, 1972) 112.

[4] Wengst, Christologische Formeln, 112.

4d; and 3d and 4c has indicated to a wide range of researchers the presence of careful, solemn composition typical for liturgical use.[5]

d. The lack of articles with many of the nouns has been suggested as a feature of traditional material here and elsewhere in the New Testament.[6]

e. The presence of non-Pauline terms like ὁρισ-θέντος and πνεῦμα ἁγιωσύνης lends itself to a theory of citation. The former appears in Acts 10:42 and 17:31, while the latter is found as an expression only in the Testament of Levi 18:11 and on a Jewish amulet.[7]

f. The expression ἐξ ἀναστάσεως νεκρῶν is used elsewhere in the Pauline letters to refer to the resurrection of the dead in a general sense in contrast to the use here in reference to Christ's resurrection.[8]

g. The terms σάρξ and πνεῦμα are used in an uncharacteristic way as compared with the other Pauline letters where they have an anthropological focus and a more clearly antithetical intent.[9]

h. Disparities with Pauline theology as visible elsewhere in the letters are quite striking. The reference to the Davidic origin of Jesus is not only unusual but also substantially in tension with references like 2 Cor 5:16.[10]

---

[5]Vernon H. Neufeld, The Earliest Christian Confessions (Grand Rapids: Eerdmans, 1963) 50.

[6]Heinrich Zimmermann, Neutestamentliche Methodenlehre: Darstellung der historisch-kritischen Methode (Stuttgart: Katholisches Bibelwerk, 1967) 198.

[7]Erik Peterson, "Das Amulett von Acre," Frühkirche, Judentum und Gnosis: Studien und Untersuchungen (Rome: Herder, 1959) 346-354, especially 351-352.

[8]Cf. Jürgen Becker, Auferstehung der Toten im Urchristentum (Stuttgart: Katholisches Bibelwerk, 1976) 23f.

[9]Cf. Egon Brandenburger, Fleisch und Geist: Paulus und die dualistische Weisheit (Neukirchen: Neukirchener, 1968); Robert Jewett, Paul's Anthropological Terms: A Study of Their Use in Conflict Settings (Leiden: Brill, 1971) 453-456.

[10]The only other reference I know to the physical descent of Jesus in the Pauline letters is Rom 9:4, which does not mention the Davidic connection. The "son of David" title is found elsewhere in Matt 1:1; 2 Tim 2:8; Rev 5:5 and 22:16 and is supported by Matt 1:2-20; Luke 1:27, 32, 69; 3:4; 3:23-31 and Acts 2:30. Cf. Christoph Burger, Jesus als Davidssohn: Eine tradi-

   i. The lack of a reference to the cross or to Jesus' death seems very distant from Paul's usual emphasis, summarized in 1 Cor 2:2.[11]
   j. The unmistakably adoptionist tone of this confession is entirely lacking in other Christological utterances of Paul, who typically stresses pre-existence.[12]
   k. Paul introduces this material in Rom 1:1-2 as a summary of the "gospel" he had been preaching, which leads one to expect the citation of traditional material, as in 1 Cor 15:1-4.[13]
   l. A primary indication of the presence of cited material is the smooth transition that would result when Rom 1:3a-4d is deleted: "...the gospel concerning his son, [delete 3a-4d] Jesus Christ our Lord, through whom we have received grace and apostleship...."[14]

   It is widely recognized that some of these observations carry more weight than others. Nevertheless the impression made by these details is that Romans 1 contains "a kind of potted creed," to use the expression that A. M. Hunter employed in 1940.[15] Even those commentators who stress the predominance of Pauline language in these lines acknowledge that traditional confessional materials are being used.[16]

---

tionsgeschichtliche Untersuchung (Göttingen: Vandenhoeck & Ruprecht, 1970).
   [11]Cf. Eduard Schweizer, "Römer 1,3f. und der Gegensatz von Fleisch und Geist vor und bei Paulus," EvTh 15 (1955) 563
   [12]Cf. Werner Kramer, Christ, Lord, Son of God, tr. B. Hardy (Naperville: Allenson, 1966) 109-111.
   [13]Cf. Poythress, "Romans 1:3-4," 182.
   [14]Cf. Heinrich Schlier, "Zu Röm 1,3f," Neues Testament und Geschichte: Historisches Geschehen und Deutung im Neuen Testament: Oscar Cullmann zum 70. Geburtstag, ed. H. Baltensweiler & B. Reicke (Zürich: Theologischer Verlag/Tübingen: Mohr-Siebeck, 1972), 208.
   [15]Archibald M. Hunter, Paul and His Prececessors, (London: S. C. M., 1961, second edition; the first edition was published in 1940) 24.
   [16]Cf. F. F. Bruce, The Epistle of Paul to the Romans: An Introduction and Commentary (London: Tyndale, 1963) 72-74.

II
The Extent of the Confessional Citation

The dilemma of Rom 1:3-4 is how to determine the extent of the cited material. A bewildering array of hypotheses must be sifted in order to clarify this dilemma. In many instances, the decisive weaknesses of individual hypotheses have been pointed out by those who sought to improve them. In order to provide a minimal sense of scholarly development and take such criticisms into account, I examine each basic option in the sequence of initial appearance, noting later adherents along the way.

a. Rudolf Bultmann's brief but incisive treatment of the confession provided a target for much of the subsequent discussion. He proposed that the original form of the pre-Pauline creed included the introductory formula of 3a, "concerning his son," but lacked 3d and 4c, the references to the flesh and the spirit of holiness. [17] These deletions of "Pauline syntax" concerning flesh and spirit were accepted by Dahl and Kuss,[18] but they left a problem that Eduard Schweizer was the first to detect. [19] The expression πνεῦμα ἁγιωσύνης is non-Pauline. While Paul uses the term "holiness" in ethical contexts (1 Thess 3:17; 2 Cor 7:1), he never otherwise attaches it to "spirit." Also when Paul uses "spirit" after κατά, he never otherwise affixes a qualifying noun as in this instance. The complex [20] and sometimes involuted [21] efforts of later

----

[17] Rudolf Bultmann, Theology of the New Testament, tr. K. Grobel (London: SCM, 1952; [1948]), vol. I, 49; the first written expression of Bultmann's analysis appeared in "Neueste Paulusforschung," TRu 8 (1936) 11.

[18] Nils A. Dahl, "Die Messianität Jesu bei Paulus," Studia Paulina in honorem Johannis de Zwaan Septuagenarii, ed. J. N. Sevenster & W. C. van Unnik (Haarlem: Bohn, 1953) 90; Otto Kuss, Der Römerbrief (Regensburg: Pustet, 1963), Lief. I, 8.

[19] Schweizer, "Römer 1,3f.," 564.

[20] Cf. C. E. B. Cranfield, A Critical and Exegetical Commentary on the Epistle to the Romans (Edinburgh: Clark, 1975) vol. I, 62-64.

[21] Cf. Bernardin Schneider, " Κατὰ Πνεῦμα Ἁγιωσύνης ," Bib 48 (1967) 359-387.

scholars to escape from this dilemma have not availed, so that an adequate account of the emergence of this peculiar formula remains a crucial task of any viable hypothesis.

b. Schweizer's hypothesis of 1955 was to retain the expressions "according to the flesh" and "according to the spirit of holiness" as part of the original creed, but to eliminate 4e, "in power." While this approach has been followed by Kramer and Burger,[22] it involves some very problematic historical and linguistic implications. In 1971, I pointed out that Schweizer explained the sphere of flesh as preliminary and obsolete, which appears to contradict the proud emphasis on Davidic origin.[23] His explanation of the historical setting of this contradictory emphasis was vague and implausible, because the antithesis of flesh and spirit appears to reflect Hellenistic Christian interests while the stress on Davidic lineage appears typical of Jewish Christianity. In the same year, Eta Linnemann pointed out the flaw in Schweizer's effort to combine the son of David/son of God motifs with a modified antithesis between flesh and spirit, suggesting two contradictory spheres of messianic honor.[24] A confession granting Jesus the status of Son of David clearly implies the messianic rank suggested by "Son of God." Clearly there is something incommensurate in the high honors of Davidic sonship and the derogatory ascription, "according to the flesh." This is an exegetical conclusion that requires an appropriate historical resolution. It appears likely that communities with antithetical interests must have been involved in the creation of the clause "born of David's seed according to the flesh."

While Schweizer did not work out the implications in detail, it is clear that his suggestion of Paul's insertion of the phrase "in power" in order to create "a concept of higher grade sonship"[25] in connection with the spirit was somehow related to the two-level messianic scheme. That such a motivation would not

---

[22]Kramer, Christ, 918; Burger, Jesus, 25-26.
[23]Schweizer, "Römer 1,3f.," 569; my discussion is in Paul's Anthropological Terms, 136-137.
[24]Eta Linnemann, "Tradition und Interpretation in Röm 1,3f," EvT 31 (1971) 266-268.
[25]Schweizer, "Römer 1,3f.," 564.

have been consistent with Pauline christology was pointed out by Ferdinand Hahn.[26] Insofar as the insertion of ἐν δυνάμει is conceived as a Pauline correction, it does nothing more than reinforce the presumed antithesis between a fleshly sphere and a spiritual sphere that Schweizer felt was part of the original confession.[27] These criticisms show how unworkable it is to hold the expressions "according to the flesh" and "according to the spirit" as original parts of the confession while simultaneously ascribing "in power" to later redaction.

   c. In 1957 C. K. Barrett attempted to improve the Schweizer hypothesis by suggesting that Paul also added the phrase "through the resurrection from the dead." Unfortunately, this failed to address the major weaknesses in the Schweizer hypothesis.[28] The contradiction between the high honors of Davidic ancestry and the derogatory emphasis on the realm of the flesh remains unresolved, and Barrett's facile translation "holy spirit" disguises the dilemma of the peculiar expression, πνεῦμα ἁγιωσύνης . While the parallelism of the lines "in the sphere of the flesh, born of the family of David; in the sphere of the Holy Spirit, appointed Son of God" appears tight in English translation, this hypothesis in fact eliminates the truly viable parallel between 3c and 4d: ἐκ σπέρματος Δαυίδ and ἐξ ἀναστάσεως νεκρῶν . These weaknesses are not resolved by Gijs Bouwman's adoption of the Barrett hypothesis.[29]

   d. In light of the difficulties encountered by the Schweizer and Barrett hypotheses, it would appear to be a step in the wrong direction to suggest that the confession ought to be viewed as a unified creation of a single early Church tradition without

---

[26]Ferdinand Hahn, The Titles of Jesus in Christology: Their History in Early Christianity, tr. H. Knight & G. Ogg (New York: World, 1969) 247.
[27]Cf. also the acute observation of Ernst Käsemann, Commentary on Romans, tr. G. W. Bromiley (Grand Rapids: Eerdmans, 1980) 12.
[28]C. K. Barrett, A Commentary on the Epistle to the Romans (New York: Harper, 1957) 18-20.
[29]Gijs Bouwman, Paulus aan de Romeinen: Een retorische analyse von Rom 1-8 (Abdij Averbode: Werkgroep voor Levensverdieping, 1980) 124-127.

any redaction by Paul or anyone else. Yet this has repeatedly been proposed with elaborate argumentation

--by J. D. G. Dunn, who believes Paul added only the preface,[30]
--by Hahn, Stuhlmacher, Käsemann and Wilckens, who believe Paul added both the preface and conclusion,[31]
--and by Hunter, Cullmann, Neufeld, Best, Bartsch and Schneider, who assert that Paul added nothing whatsoever.[32]

In whatever form one wishes to advance this option, it labors under insuperable burdens. It requires advocates to downplay the tension between flesh and spirit in order to preserve the honor attached to the Davidic descent, to invent implausible explanations for the peculiar expression "spirit of holiness," and to provide endless alibis for the seeming heightening of adoptionism in the inclusion of the expression "in power." None of these hypotheses provides a convincing historical Sitz im Leben for a pre-Pauline formula bearing all these contradictory features; in fact, the greatest concern in most of these hypotheses is theological rather than historical. To find ways to bring theology into consonance with this highly

---

[30]James D. G. Dunn, "Jesus--Flesh and Spirit: an Exposition of Rom 1.3-4," JTS 24 (1973) 40-68.

[31]Hahn, Titles, 246-252; Peter Stuhlmacher, "Theologische Probleme des Römerbrief-präskripts," EvT 27 (1967), 374-389; Käsemann, Romans, 13; Ulrich Wilckens, Der Brief an die Römer (Zürich: Benziger/Neukirchen: Neukirchener, 1978) vol. I, 56-61; Wilckens' position is somewhat difficult to determine, because he prints out the confession on p. 56 as if the phrase "in power" did not originally belong, but when discussing this detail, he claims that "in power" stands parallel to "according to the spirit of holiness," which would seem to imply that it was original, 65.

[32]Hunter, Paul, 25-28; Oscar Cullmann, The Earliest Christian Confessions, tr. J. K. S. Reid (London: Lutterworth, 1949) 55-56; Vernon H. Neufeld, The Earliest Christian Confessions (Grand Rapids: Eerdmans, 1963) 50-51; Ernest Best, The Letter of Paul to the Romans (Cambridge: University Press, 1967) 10f.; Hans-Werner Bartsch, "Zur vorpaulinischen Bekenntnisformel im Eingang des Römerbriefes," TZ 23 (1967) 329-339; Schneider, " Κατὰ Πνεῦμα," 360-369.

ambivalent creed requires immense inventiveness.
But even the least problematic of these explanations
does nothing to render the creed historically plausible. One cannot avoid the impression that the ground-
clearing start of Bultmann offered a more satisfactory
foundation for reconstructing the original creed,
and that the effort to avoid his incisive critique
raises far more problems than it solves.

    e. It is with some relief that we turn in the
sections that follow to the hypotheses that responded
to the Bultmann and Schweizer efforts by addressing
the internal contradictions in the creed rather than
attempting to eliminate them. In 1967, Heinrich Zimmermann proposed that the present confession began with
the fusion of two separate formulas, one stressing
the seed of David and the other the resurrection.
The Hellenistic congregations added to this fusion
the antithetical expressions κατὰ σάρκα and κατὰ πνεῦμα
ἁγιωσύνης to heighten the significance of the resurrection as compared with Davidic ancestry. Paul took
over the formula that had been combined by the Hellenistic church, and added the phrase "in power."[33]
In addition to downplaying the original symmetry between
ἐκ σπέρματος Δαυίδ and ἐξ ἀναστάσεως νεκρῶν, the problem
with this hypothesis is in conceiving a confession
of Davidic sonship without a corresponding stress
on the resurrection. Zimmermann cannot suggest a
plausible setting for such a truncated Christology
in the branches of early Christianity that are known
to us. Further his theory does not provide a satifactory
explanation for the origin of the peculiar phrase
"according to the spirit of holiness," which as we
have seen is a crucial problem to be addressed.

    f. A more intriguing solution was presented
by Eta Linnemann in 1971.[34] After a trenchant critique
of Bultmann, Schweizer and Stuhlmacher, she returns
to Bultmann's contention that the phrases "according
to the flesh...and spirit" do not fit the original
rhetoric of the confession concerning Jesus as born
of the seed of David. But since the expression κατὰ
πνεῦμα ἁγιωσύνης is non-Pauline, she suggests that
it was created by Paul's addition of κατὰ to the ori-

_____

[33]Zimmermann, <u>Neutestamentliche Methodenlehre</u>, 200-202.

[34]Linnemann, "Tradition," 264-275.

JEWETT

ginal formulation ἐν δυνάμει πνεύματος ἁγιωσύνης . Paul
changed the genitive of "spirit" to the accusative
in order to reduce the significance of the seed of
David to the realm "according to the flesh" and to
make clear that the appointment to sonship involved
"power" prior to the resurrection, which makes room
for Paul's characteristic emphasis on a preexistent
Christology.35 The original confession therefore ran
as follows:

> Πιστεύω εἰς 'Ιησοῦν ,
> τὸν γενόμενον ἐκ σπέρματος Δαυίδ ,
> τὸν ὁρισθέντα υἱὸν θεοῦ
> ἐν δυνάμει πνεύματος ἁγιωσύνης
> ἐξ ἀναστάσεως νεκρῶν .

A brief response by Eduard Schweizer in the same
issue of Evangelische Theologie indicated several
problems with this ingenious hypothesis.36 Reiterating
his earlier critique of Bultmann, the ascription of
the κατὰ σάρκα / κατὰ πνεῦμα antithesis to Paul remains
implausible because of their peculiar theological
implications in this confession and because Paul never
otherwise adds a qualifying noun to πνεῦμα in such
an antithesis. Even if Paul's contribution were limited
in the latter instance to adding the word κατά , he
nonetheless becomes responsible for the resultant
expression, "according to the spirit of holiness."
One could add that Linnemann's reconstruction erodes
the neat antithesis between ἐκ σπέρματος Δαυίδ and
ἐξ ἀναστάσεως νεκρῶν and lacks a plausible Sitz im
Leben in a particular branch of early Christianity.
Furthermore, the insertion of κατά into the phrase
ἐν δυνάμει πνεύματος ἁγιωσύνης allegedly implies so
extremely subtle an implication of preexistent Christology that neither Paul nor his audience can plausibly
be thought to have understood it.37 Nevertheless,
Linnemann cogently addresses one of the crucial problems
in the confession, the peculiar expression κατὰ πνεῦμα
ἁγιωσύνης, thus making a decisive contribution to
the evolution of the discussion.

g. A second contribution to the discussion appearing
in 1971 was Paul's Anthropological Terms, the printed

35Ibid., 275.
36Untitled critique following Eta Linnemann's article
on pp. 275-276 of EvT 31 (1971).
37Cf. Wengst, Christologische Formeln, 114.

version of a Tübingen dissertation of 1966.[38] Like
Linnemann, I attempted to refine the Bultmann hypothesis
by explaining the origin of the phrase κατὰ πνεῦμα
ἁγιωσύνης . Unlike her, I accepted elements of Schweizer's argument that the antithesis "according to the
flesh/according to the spirit" did not stem from Paul.
Since the term "holiness" points to a Judaic context
and the phrase "according to the spirit" to a Hellenistic
Christian context, I suggested the emergence of the
confession involved an original Jewish-Christian confession and two levels of redaction. The original confession
was similar to the confessional summaries in Acts,
stressing Davidic descent, an adoptionist Christology,
and an important role for the resurrection. Its wording
was as follows:

$$τοῦ \quad γενομένου$$
$$ἐκ \quad σπέρματος \quad Δαυίδ$$
$$τοῦ \quad ὁρισθέντος \quad υἱοῦ \quad θεοῦ$$
$$ἐν \quad δυνάμει$$
$$ἐξ \quad ἀναστάσεως \quad νεκρῶν,$$
$$'Ιησοῦ \quad Χριστοῦ \quad τοῦ \quad κυρίου \quad ἡμῶν.$$

The first level of redaction occurred at the hands
of Hellenistic Christians seeking to depreciate the
Davidic descent and emphasize the spiritual power
of Christ. They added the phrases κατα σάρκα and
κατὰ πνεῦμα , implying an ontological antithesis between
the material and the immaterial realms. Since a similar
kind of materialistic dualism was present in the Corinthian church and since the Pauline antithesis between
flesh and spirit originated approximately in A.D. 52,
the suggested Sitz im Leben for the interpolated confession was the gnostic branch of the Corinthian congrega-
tion. The second stage of redaction, the addition
of ἁγιωσύνης, occurred at the time Paul dictated Romans
and was intended as a correction to dualistic, libertinistic Christology.

This hypothesis had the advantage of explaining
the tension between the depreciatory terms "according
to the flesh/spirit" and the honorific reference to
the "seed of David," providing a plausible setting
for each Christological emphasis. It provided a more
believable explanation for the peculiar expression
κατὰ πνεῦμα ἁγιωσύνης than Linnemann's. It also offered
a preliminary approach to the motivation of Paul's
use and redaction of the confession in the purpose

[38]Jewett, Anthropological Terms, 136-139.

of Romans, but without taking sufficient account of
the rhetoric of Romans. The hypothesis did not deal
explicitly with the question of the parameters of
the confession, the origins of Rom 1:3b and 4h, and
it failed to discuss the question of the origin of
the phrase ἐν δυνάμει.

h. From a form-critical point of view, the most
adequate analysis of the original confession eliminates
both the phrase ἐν δυνάμει and the antithesis between
"flesh and spirit." This rigorous refinement of the
Bultmann viewpoint first surfaced in the 1965 monograph
by Reginald Fuller.[39] He followed Schweizer in deleting
"in power" from the original confession, but apparently
misread Schweizer in believing that he had advocated
"according to the flesh/spirit" as Hellenistic additions.[40] But the resultant antithesis is highly plausible:

   γενομένου ἐκ σπέρματος Δαυίδ ,
   ὁρισθέντος υἱοῦ θεοῦ ἐξ ἀναστάσεως νεκρῶν .

Fuller argued for a Palestinian origin of this confession on grounds of close parallels with Acts 3:20
and 10:42. "The Davidic descent of Jesus serves the
purpose of legitimating his destined appearance as
the eschatological judge and saviour at the parousia."[41] Fuller went on to show how the addition of
the phrases "according to the flesh/spirit" transformed the original confession. "The Davidic sonship
now characterizes his whole historical ministry...,
while the divine sonship from the time of the resurrection becomes one of active rule in an exalted
state...."[42]

What this hypothesis fails to explain is the
origin of the peculiar phrase "according to the spirit
of holiness," which is unlikely to have originated
in the Hellenistic circle that wished to depreciate
the Davidic sonship. The same weakness is found in
Klaus Wengst, who independently came to Fuller's con-

---

[39]Reginald H. Fuller, The Foundations of New Testament
Christology (New York: Scribners, 1965) 165-167.
[40]Fuller's description of Schweizer's view of the
κατὰ σάρκα / κατὰ πνεῦμα would match the hypothesis
presented in Jewett, Anthropological Terms, but this
book is not referred to in his notes.
[41]Fuller, Foundations, 166.
[42]Ibid.

clusion in 1972 about the content of the original confession.[43] He provides a convincing argument in favor of assigning ἐν δυνάμει to Pauline redaction, not to create a concept of higher grade sonship as Schweizer had suggested but to reinforce Jesus' status as "son of God with power." But he fails to overturn the assessment of Schweizer that the expressions "according to flesh/spirit" were not added by Paul. On this point Fuller's suggestion of a non-Pauline, Hellenistic circle redacting the original confession appears more plausible.

A more extensive presentation of this hypothesis appeared in the same year, 1972, from the pen of Heinrich Schlier.[44] That Paul added the phrase ἐν δυνάμει is indicated by its lack of parallelism in the first half of the confession as well as its consistency with Pauline references to Christ as living from the power of God. In his judgement, Schweizer was correct in seeing that the phrases κατὰ σάρκα / κατὰ πνεῦμα ἁγιωσύνης did not originate with Paul. But they also do not belong to the original confession, having been added by Hellenistic Jewish Christians interested in reducing the importance of descent from David and laying greater emphasis on the resurrection as the revelation of divine glory. On the basis of parallels in the Testament of the Twelve Patriarchs and the amulet from Acre discussed by Erik Peterson,[45] Schlier argues that ἁγιωσύνης is used in the sense of "glory." The original confession therefore emphasized that Jesus was "appointed Son of God with glory, which is effective in the resurrection of the dead."[46]

The problem with this conclusion is that while ἁγιωσύνης is closely associated with δόξα , neither in the amulet nor in the Testament of the Twelve Patri-

---

[43]Wengst, Christologische Formeln, 112-117; Fuller's study is not cited in the notes or bibliography.
[44]Schlier, "Zu Röm 1,3f," 207-218.
[45]Erik Peterson, "Das Amulett von Acre," Frühkirche, Judentum und Gnosis: Studien und Untersuchungen (Rome: Herder, 1959) 346-354.
[46]Schlier, "Zu Röm 1,3f," 212.

archs are these terms actually used as synonyms.[47] Schlier is able to retain the antithetical quality of "according to the flesh/spirit" only by treating "holiness" essentially as something else. "Κατὰ σάρκα and κατὰ πνεῦμα ἁγιωσύνης do not imply higher and lower levels but a strict opposition. Both together imply a paradoxical circumstance. Particularly since ἁγιωσύνης equals δόξα, the first member of the sentence does not contain a confession of the earthly messiah as a preliminary phase of the heavenly, but rather a confession of the earthly as the Jesus Christ who in his power has been appointed son of God."[48] While the construal of holiness as glory appears strained, Schlier's basic idea of a double redaction of an original Jewish Christian confession is on target. However, it remains more likely that the first redaction occurred with Hellenistic Christians inserting the flat antithesis "according to the flesh/spirit" and that Paul was responsible for the insertion of both "in power" and "of holiness."

i. The final option that I know about was worked out by Jürgen Becker in 1976.[49] He hedges on the question of whether "in power" was added by Paul and concentrates his critical attention on the puzzling antithesis between "according to the flesh" and "according to the spirit of holiness." Rejecting the option that Paul created this uncharacteristic antithesis, he suggests that the original confession contained only the second half. To avoid adding more ambiguity to a somewhat confusing discussion, I provide Becker's wording of the reconstructed credo:
(Wir glauben an Jesus,)
geboren aus dem Samen Davids,
eingesetzt zum Sohn Gottes im (oder:in der Macht des) heiligen Geist(es) aufgrund der Auferstehung von der Toten.[50]

In light of our previous discussion, it is clear that this alternative should be set aside even though

---

[47]Peterson, "Das Amulett," 349, fails to make a convincing case for synonymous usage in the amulet found at Acre.
[48]Schlier, "Zu Röm 1,3f," 213.
[49]Jürgen Becker, Auferstehung der Toten im Urchristentum (Stuttgart: Katholisches Bibelwerk, 1976) 20-31.
[50]Ibid., 24.

it correctly identifies one of the crucial problems
to be resolved. Becker's retention of multiple qualifications in the second line erodes the balance between
ἐκ σπέρματος Δαυίδ and ἐξ ἀναστάσεως νεκρῶν ; no explanation is provided for the phrase "according to the
spirit of holiness," which Becker translates here
differently than in his supporting discussion;[51]
no <u>Sitz im Leben</u> is provided for the original confession,
with its peculiar tension between Davidic origins
and spiritual power; and no motivation is suggested
for Paul's addition of the κατὰ σάρκα qualification,
which makes Paul the author of the antithesis after
Becker had concluded that this was unlikely.

    j. The result of this debate is that a three-
level development of the confession emerges as the
most likely option. My earlier espousal of a three-
level redactional scheme required the correction of
Fuller, Wengst and Schlier. The earliest level was
a Jewish Christian confession of Jesus:

    3b   τοῦ γενομένου
    3c   ἐκ σπέρματος Δαυίδ
    4a   τοῦ ὁρισθέντος υἱοῦ θεοῦ
    4d   ἐξ ἀναστάσεως νεκρῶν.

The second, or redacted, level of the confession included
the antithesis, "according to the flesh/spirit":

    3b   τοῦ γενομένου
    3c   ἐκ σπέρματος Δαυίδ
    3d   κατὰ σάρκα,   ,
    4a   τοῦ ὁρισθέντος υἱοῦ θεοῦ
    4c   κατὰ πνεῦμα
    4d   ἐξ ἀναστάσεως νεκρῶν.

The third level of the confession is the one found
in Rom. 1:3-4, including Paul's insertions of the
phrase ἐν δυνάμει and the qualifying genitive ἁγιωσύνης .

III
The Meaning of the Original Confession
and Its Initial Redaction

    There are elements in the original confession

---

[51]On pp. 20-23, Becker refers consistently to the "Geist
der Heiligkeit" and nowhere does he provide the basis
for his concluding translation, "im heiligen Geist(es)."

that bear the marks of the primitive Aramaic speaking church. It is generally agreed that the interest in Davidic descent points in this direction.[52] Leslie C. Allen,[53] following suggestions by Fuller and Kramer,[54] has shown that ὁρισθέντος in Rom 1:4 is derived from the royal decree language of Psalm 2:7, with its closest analogues in the Aramaic section of Daniel. There is a strong likelihood that this component in the confession derived from "the Aramaic-speaking primitive church,"[55] so it should be interpreted in light of the interests of that group.

At the core of the original confession, therefore, is the affirmation of Jesus as the traditional Davidic messiah, who was adopted and enthroned as the Son of God on the basis of his resurrection. The popular Jewish expectation of a Son of David as found in Cant 17:21 and elsewhere is reflected here, with the traditional expectation of national restoration, victory over the Gentile nations and governance of the world.[56] The potentially chauvinistic element in the first line of the credo is not diminished by the second line, which affirms the divine appointment of Jesus as the heavenly Son of God. The adoptionist christology of primitive Palestinian Christianity surfaces in this formulation, consistent with the confessional materials in Acts 2:36 and 13:33.[57] But it appears clear that no diminution of authority is intended by this primitive formulation: the Son of God is empha-

---

[52]Cf. A. J. B. Higgins, "The OT and Some Aspects of NT Christology," CJT 6 (1960) 200-202; Otto Michel, Der Brief an die Römer (Göttingen: Vandenhoeck & Ruprecht, 1963, twelfth edition) 38; Burger, Jesus, 28; Wilckens, Römer, 60.
[53]Leslie C. Allen, "The Old Testament Background of (προ-) ὁρίζειν in the New Testament," NTS 17 (1970-71) 104-108.
[54]Cf. Fuller, Foundations, 166; Kramer, Christ, 112ff.; M.-E. Boismard indicates less interest in the source of the term in "Constitue Fils de Dieu (Rom., I, 4)," RB 60 (1953) 5-11.
[55]Allen, "Background," 104-105.
[56]Becker, Auferstehung, 29, cites Ps 2:8 and Cant 17:3 in this connection.
[57]Cf. Käsemann, Romans, 12.

tically appointed as ruler of the world.[58] The precise
implications of the phrase "from the resurrection
of the dead" depend on whether one accepts Hans Lietzmann's suggestion that this is an aesthetically motivated
abbreviation of a formula referring more precisely
to Christ's resurrection.[59] In light of the compelling
evidence Bartsch assembled to show that this reference
to the general resurrection from the dead is typical
of early Christian apocalyptic, there is no reason
to provide a less than literal interpretation.[60]
As Käsemann writes, "The hymnic tradition does not
isolate Christ's resurrection, but views it in its
cosmic function as the beginning of general resurrection."[61] At the somewhat primitive level of the
original credo,[62] no distinction is made between Christ's
resurrection and the dawn of the age of the general
resurrection. Both are apparently associated as the
inbreaking of the new age.[63] This leads to a significant
conclusion: the original, Jewish Christian confession
contained an emphasis on the apocalyptic hinge between
the two ages even before the insertion of the clearly

---

[58]Cf. Anton J. Fridrichsen, The Apostle and His Message
(Uppsala: Lundequistska, 1947) 10: "In other words,
through His resurrection from the dead, Jesus, formerly
the Messiah of the Jews, has been enthroned as Lord
and Saviour of the whole world."
    [59]Hans Lietzmann, An die Römer (Tübingen: Mohr, 1933,
fourth edition) 25.
    [60]Bartsch, "Bekenntnisformel," 330-335, shows the close
parallels to Acts 26:23; Matt 27:51-53 and 1 Cor 15:20.
Dunn, "Jesus," 56 follows this approach, citing a
number of scholars including S. H. Hooke, "The Translation of Rom. i.4," NTS 9 (1962-63) 370-371. Jürgen
Becker overlooks this evidence in concluding that
Rom 1:4 refers exclusively to Jesus' individual resurrection, Auferstehung, 30-31.
    [61]Käsemann, Romans, 12.
    [62]Schlier, "Zu Röm 1,3f," 214, speaks of "a certain
archaic quality" in the wording of ἐξ ἀναστάσεως νεκρῶν .
    [63]It therefore appears inappropriate to conclude with
Ferdinand Hahn that the credo features "the de-eschato-
logization of the messianic office of Jesus...," Titles, 251. For a detailed critique on this point,
cf. Philipp Vielhauer, "Ein Weg zur neutestamentlichen
Christologie? Prüfung der Thesen Ferdinand Hahns,"
Aufsätze zum Neuen Testament (Munich: Kaiser, 1965)
141-198, esp. 187.

antithetical expressions, "according to the flesh/ spirit."

When the original confession was edited by the insertion of references to σάρξ and πνεῦμα, the implicit antithesis between the ages was developed in a radical direction. As Eduard Schweizer has pointed out, Hellenistic thought tended to conceive the flesh/spirit dualism in material terms, as counterposed realms of damnation/salvation.[64] Human destiny was thought to be determined by the realm to which one was subordinate. Bondage to the realm of the flesh could be overcome only by divine means. When flesh and spirit are combined with the preposition κατά, the thought of being limited or dominated by a particular sphere is strongly implied.[65] The antithesis thus has a negative as well as a positive set of implications. On the negative side, there is a clear deprecation of the significance of the Davidic origin of the messiah and all that it implied. The Hellenistic Christians who inserted this line probably stood close to the radicals refuted in Rom 11:11-25, who vaunted their superiority as divinely grafted branches that displaced the original Jewish branches of the olive tree. They appear to have shared the outlook of the Corinthian radicals who devalued the fleshly, historical Jesus (1 Cor 12:3; 15:44-46). Insofar as Jesus descended from the fleshly seed of David, this insertion implies, he was bound to a realm of material bondage that was opposed to the power of salvation.

The positive implication of the phrase κατὰ πνεῦμα is that the redemptive power of Christ derives from his spiritual authority rather than his Davidic origin. Divine sonship is here qualified in terms of spirit, which means that the ecstatic experiences of early Christians could be seen to derive directly from him. In place of the apocalyptic expectation of the dawn of the age of bodily resurrection, this phrase implies that the salvation brought by the Son of God is pneumatic and experiential. To belong to the sphere of the spirit was to be set free from bondage to the flesh,

---

[64]Eduard Schweizer, "πνεῦμα, πνευματικός," TWNT, 6. 387-453, esp. 390; idem, "σάρξ," TWNT, 7.98-151, esp. 123.
[65]Cf. Rudolf Bultmann, Theology of the New Testament, tr. K. Grobel (London: SCM, 1952) vol. I, 236-237.

to partake in a superior world of divine power. In
short, the insertions of the phrases κατὰ σάρκα and
κατὰ πνεῦμα move the credo unmistakeably in the direction
of Hellenistic dualism, with all its appeals, powers,
and dangers.

IV
Pauline Use of the Confession

I believe that it was to contend with the dangers
of the Hellenistic Christian redaction as well as
of the original Jewish Christian wording of the credo
that Paul inserted the phrase ἐν δυνάμει and the modi-
fying term ἁγιωσύνη. Aside from the use in Rom 1:4,
the only two other New Testament uses of "holiness"
are in Pauline passages where ethical obligations
are being stressed. These passages provide an initial
clue to Paul's intention here as well. In 1 Thess 3:13,
the homiletic benediction that summarizes the argument
of the first portion of the letter, the action of
God is described as establishing "your hearts unblamable
in holiness before our God and Father, at the coming
of our Lord Jesus with all his saints." The specific
reference of ἁγιωσύνη is developed in the succeeding
section which argues for sexual fidelity (1 Thess 4:1-
8). A similar context is visible in 2 Cor 7:1, which
refers to cleansing of "every defilement of body and
spirit" so that "holiness" might be made "perfect
in the fear of God." In both instances congregational
tendencies toward libertinism motivated by freedom
in the spirit are countered by the use of ἁγιωσύνη.
One suspects a similar concern in Rom 1:4, because
the belief in having transcended the realm of σάρξ
by virtue of one's adherence to the realm of πνεῦμα
easily led to libertinistic excesses. The qualification
of spirit as the "spirit of holiness" made clear that
the divine power celebrated in the confession entailed
moral obligations. This is in fact a theme developed
at length in Romans 5-8, which shows that the new
life involves righteousness, a repudiation of fleshly
passions, and walking "according to the spirit."
Paul makes plain that the spirit given to Christian
believers is the "holy spirit" (Rom 5:5), and that
the law remains "holy" even for members of the new
age (Rom 7:12). The key to the new ethic is giving
oneself as a holy sacrifice for others (Rom 12:1).
In this sense, the insertion of the term "holiness"
prepares the reader for a major emphasis in the letter.

117

Paul's insertion of the phrase ἐν δυνάμει appears to be a correction of the Christology of the original confession, and thus to be directed more against the Jewish Christian than the Hellenistic Christian theology. It counters the adoptionism of the original confession by asserting that Christ bore the "power" of God prior to the resurrection, [66] thus bringing the confession more nearly in line with Paul's typical interest in the doctrine of pre-existent κύριος .[67] But as the subsequent argument of Romans indicates, the interest in "power" is more than christological. The thesis of Romans is that the gospel about Christ is "the power of God for salvation" (Rom 1:16). Insofar as Romans serves the task of world mission, aiming to elicit support for proclaiming the gospel in Spain, the entire letter can be understood as elaborating this thesis. It is consistent that the benediction wrapping up the formal argument of Romans reiterates this theme: "May the God of hope fill you with all joy and peace in believing, so that by the power of the Holy Spirit you may abound in hope" (Rom 15:13; cf. also 15:19). To return to the context of the confession, the insertion of ἐν δυνάμει therefore reiterates a motif that was implicit in the Hellenistic Christian insertion of the flesh/spirit dualism: the power of God resides not in Davidic descent but in direct, divine appointment of Christ as Son of God, so that the proclamation of the gospel about him is to be the powerful means by which the "righteousness of God" is restored.

It would be a mistake, however, to interpret Paul's citation of the credo merely on the basis of two, relatively minor, corrections. The introductory and concluding formulations need to be taken into account, and above all, the fact that Paul selected a composite creed should be reflected upon in light of the purpose of the letter as a whole.

The characteristic assumption of form and redac-

---

[66]Cf. Schlier, "Zu Röm 1,3f," 210; Oscar Cullmann infers from the phrase "in power" that "Jesus is the 'Son of God' from the beginning," The Christology of the New Testament, tr. S. C. Guthrie & C. A. M. Hall (Philadelphia: Westminster, 1959) 292.
[67]Cf. Burger, Jesus, 31f; Wengst, Christologische Formeln, 114.

tion criticism is that introductory and concluding
formulas should be ascribed to redactors rather than
to the original scope of cited material. That Rom 1:3b,
περὶ τοῦ υἱοῦ αὐτοῦ , was probably not part of the
original credo has been assumed in this study. Klaus
Wengst has pointed out that if this line belonged
to the credo, the reference to appointed sonship in
verse 4 would lose its emphatic quality through anticipation and redundancy.[68] By introducing the credo
with these words, however, Paul thwarts adoptionist
inferences and qualifies the Davidic sonship by stressing that Jesus was the Son of God prior to his earthly
appearance.[69] The line that Paul provided to close
the confession, Ἰησοῦ Χριστοῦ τοῦ κυρίου ἡμῶν , employs
distinctively Pauline language that differentiates
it from the cited material.[70] These words explicitly
state the lordship theme that we detected both in
the insertion of ἐν δυνάμει and ἁγιωσύνης . The pre-
existent Son of God celebrated in the credo is to
be seen as the Lord of the world, a theme closely
related with the thesis concerning the revelation
of the "righteousness of God" (Rom 1:16-17) and the
anticipated acknowledgement by the nations (Rom 15:10-
12). In Käsemann's words, "For Paul the kyrios is the
representative of the God who claims the world and who
with the church brings the new creation into the midst
of the old world that is perishing."[71] With this
introduction and conclusion, Paul effectively encloses
the credo within the framework of his own theology.

The most significant feature of all, however,
is that Paul selects a credo that bears the marks
of both "the weak and the strong," the Gentile and
the Jewish Christian branches of the early church.
Despite the careful framing with typical Pauline language, and regardless of the correcting insertions,
the prominent location of this creed indicates Paul's
acceptance of a common faith and his effort to be
evenhanded. He is willing to cite the Jewish Christian

---

[68]Wengst, Christologische Formeln, 112; cf. also Käsemann,
Romans, 10.
[69]Cf. Stuhlmacher, "Probleme," 382; Dunn, "Jesus," 55-56.
[70]Cf. Schlier, "Zu Röm 1,3f," 208; Käsemann, Romans,
13-14; Bouwman, Paulus, 128.
[71]Käsemann, Romans, 14.

affirmation of Jesus as coming from the "seed of David,"
despite his opposition to Jewish zealotism (Rom 10:1-
3) and pride (Rom 2:17-24). He is willing to accept
the Hellenistic Christian dialectic of flesh versus
spirit, despite his subsequent effort to insist upon
moral transformation (Rom 6-8) and to counter the
results of spiritual arrogance (Rom 14:1-15:7). Yet
none of these points are scored overtly; the credo
is cited with respect, edited with skill, and framed
effectively in language that various branches of the
early church would have understood. The overwhelming
impression one has after reflecting on the implications
of Paul's use of the credo is his irenic style. He
is obviously seeking to find common ground, which
brings the confession into the context of Paul's ambassadorial strategy in the letter as a whole.[72]

For this reason I find it necessary to qualify
the formulation of Peter Stuhlmacher, that Paul is
attempting primarily to prove to the Romans that he
shares an essentially salvation-historical Christology.[73] Schlier pointed out that the first level
editing of the formula had severely qualified this
salvation history point of view by the insertion of
the "flesh/spirit" antithesis, and that it was likely
this edited credo that was known in Rome. What Paul
provides, in Schlier's perspective, is Paul's own
edited version which means that it functions as part
of the firming up of their faith (Rom 1:11-12), an
apostolic correction so to speak. "He practices the
spiritual relation between apostle and church,"[74]
which, if understood in a traditional manner, might
involve some rather authoritarian implications. It
seems to me that Paul's use of the credo transforms
the features of both Stuhlmacher's and Schlier's perspectives. The christological parameters are drawn
broadly enough to incorporate the insights both of
the salvation-history advocates and the Hellenistic
dualists. And apostolic authority is used here not
to discredit theological options that Paul happens
to dislike but rather to find common ground in the
faith for a variety of cultural, theological and ethical
alternatives.

---

[72]Cf. Robert Jewett, "Romans as an Ambassadorial Letter,"
Int 36 (1982) 12-20.
[73]Stuhlmacher, "Probleme," 378-386.
[74]Schlier, "Zu Röm 1,3f," 218.

V
Implications

This analysis of a "living word" throws light on the rhetoric and the interpretation of Romans as well as on the evolution of early Christian credal materials and their significance for the church today. A few words will have to suffice on each of these points.

The study of classical rhetoric reveals the crucial role of the exordium for the understanding of a subsequent argument. It not only introduces the speaker in a manner calculated to appeal to the audience and lend credence to the speaker's cause, but it also frequently introduces the topics to be addressed in a letter or speech.[75] Only in Romans is there a confession included in the exordium, which has led exegetes to suggest that Paul was attempting to demonstrate his orthodoxy to the Romans by citing a creed in use there.[76] The fact that this is a composite creed could lend precision to this suggestion. Insofar as the creed contains components contributed by branches of the early Church that are in competition in Rome,[77] its use signals the intent to find common ground in the letter as a whole. The argument for early Christian

---

[75]Cf. Heinrich Lausberg, Handbuch der literarischen Rhetorik (Munich: Max Hueber, 1973) 1. 150-163; George A. Kennedy, New Testament Interpretation through Rhetorical criticism (Chapel Hill: University of North Carolina, 1984) 23-24; 142, 153; Frank Witt Hughes, "Second Thessalonians as a Document of Early Christian Rhetoric," (Ph.D. dissertation, Garrett-Northwestern, 1984) 91-95.

[76]Cf. Neufeld, Confessions, 51, citing Dodd, Bultmann, Michel and Barrett; Kuss, Römerbrief, 8.

[77]Cf. Wolfgang Wiefel, "The Jewish Community in Ancient Rome and the Origins of Roman Christianity," The Romans Debate, ed. K. P. Donfried (Minneapolis: Augsburg, 1977) 100-119; Dieter Zeller, Juden und Heiden in der Mission des Paulus: Studien zum Römerbrief (Stuttgart: Katholisches Bibelwerk, 1973); Halvor Moxnes, Theology in Conflict: Studies in Paul's Understanding of God in Romans (Leiden: Brill, 1980).

pluralism that has been detected in Rom 14:1-15:7 is thus integral to the letter as a whole as the exordium makes plain.[78]

It is worth pointing out that the use of the credal material in Rom 1:3-4 is rather different from the litmus test of orthodoxy that became typical for the later church. Paul's purpose appears to be inclusive rather than exclusive. He does not discard the adoptionist language, despite his preference for affirmations of pre-existence. He does not eliminate the flesh/spirit dualism even though he had struggled in several congregations to counter the resultant libertinism. The interest in ideological, racial and theological unification manifest in this creed is an admirable model for the church today.

Finally, there is a remarkable element of fluidity in this early Christian confession. Heinrich Schlier commented that this was an example of "the steadfastness and changeability of early Christian confessional forms," arguing that this was the "changing of what holds fast."[79] To use the terms of this Festschrift, the word only remains living as it transforms itself to meet new cultural circumstances and challenges. If it stops changing, it dies. The confession of Rom 1:3-4 thus stands as an abiding invitation to theological reflection and indoctrination, not in a static sense of providing formulas that transcend time but in the sense of inviting others to join in the confessional process themselves. Neither the first century conservatives nor liberals, neither the Jewish Christians nor the Gentile Christians, could hope adequately to confess Jesus as Lord by using their preferred language alone. They needed each other, and they needed Paul to help them retain common ground despite all of their tensions. What was true for them is surely true for us as well, as we seek to serve a church and world whose pluralism is more diverse with every passing year.

---

[78]Cf. Robert Jewett, Christian Tolerance: Paul's Message to the Modern Church (Philadelphia: Westminster, 1982).
[79]Schlier, "Zu Röm 1,3f," 216.

CHAPTER NINE

THE SEARCH FOR THE LIVING TEXT OF THE LUCAN
INFANCY NARRATIVE

P. Boyd Mather

Twenty-five years ago, working under the direction
of Professor Ernest Saunders, I completed a thesis
on the hymns of the nativity that are found in the
first two chapters of the gospel according to Luke.[1]
The occasion of this essay affords an appropriate
opportunity to return to these opening chapters of
the Third Gospel for the purpose of searching for
the living text of the Lucan infancy narrative. The
operative question has been, What is the history of
the tradition of Luke 1-2 in the first two centuries
of the Common Era? The beginning assumption was that
in the past two decades Lucan studies have made a
quantum leap forward and new windows of research are
now open. The assumption has proved to be half right.

The early '60s became the watershed of English
publications related to Luke. In 1961 the English
translatin of Conzelmann's Die Mitte der Zeit (German
edition, 1953) was published.[2] The same year Barrett's
Luke the Historian in Recent Study summarized the
state of the study of Luke-Acts, especially the work
of six 20th-century scholars: Martin Dibelius, Bertil
Gärtner, Arnold Ehrhardt, Robert Morgenthaler, Ernst
Haenchen, and Conzelmann.[3] Then in 1966 the Keck-Martyn
volume honored Paul Schubert with its Studies in Luke-

---

[1]P. B. Mather, "A Literary-Linguistic Analysis of the
Hymns of the Nativity," M.A. Thesis (Northwestern
University, 1959).
[2]Hans Conzelmann, The Theology of St. Luke (London:
Faber & Faber, 1961).
[3]C. K. Barrett, Luke the Historian in Recent Study
(London: Epworth, 1961).

Acts.[4] Since that time a renewed study of Luke-Acts
has flowed from the scholarly pens in an ever widening
stream. Especially noteworthy has been the production
of the Luke-Acts Seminar of the Society of Biblical
Literature, which was chaired by Charles Talbert,
and a constellation of other scholars who have related
to that work, both positively and negatively, during
the past decade.

The study of the infancy narrative, however,
has not kept pace with the stream of scholarship.
Raymond Brown, using another metaphor, describes the
matter accurately:

> For Roman Catholicism the narrative of Jesus'
> birth and infancy found in Matthew and Luke may
> well constitute the last frontier to be crossed
> by biblical criticism. . . While Protestant
> biblical criticism breached this frontier a long
> time ago, it never really settled the territory
> and made the desert bloom.[5]

Brown's own The Birth of the Messiah[6] along with several
recent commentaries, that of Joseph A. Fitzmyer being
the most notable, have taken the longest steps across
the frontier.[7] Bibliography has continued to grow;
the basic critical question, however, remain either
unsolved or their proposed answers continue to be
debated. The basic bibliographic references on Luke
1-2 remain amazingly similar to what my own cards
recorded twenty-five years ago.

In the following pages I shall offer a prolegomenous
survey of the methodological questions that surround
the search for the living text of the infancy narrative
in Luke, define the limited perspective through which
one might approach the history of the tradition, and
attempt a constructive statement from that perspective.

---

[4]L. E. Keck and J. L. Martyn, eds., Studies in Luke-Acts
(Nashville: Abingdon, 1966).
    [5]Raymond E. Brown, "Luke's Method in the Annunciation
Narrative of Chapter One," in Perspectives on Luke-Acts,
ed. Charles H. Talbert (Danville, VA: Association
of Baptist Professors of Religion, 1978), 126.
    [6]Raymond E. Brown, The Birth of the Messiah (Garden
City, NY: Doubleday & Company, 1979), Book Two:
The Lucan Infancy Narrative.
    [7]Joseph A. Fitzmyer, The Gospel According to Luke I-IX
(Garden City, NY: Doubleday & Company, 1981).

*

The problems of approaching Luke 1-2 cluster around four questions:

1. What is the literary relationship of these chapters, and especially 1:5-2:52, to the whole of the Third Gospel?
2. What, if any, sources can be posited for Luke 1-2?
3. What is the internal structure of the Lucan infancy narrative?
4. What, if any, corroborative material outside of the Third Gospel gives credence to the various hypotheses related to these questions?

The fourth question can be answered most easily and with the least dispute. Unlike much of the Third Gospel, which finds parallels in Mark and Matthew, the infancy narrative has no synoptic relationship and has no extant first-century documents with which its own text finds literary reference. In the ante-Nicene fathers, Ignatius has one reference, and Justin Martyr two, to Luke's infancy narrative. Only with Irenaeus does one find discussion of its narratives, by both Irenaeus and the "heretics" he seeks to refute. These are references to Luke, however, rather than to an independent or separate tradition or document.

Fitzmyer suggests that Matthew and Luke both depend "on a certain body of information in the tradition that existed perior to their writing." He says of the common details which they share that he tends "to regard them as the historical nucleus of what the evangelists worked with."[8] Fitzmyer outlines the following common details:

1) Jesus' birth is related to the reign of Herod (Luke 1:5; Matt 2:1).
2) Mary, his mother to be, is a virgin engaged to Joseph, but they have not yet come to live together (Luke 1:27, 34; 2:5; Matt 1:18).
3) Joseph is of the house of David (Luke 1:27;

---

[8]Fitzmyer, Luke, 306-307.

2:4; Matt 1:16, 20).

4) An angel from heaven announces the coming birth of Jesus (Luke 1:28-30; Matt 1:20-21).

5) Jesus is recognized himself to be a son of David (Luke 1:32; Matt 1:1).

6) His conception is to take place through the Holy Spirit (Luke 1:35; Matt 1:18, 20).

7) Joseph is not involved in the conception (Luke 1:34; Matt 1:18-25).

8) The name "Jesus" is imposed by heaven prior to his birth (Luke 1:31; Matt 1:21).

9) The angel identifies Jesus as "Savior" (Luke 2:11; Matt 1:20-21).

10) Jesus is born after Mary and Joseph come to live together (Luke 2:4-7; Matt 1:24-25).

11) Jesus is born at Bethlehem (Luke 2:4-7; Matt 2:1).

12) Jesus settles, with Mary and Joseph, in Nazareth in Galilee (Luke 2:39, 51; Matt 2:22-23).[9]

Brown's evaluation of these details, which he calls "common points," is correct in showing that nearly all of them are confined in Matthew to one section (1:18-2:1), that even within the parallels there are significant differences (e.g., the angelic visit to Joseph in Matthew hardly compares to the angelic annunciation to Mary in Luke), and that some details can be deduced from Jesus' public ministry separate from the infancy narratives. Brown's terminology is also better, for these are "common points" that hardly demonstrate that we have found details of a common or single tradition. In fact, the remainder of the Matthean infancy narrative differs markedly from Luke's, to the point that Brown makes the "observation that the two narratives are not only different -- they are contrary to each other in a number of details."[10]

The evidence probably indicates separate traditions that have commonality because they treat the same subject rather than because of common sources or interdependence. Matthew's tradition was formulated around OT quotations that find no parallel in the Lucan ma-

---

[9]Fitzmyer, Luke, 307.
[10]Brown, Birth, 36; see whole of pp. 33-37.

terial.[11]   Luke's own tradition is less clear as to
its source and methodology, and it remains the subject
of this paper's search. For the historian the common
points are useful to summarize what we can safely
say about Jesus' birth, but they tell us little or
nothing of the narratives' pre-histories.

Question four, therefore, must be answered with
a single word, None. No corroborative material is
available to test our various theories as to the history
of the tradition in Luke either outside or within
the NT.

What then of the second question, regarding sources? It is commonly known that Luke uses sources
of some sort. The Anti-Marcionite prologue said of
the author:

He shows by means of the preface . . . that before
him other Gospels had been written, and that
it was necessary to set forth, for those of the
Gentiles who believed, the accurate narrative
of the dispensation, that they should not be
distracted by Jewish fables nor miss the truth
by the heretical and vain fantasies. So we have
received as the most necessary at the beginning
the birth of John, who is the beginning of the
Gospel, in that he was the forerunner of the
Lord and a sharer both in the preparation of
the Gospel and the fellowship of the Spirit.
This dispensation a prophet among the Twelve
calls to mind.[12]

Cadbury's comment, also based on the information of
Luke's preface and the nature of the material which
follows it, remains relevant. Namely, for large sections
of the Third Gospel -- altogether nearly half of it
-- "we have good reason adduced from the existence
of parallel records to assert the author's reliance
on earlier writings."[13]   The probability that the
infancy narratives depend on written sources is not
lessened because parallel passages are not extant.
"The means of demonstration are less available, but

---

[11]Norman Perrin, The New Testament: An Introduction
(New York: Harcourt Brace Jovanovich, 1974), 172-174.
[12]Translation of R. G. Heard, "The Old Gospel Prologues,"
JTS n.s. 6 (1955) 1-16.
[13]Henry J. Cadbury, The Making of Luke-Acts (New York:
Macmillan Company, 1927), 63.

the probability is still very great."[14]

Three theories of sources have been set forth with regard to Luke 1-2, with the theories sometimes mixed.

1. A special source, or sources, is posited for the hymns of the Nativity. The basic thesis common to all these theories is that the hymns and canticles, especially the Magnificat (Luke 1:46-55), the Benedictus (1:67-79), and the Nunc Dimittis (2:29-32), can be separated from their narrative settings as pre-Lucan units in a manner similar to the isolation of pre-Pauline hymnic sections in the epistles. Further, these hymns and associated poetic sections can be reconstructed in an earlier, often pre-translated form that, in turn, indicates something of the pre-history of the text. No one claims that the hymns can be isolated in a separate, non-Lucan form prior to Luke's usage of them, although it is commonly known that several appear at the end of the Psalms in Codex Alexandrinus as separate Odes of the Church.[15]

R. A. Aytoun argues that ten such hymns are to be found in Luke 1-2 and that their original language is Hebrew.[16] Building his case on Franz Delitzsch's 19th-century Hebrew translation of the NT, a translation made prior to the rediscovery of the canons of Hebrew poetry that were assumed by Aytoun himself, Aytoun attempted to demonstrate the Hebraic poetic form of these passages: "That the speeches and songs . . . were originally in the Hebrew language; and further, that in metre, balance, and structure they must have been composed in accordance with what are now generally agreed to have been the canons of ancient prosody."[17]

---

[14]Cadbury, Making, 66; see whole of chap. VI, "The Immediate Sources."

[15]To my knowledge, no one has been able to establish the history of the use of Lk. 1:46-55, 68-79 and Luke 2:29-32 as separate odes (No. 9 & 13) and Lk. 2:14 as the opening verse of Ode 14 in the period prior to their appearance in the 5th century manuscript, Codex Alexandrinus.

[16]R. A. Aytoun, "The Ten Lucan Hymns of the Nativity in Their Original Language," JTS 18 (1917) 274-288.

[17]Aytoun, "Lucan Hymns," 287.

Aytoun's hypothesis found both support and opposition in the '50s. A. H. McNeile, who stated that the style and language of these two chapters are its only guides to its sources, argued that Burney had demonstrated that the passages could be translated into Aramaic and be no less poetic.[18] Turner likewise argued for an Aramaic background.[19] But Paul Winter, beginning with the question, "Magnificat and Benedictus--Maccabaean Psalms?"[20] published a series of essays in which he maintained that Hebrew was the base language and the sources were Jewish and Jewish-Christian redactions.[21] Laurentin, likewise, argued that the first two chapters of Luke emanated from a Judaeo-Christian atmosphere where the knowledge of Scripture, Jewish culture and midrashic exegesis had attained a high degree of development and where the redaction of the "Gospel of the Infancy," to use his term, is Luke's, who translated and utilized a Hebrew document.[22]

If sources can be isolated, the case for a Hebrew, Judaeo-Christian source is probably the strongest. Therefore, I have offered a rather long summary of the main hypothesis. Theories of written sources are often built on vocabulary, but Luke's method of recasting his material, paraphrasing it into his own style in a manner he shares with Greek and Latin writers generally, prevents the determination of his sources by the criterion of vocabulary. Comparative studies of the Lucan usage of Mark and Q were well summed up long ago by Cadbury:

---

[18]A. H. McNeile, An Introduction to the New Testament (2nd ed.; Oxford: Clarendon, 1953), 89; citing C. F. Burney, The Poetry of Our Lord (Oxford: Clarendon, 1925).
[19]N. Turner, "The Relation of Luke I and II to Hebraic Sources and to the Rest of Luke-Acts," NTS 2 (1956) 100-109.
[20]BJRL 27 (1954-1955) 335-335.
[21]Cf. esp., Winter, "Some Observations on the Language in the Birth and Infancy Stories of the Third Gospel," NTS 1 (1954) 111-121; "On Luke and Lucan Sources," ZNW 47 (1956) 217-242; and "The Main Literary Problem of the Lucan Infancy Story," Vox Theologica 28 (1957-1958) 117-122.
[22]Rene Laurentin, Structure et Theologie de Luc I-II (EBib; Paris: J. Gabalda, 1957), esp. 12-21.

His own style is more obvious at some times than at
others, but it is never so totally wanting as to prove
alien origin for a passage, and it is never so pervasive
as to exclude the possibility that a written source
existed, although the source be no longer capable of
detection by any residual difference of style.[23]

When the attempt is made to define a special
source or sources for the hymns of the nativity, Luke's
own style and his known use of sources make such con-
jecture appealing. It must be said, however, that
the evidence is thoroughly ambiguous and the analysis
highly speculative.

2. A special source, or sources, is posited
for the stories of John the Baptist and Jesus in Chapter
1. A special note is needed here because I normally
mean by "sources" written materials, while discussion
of these theories often speak of oral traditions as
well. Hence, due to the intimate details about the
conception of each child, a family tradition has been
suggested.[24] Others have set forth a Baptist source
for several of these stories, not only those that
have particular reference to John the Baptist but
also to material that has been modified, either in
the pre-Lucan material or by Luke, to be applied to
Jesus. The Magnificat, for example, is often suggested
to have been originally spoken to Elizabeth.[25]

The absence of corroborative materials to demonstrate "Baptist sources" has necessitated that several
of the theories arguing this background for Chapter
1 remain very speculative. It is well to remember,
also, that form-critical approaches to these materials
have often supported the Baptist source theory. Given
the great variety of theories and reconstructions,
the more one compares them, the less convincing they
are. It should be noted as well, that form criticism
has been of very little value for these chapters.
To use Taylor's term, the infancy narratives have
been placed among the "stories about Jesus" (Dibelius'

---

[23]Cadbury, Making, 67.
[24]Summary in Brown, Birth, 244-245.
[25]See, e.g., Winter, "Magnificat and Benedictus."

Mythen; Bultmann's Geschichterzählung und Legende).[26]
These classifications have lacked a definite structural
form and, as Fascher has said, are very elastic
(kautschukartig), allowing their usage for a catch-all
category with interpretive connotations but little
objective value.[27] With regard to sources, I find
no value at all.

3. A special source, or sources, is posited
for one or more units in Chapter 2. The primary internal
support for these suggestions comes from the analysis
which says that Chapter 2 is completely separable
from Chapter 1.

> It has its own introduction, and presupposes
> nothing from Chapter 1, neither the virginal
> conception nor the identity of the parents.
> Although prominent in Chapter 1, JBap has completely
> disappeared from the scene. Within Chapter 2
> itself, the story in 2:41-51 is quite separable
> from the rest. . . One could argue that 2:40
> was the original conclusion and that a story
> of different provenance was added, requiring
> a second and duplicate conclusion in 2:52.[28]

The primary difficulties with such a source theory,
however, derive from the same problems already discussed
about either written or traditional (i.e., oral) sources. Further, structural analysis, which shall be
discussed below, makes the separate-unit concept doubt-
ful.

Brown has rightly observed that "Inevitably,
the source proposals have been combined in complicated
theories."
C. A. Briggs thought he could detect a pattern
of seven poems, reflected not only in the obvious
poetry of the canticles, but also in the prose
account. K. L. Schmidt has found seven separate
traditions or narratives cemented together by
Lucan additions. Most recently, H. Schürmann
has found five separate tales about Jesus, in

---

[26]Vincent Taylor, The Formation of the Gospel Tradition
(2nd ed.; London: Macmillan & Company, 1957) 159-163.
[27]Rudolf Bultmann, Die Geschichte der synoptischen Tradition (2nd ed.; Göttingen: Vandenhoeck & Ruprecht,
1931) 32.
[28]Brown, Birth, 244.

addition to a JBap narrative and at least three different hymns.[29]
To this list could be added Aytoun, Winter, my own earlier work, and many other attempts to explain the current form of the materials, at least in part, by theories of putative sources. On the basis of my review of such attempts, I must answer my second question, None with any certainty. That is to say, it remains a probability that sources of some sort are behind Luke 1-2, but the lack of external evidence and the pervasive nature of Lucan style to obscure the analysis of sources make the possibility of discovering such sources nil.

*

The negative answers arrived at for the first two questions bring the other two into crucial focus. For they are questions pertaining to analysis of the literary structure of the text itself, which in fact may be the living text. Methodologically, the known text is far more important than the text "behind" or "before" it, which is, at best, a reconstruction. As one of my former professors said, It is time we give up efforts to explain the known by the unknown, the obscure by the more obscure.

What then of the literary relationship of Luke 1-2 and the whole of the Third Gospel? Two well known characteristics found within the history of the interpretation of the Third Gospel illustrate the commonly held assumption that Luke 1 and 2 lack essential connection with the remainder of the gospel. On the one hand, while the Proto-Luke Theory, which saw portions of Mark and most of Luke 1-2 added subsequently to a gospel formed from Q and L (note: Luke 1-2 does not belong even to the Lucan special source L!), is generally not accepted as an explanation for the Synoptic Problem, the memory lingers on that the infancy narrative was the last portion of the Third Gospel to be included

---

[29]Brown, _Birth_, 245.

in the text.[30]   On the other hand, Conzelmann is not alone among the commentators as he basically ignores these chapters in his _Theology of St. Luke_.[31]   The reasons for the separation are also well known:

1. The dramatic change of language between the prologue (1:1-4) and the infancy narrative from pseudo-classical to highly semitic Greek. Since Harnack, many have suggested a deliberate attempt to imitate the LXX begins at vs. 5; others have said that this change is a clear indication of a translated source. Regardless of explanation, the language is distinctively different from that which precedes and, to a lesser degree, from that which follows.

2. The sixfold synchronism of Luke 3:1 has the appearance of an elaborate opening of a gospel. That appearance plus the use of   in Luke 1:4 as an equivalent to   in 1:2, as Acts 26:4-5 suggests, leads many to see the reference of Luke's beginning the Gospel itself with the apostolic tradition.[32]

3. Some early text types, namely that of Marcion and that of Tatian's Diatessaron the Gospel of

---

[30]See Fitzmyer, _Luke_, 305ff., for summary of current discussion which is built on the formulation of the original _kerygma_ from "fragments" found in I Cor 15:3-4, Rom 1:3-4, I Thes 1:9-10, plus the preaching in Acts; thus, the conclusion that the infancy narratives represent "the latest part of the gospel tradition to take shape" is derivative of a hypothetical reconstruction of the tradition rather than, as with Streeter, a hypothetical theory as to redaction. It remains to be seen how much the latter remains a presupposition of the former.

[31]Conzelmann calls Luke 1-2 a "prologue" and can speak of statements found there as "plainly contradicted" by Luke's own view; see Conzelmann, _Theology_, 22 and 24 on John the Baptist.

[32]Brown, _Birth_, 240; Fitzmyer, _Luke_, 450-454; see Oscar Cullmann, "Infancy Gospels," in Hennecke-Schneemelcher, _New Testament Apocrypha_ (Philadelphia: Westminster, 1963), I., 363-369.

Luke began with what we know as 3:1.[33]

The third of these observations is the least
troublesome, since the omission from Marcion's text
of Luke 1-2 is quite consistent with his rejection
of the Jewish Old Testament in his highly modified
canon and the contents of the _Diatessaron_ are only
hypothetically reconstructed and hardly normative.

What then of the second observation? Brown speaks
for many when he says that "the solemn beginning of
the ministry in 3:1-2 has proved an almost insurmountable
obstacle."[34]   The support he cites from Cadbury and
Streeter, however, is not very convincing since both
of them refer to other authors who have parallels
but who, in turn, do not have these parallels at the
physical beginning of the books. As Cadbury says,
"The completest parallels . . . occur, however, in
special passages in other historians where they are
marking like the evangelist the real starting-point
of the narrative."[35]   That real starting-point in
Luke, according to this theory, is enhanced by Mark's
beginning the gospel with the baptism of Jesus and
the reference in Acts 1:22 to the baptism by John
the Baptist as a beginning.[36]

The primary argument against Luke 3:1 as the
actual beginning of the gospel, with perhaps Luke
1-2 added after the completion of Acts,[37] is found
in an examination of the genre of Luke. Talbert's
studies of the Mediterranean biographical writings
of antiquity has demonstrated not only that Luke belongs
to that genre but also that this genre was characterized
by an account of the prepublic career of the person
who is presented to the readers.
In this convention one found an account of the
hero's career, before the public activity was
begun, which included material on family background, perhaps a reference to a miraculous con-

[33]Fitzmyer, _Luke_, 311, on Conybeare's comments on Luke
based on the _Diatessaron_ and on Marcion as possibly
the preserver of "the original text of the Gospel."
[34]Brown, _Birth_, 240.
[35]Cadbury, _Making_, 206.
[36]Fitzmyer, _Luke_, 310.
[37]Against such a view, see Paul S. Minear, "Luke's Use
of the Birth Stories," _Studies in Luke-Acts_, 111-130.

ception, along with omens and other predictions of future greatness, including childhood pro-digies.[38] Suetonius' biography of Augustus in his **Lives of Twelve Caesars** is a good example of this genre. The function of such a section is to provide a foreshadowing of the character of the public career to follow. In Luke, then, "the first section of the gospel . . . should be read as an anticipations/prophecies/foreshadowings of the future career of Jesus."[39]

A structural analysis of Luke reinforces this argument. Although there may be no general agreement to the structure of Luke 1-2 among the commentators,[40] most would agree that the literary structure is used to present the parallels and contrasts of the two principal characters, John and Jesus.[41] Once we allow ourselves to go beyond 3:1 without prejudging the first chapters' relationship to what follows, it is clear that the parallelism and contrast continues until John disappears from the scene.[42] Basing my study on the materials that are peculiar to Luke, I found a surprising continuance of the structure going far beyond the infancy narrative:

3:1-2	Dating of John's ministry
3:4-6	OT Identification of John
3:10-14	John and the People
(3:15-17	John the Prophet)
(3:18-20	John's Imprisonment)
3:23-38	Dating of Jesus' ministry
4:16-30	OT Identification of Jesus

---

[38]Charles H. Talbert, **Reading Luke** (New York: Crossroad, 1982), 15-16.

[39]Talbert, **Reading Luke**, 17; for full discussion of his genre theory and its basis as found in biographies of the Mediterranean world, see his **What Is a Gospel?** (Philadelphia: Fortress Press, 1977).

[40]See text below.

[41]See Fitzmyer, **Luke**, 313-316, for excellent summary, plus his own helpful charting of the structure within Luke 1-2 itself, following Dibelius, Lyonnet, and Laurentin. I basically agree with his table.

[42]Note, e.g., the parallel discussions of John and Jesus in Luke 7:18-35; when Luke presents details of John, so also of Jesus.

7:11-17   Jesus and the People
(7:13-23   Jesus the Messiah)
(16:16   Jesus' Interpretation)[43]

Preceding Luke 9:57, only three other brief sections
peculiar to Luke -- 5:1-11; 7:36-50; and 8:1-3 --
are omitted, and I have added two Lucan summaries
in the bracket "final entry." When this material
peculiar to Luke is read along with material the author
has in common with Matthew and Mark, it is clear that
the pattern of parallelism and contrast is not built
on a Lucan source (L), but on the author's plotting
which places the two of them in juxtaposition to each
other from their conceptions until their deaths.
The literary structure demonstrates this more clearly
than source theory and has led Talbert, Perrin, Kümmel
and others to show that the first section of the gospel
goes beyond 2:52, to at least 4:15, or as I would
suggest, to 4:30, when Jesus is delivered miraculously
from death.

So, although the sixfold synchronism of Luke
3:1 has the appearance of an elaborate opening of
a gospel, structurally it is the dating of the opening
of John the Baptist's ministry, a secular event in
the public arena of the Roman Empire, while Jesus'
public ministry also received an elaborate dating
in 3:23-38, the sacred event of the son of God. It
is clear that a genealogy can be the elaborate opening
of a gospel (cf., Matthew), but for Luke the function
of both systems of dating are preceded in a prehistory
by events dated (ἐγένετο plus "days") in the days
of Herod and in the days of Caesar Augustus, events
that serve as portents and omens of the lives to come.

What then of the first observation, about the
language? It has already been seen that many of the
source theories for the infancy narrative are based,
at least in part, on an explanation for the language
change. Many have followed the suggestion that is
at least as old as Harnack that we have in these chapters
Greek that deliberately imitates the LXX.[44] More

---

[43]These parallels include material that is not uniquely
Lucan, but I am outlining Lucan usage.
[44]See B. M. Metzger, "The Language of the New Testament,"
IB 7, 47.

recently, several attempts have been made to show that Luke's writing here is just as deliberately midrashic. As Fitzmyer has put the matter:

> Because the Lucan infancy narrative is heavily Semitized in language and the Matthean is structured about five OT quotations, the question has been raised whether the NT infancy narratives could be midrashic, especially in the story-telling sense.[45]

Gouldner and Sanderson called these chapters "St. Luke's Genesis" that present a midrash on two themes:

> (1) A fulfillment of the lives of the Old Abraham, Isaac, and Jacob, elaborated with other fulfillments from the prophets; and
> (2) a chain of prophecy as the Holy Spirit is released at the Incarnation.[46]

They attempt through the use of seven OT passages to show that Zechariah and Elizabeth were the beginning of the New Israel as Abraham and Sarah were the beginning of the Old Israel. Unfortunately for the argument, none of the seven passages were normally considered messianic,[47] and so Gouldner and Sanderson depend very heavily on typology for their argument. I agree with Fitzmyer at this point when he suggests that a theory of midrash, when there is no obvious OT text behind the passage in question (Fitzmyer: "Matthew at least quotes the OT."), has more problems than merit. Incidentally, Gouldner and Sanderson do not deal with the language issue.

No real consensus is found among today's scholars to explain the change of language following the prologue in Luke. It might be noted that the contrast between the semitized Greek of Luke 1-2 and what follows in the Third Gospel or in parts of Acts is not nearly as great; and it is seldom commented on. Perhaps the best explanation is to suggest that it is imitative of the LXX, but this should not imply any evidence then of division from the remainder of the gospel. In fact, the concept that Luke has freely composed the infancy narratives is enhanced by the idea.

---

[45]Fitzmyer, _Luke_, 308.
[46]M. D. Gouldner and R. L. Sanderson, "St. Luke's Genesis," JTS 8 (1957) 14.
[47]Mather, "Literary-Linguistic Analysis," 17-18.

To summarize, the literary relationship of the infancy narrative to the whole of Luke-Acts is one that has more continuity than has often been projected. The genre of the gospel clearly makes use of this type of prehistory to indicate what kind of person the reader may anticipate in the presentation. The links between these anticipations and what follows are much stronger than many have suggested, with John developed by Luke as the prophet who is finally killed by his people and with Jesus presented as the Son of God. The omens, and specifically here, the prophecies of Mary, Simeon and Anna, come true. The literary structure of parallelism, often to show contrast, begins in Luke 1-2 and continues into the remainder of the gospel in such a manner as to suggest that the infancy narratives were not an afterthought added late to the tradition, but part and parcel of the presentation in Luke-Acts from the beginning of its author's literary effort.

*

What then of the internal structure of the Lucan infancy narrative?

A variety of diagrams have been suggested by contemporary scholars. They do not all agree with each other; in fact, it would be difficult to print a consensus, for there is none. Brown provides a two-page table that charts how Galbiati, Burrows, and Dibelius break the material into three divisions, while the analyses of Gaechter and of Laurentin set the material into two divisions.[48] Brown then does his own! Rather than adding one more offering of my own to the list, I offer the following observations about the current approach to the passages which do provide some methodological consensus to guide our search for the living text.

Most analyses of Luke 1-2 recognize the literary structure of parallelism in the presentation of John the Baptist and Jesus, and this structure is seen as Luke's purposeful authorship. The literary formation of the infancy narrative is, therefore, clearly consistent with the remainder of Luke-Acts. The Lucan

---

[48]Brown, _Birth_, 248-249.

text is itself the living text.

Most analyses of Luke 1-2 recognize the presence of narrative units that are formed from the Gattungen of biblical oral and written tradition. The elastic form-critical categories of legends and stories about Jesus have given way to more specific forms. For example, Talbert, following in part G. F. Wood, outlines the "stereotyped pattern for theophanies" and then asserts that "Luke's two annunciations in 1:5-38 correspond to this stereotyped pattern."[49] Whether such type-scenes come from the oral tradition or are the result of literary structuring is most difficult to say, but that they are the substructure of the infancy narrative is quite clear.

Most analyses of Luke 1-2 recognize a biblical mystique about these narratives. These chapters, of all the NT writrings, remain the closest in feeling to their author's Scriptures, especially the LXX. As it has already been said, there is no consensus of explanation, in part because there is no way to know if that impression of "imitative historiography," to use Burrows' phrase,[50] has anything to do with the intention of the author, Luke. A more reasonable explanation for the relationship between Luke and the earlier writers of Scripture is to be found in the centuries of continuity already found among the Hebraic historiographers and story tellers. As Alter has said, "There is a series of recurrent narrative episodes attached to the careers of biblical heroes" and the biblical type-scenes occur "not only in the rituals of daily existence but at the crucial junctures in the lives of the heroes, from conception and birth to betrothal to deathbed."[51] I would suggest that in the scene of theophanies, conception, and birth, the art of the biblical narrative is Luke's.

Finally, most analyses of Luke 1-2 have not crossed the frontier and made the desert bloom. Probably Brown, with his attention to the structure of the

---

[49]Talbert, Reading Luke, 18; G. F. Wood, "The Form and Composition of the Lucan Annunciation Narratives," (S.T.D. thesis, Catholic University of America, 1962).
[50]Fitzmyer, Luke, 309.
[51]Robert Alter, The Art of Biblical Narrative (New York: Basic Books, 1981), 51.

narrative, and Talbert, with his emphasis upon genre-criticism, have brought us back closer to the living text than most. So much of the past study of the infancy narratives has been excavation, a digging to get behind what we have, back to something more authentic. It is extremely interesting to me that the brightest future today seems to be in the direction of reading Luke 1-2 as fictionalized history, in appreciation of the story telling of Luke.

CHAPTER TEN

THE PHARISEES IN LUKE-ACTS

Jack T. Sanders

Exactly how the author of Luke-Acts intended
to portray the Jews in his two-volume work is something
of a puzzle. On the one hand, one has the opinion
of Ernst Haenchen that "Luke has written the Jews
off,"[1] while, on the other hand, Jacob Jervell has
maintained that Luke's theology of salvation for the
Gentiles is built upon and is, indeed, a part of his
understanding of the salvation of the Jews.[2] Even
a casual reading of Luke-Acts, however, will reveal
that the author's attitude toward Jews cannot be described in a few words, but that the way in which
he presents them is, in fact, quite complex. A major
part of the complexity is the role--or roles--that
the Pharisees play in Luke-Acts, and it is to an investigation of the way in which that group appears in Luke's
work that we now turn. Inasmuch as no thorough study
of the Pharisees in Luke-Acts has ever been undertaken
before,[3] we shall be, to some extent, breaking new
ground.

---

[1]E. Haenchen, "The Book of Acts as Source Material
for the History of Early Christianity," in Studies
in Luke-Acts, ed. L. E. Keck and J. L. Martyn (Philadelphia: Fortress, 1966) 278.
    [2]J. Jervell, Luke and the People of God (Minnea-
polis: Augsburg, 1972) 41-74.
    [3]The short article by J. A. Ziesler, "Luke and the
Pharisees," NTS 25 (1979) 146-57, briefly recites
the evidence and then moves directly to questions
about the relation of Pharisees to Jesus. The TWNT
article on the Pharisees, altogether too brief on
Acts (H. F. Weiss, " Φαρισαῖος , " TWNT 9 [1973] 47),
notes simply that, whereas in the Gospels the Pharisees
were enemies of Jesus, in the Acts they are not--thus
reveals how superficially the author has read both
Luke and Acts.

It may be instructive to begin by reminding ourselves of how modern scholars generally characterize
the Pharisees in the early Christian period. A few
lines from a standard reference work will suffice.

Although [the Pharisees] recognized [Jesus] as
a teacher and although they were pleased with
his refutation of the Sadducees and his affirmation
that God was one and that one should love one's
neighbor as oneself, they were hostile to his
teaching of doctrines they had not authorized;
to his taking the law in his own hand; to his
forgiving sins; to his exorcising demons; and,
above all, to his affirming, or allowing his
disciples to affirm of him, that he was the Son
of man, the Messiah. The Pharisees were especially
angry over his unwillingness to heed them when
they confronted him with his deviations.[4]

However accurate <u>historically</u> such a summary may be--and
we remind ourselves that our interest here is not
a "quest of the historical Pharisees"--the information
on which it relies is drawn almost entirely from Mark
and Matthew and has very little to do with Luke-Acts,
where the Pharisees take, nevertheless, a significant
role. How does Luke portray the Pharisees, and why?

John Reumann begins his introduction to the Facet
Book edition of W. D. Davies's <u>Introduction to Pharisaism</u>
with these words: "The Pharisees have had 'bad press'
ever since the first Christian century."[5] Yet in
Luke the situation is otherwise. Perhaps the most
striking difference between Luke and his (surviving)
predecessors in this matter is that he indicates that
some Pharisees were Christians. Not only does he
agree with Paul himself that Paul was a Pharisee,[6]
he has Paul state the fact twice (more often, therefore,
than the real Paul does in his surviving letters)
in emphatic terms. Before the Sanhedrin (Acts 23:6)
Paul declares that he is a Pharisee from a Pharisaic
family, and before Agrippa (26:5) he claims that he has

[4]E. Rivkin, "Pharisees," IDBSup (1976) 662.
[5]W. D. Davies, <u>Introduction to Pharisaism</u> (Facet Books--
Biblical Series; Philadelphia: Fortress, 1967) v.
[6]Cf. Phil 3:5.

been a Pharisee, which means belonging "to the very best party" among the Jews. Beyond this, however, Luke even tells us that there were "some believers from among the party of the Pharisees" (Acts 15:5), so that Paul is by no means represented as unique in his having been a Pharisee before having converted to Christianity; there were Pharisees among the Christians, Christians among the Pharisees (according to Luke's account).[7] That is quite remarkable in view of the picture of the Pharisees drawn from Mark and Matthew.

But still more. Even those Pharisees who are not Christians are routinely friendly to Christianity.[8] In Acts 5:34-39 it is a Pharisee, Gamaliel,[9] who talks sense to his colleagues in the Sanhedrin and who persuades them not to hinder the nascent Christian movement, since "if it is from God you will not be able to destroy them. (v 39). Later, then, when Paul is in the Sanhedrin announcing that he is a Pharisee, he does so deliberately in order to appeal to the sympathies of Pharisees in the Sanhedrin, who pronounce him innocent in the same

---

[7]J. Munck, The Acts of the Apostles, rev. by W. F. Albright and C. S. Mann (AB; Garden City, N.Y.: Doubleday, 1967) 49, thinks of "former Pharisees." While Luke's syntax makes this possible, he apparently thinks rather of Christians who are also Pharisees, as we shall yet see--or in any case, if they are somehow no longer Pharisees, the "no longer" is of little moment.

[8]This Pharisaic friendliness, however, is not the same thing as accepting the gospel, as A. George, "Israël dans l'oeuvre de Luc," RB 75 (1968) 507-508, understands it.

[9]Luke was surely aware that he had chosen a particularly famous Pharisee for this role, since he also has Paul claim, in Acts 22:3, that he himself had been a pupil of Gamaliel. A. Loisy, Les Actes des Apôtres (Paris: Nourry, 1920) 284 writes that "for a little one could make of [Gamaliel] the grandfather of Christianity."

SANDERS

terms that Pilate had earlier used for Jesus,[10] and who
become so vigorous in their defense of his cause that
the Tribune is forced to intervene and to remove Paul
from the tumult for his own safety (Acts 23:10). These
two attempts by Pharisees in Acts to save Christians
from punishment at the hand of the Jewish authorities
surely, then, provide the necessary perspective for
interpreting the Pharisaic motive in warning Jesus that
Herod wanted to kill him (Luke 13:31).

Some authors have thought that Luke intends for
his readers to see through this last mentioned display
of Pharisaic friendliness to an underlying hostility
or deceit. Thus Loisy writes that
> the Pharisees act not in the interest of Jesus,
> but in that of Herod. The information that they
> give to the Savior is something quite different
> from a witness of sympathy; the advice that they
> put to him corresponds to a desire that they
> would not dare express otherwise. Jesus does
> not give the impression of thinking of them in
> his response.[11]
Certain aspects of the episode as Luke presents it,
however, weigh on the side of realizing that he intends
to show the Pharisees attempting to do Jesus a friendly
service here.[12] In the first place, such is the obvious
meaning of what they say: "Leave and go elsewhere,
for Herod wishes to kill you" (Luke 13:31). This
admonition is, on the face of it, a plain warning.
While it is possible to interpret this warning as
a "scare tactic," a threat that Herod does not really
intend to carry out but that will nevertheless serve
the function of restricting Jesus' activity,[13] neverthe-

---

[10]Acts 23:9: "We find no guilt (nothing bad) in this
person"; Luke 23:4: "I find no cause [s.c., for a
guilty verdict] in this person." On this point cf.
G. W. H. Lampe, "Acts," in Peake's Commentary on the
Bible, ed. M. Black and H. H. Rowley (London, et.al.:
Nelson, 1962) 921.
[11]Loisy, Les Evangiles synoptiques (Ceffonds, pres Monti-
er-en-Der [Haute-Marne]: published by the author,
1907-1908) 2.126. Other commentators make the same
or a similar point.
[12]So also Ziesler, "Luke and the Pharisees," 150.
[13]So, e.g., G. B. Caird, Saint Luke (Westminster Pelican
Commentaries; Philadelphia: Westminster, 1977) 173.

less, in view of the role that Herod shortly plays
in the Lucan Passion Narrative, such a motivation
appears unlikely; but, in any case, however, we are
to understand Herod's motive here, it is difficult
to see how a deceitful motive can be attributed to
the Pharisees, since, furthermore--Loisy's remark
about Jesus' response to the Pharisees notwithstanding--
nothing in his response indicates anything about the
Pharisees other than that they are serving the role
of neutral and innocent ambassadors and have, in fact,
his interest at heart.[14] Jesus' criticism falls on
Herod,[15] not on the Pharisees. When one then brings
the evidence of the Pharisees' behavior in Acts to
bear on Luke 13:31, one is left really with only one
possible understanding of the Pharisees' motive in
warning Jesus. It is sincere.

Luke goes quite beyond this one warning to Jesus,
however, in representing the Pharisees as friendly
not only to the church but to Jesus as well, for in
Luke Jesus is a regular dinner guest of Pharisees.[16]

---

[14]So also W. Grundmann, Das Evangelium nach Lukas (THKNT;
7th ed.; Berlin: Evangelische Verlagsanstalt, 1974)
288. S. MacL. Gilmour, "The Gospel According to Luke,
Introduction and Exegesis," IB 8 (1952) 248; and
G. Schneider, Das Evangelium nach Lukas (ÖTKNT: Gütersloh: Mohn; Würzburg: Echter Verlag, 1977) 309,
take the Pharisees of Luke 13:31 to be friendly to
Jesus.
[15]Cf. also E. Buck, "The Function of the Pericope 'Jesus
Before Herod' in the Passion Narrative of Luke," in
Wort in der Zeit. Festgabe für Karl Heinrich Rengstorf,
ed. W. Haubeck and M. Bachmann (Leiden: Brill, 1980)
177. Whatever "fox" means to Luke, it is clear that
it is not intended to be a complimentary term. Cf. the
discussion of the term in Schneider, Lukas, 309-310.
[16]This remarkable trait is hardly to be explained as
a part of Luke's universalism, as if "Tischgemeinschaft"
represented "Lebensgemeinschaft," for Pharisees as
for all (so J. Schmid, Das Evangelium nach Lukas [RNT;
4th ed.; Regensburg: Pustet, 1960] 147); nor are
we to think that the purpose of the Pharisaic invitations
is to "test" Jesus (so S. Kealy, The Gospel of Luke
[also known as J. P. Kealy, Luke's Gospel Today; Den-
ville, N. J.: Dimension, 1979] 237). Nevertheless,
there is a certain two-sidedness to the repeated Pharisaic hospitality, so that A. Denaux, "L'hypocrisie

In Luke 7:36 and in 11:37 a Pharisee invites Jesus
to dinner (which invitations he accepts), and in 14:1
he is found again going to dine at a Pharisee's house,
presumably by invitation. Thus, of the six meals
that Jesus takes in others' homes in Luke, half are
in the homes of Pharisees! Frequent invitations to
dinner are not a sign of hostility. In addition,
furthermore, Luke has scrupulously kept the Pharisees
out of the Passion Narrative.[17] Their pronounced
appearance at the Triumphal Entry into Jerusalem (Luke
19:39) is their last appearance in Luke-Acts until
Acts 5, where Gamaliel plays his aforementioned role.
Thus the Pharisees seek to defend the early Apostles
and Paul, and they have nothing to do with the crucifixion of Jesus. It is therefore not surprising that
they also have nothing to do with the martyrdoms of
Stephen (Acts 7-8) and of James (Acts 12), the other
Christian martyrdoms reported in Acts. Thus the Pharisaic friendliness to Jesus and to the church in Luke-Acts
has two sides, an active and a passive. On the active
side, they display overt friendliness and attempt
to protect Jesus and his followers; on the passive
side, they have nothing to do with any of the martyrdoms. No wonder that F. C. Baur could note that Luke
"almost . . . make[s] the Pharisees into Christians."[18]

Baur's remark, of course, also had another facet
of the Lucan portrayal of the Pharisees in view, one
which we have barely avoided mentioning above; that
is that the Pharisees, like the Christians, believe in

---

des Pharisiens et le dessein de Dieu. Analyse de
Lc., XIII, 31-33," in L'Evangile de Luc. Problèmes
littéraires et théologiques. Mémorial Lucien Cerfaux,
ed. F. Neirynck (BETL; Gembloux: Duculot, 1973) 262,
observes that the Pharisees "acceptent [Jésus] froide-
ment, ils l'observent, ils le jugent sévèrement."
Cf. further below in this essay.
    [17]Cf. H. Conzelmann, The Theology of St. Luke (New York:
Harper & Row, 1961) 78.
    [18]F. C. Baur, Paul the Apostle of Jesus Christ. His
Life and Works. His Epistles and Teachings, ed. E. Zeller
(London and Edinburgh: Williams and Norgate, 1873-
1875) 1.217.

the resurrection.[19]   It was this chord that Paul struck
when he was being examined in the Sanhedrin in Acts 23;
for, not only did he announce (v 6) that he was a
Pharisee, he also played on the sympathies of the
Pharisees in the Sanhedrin by claiming that he was on
trial "concerning the hope and the resurrection of the
dead." When he then tells Herod Agrippa that he is in
custody "because of the hope of the promise to [the
Israelite] fathers" (26:6), just after announcing
that he is a Pharisee (v 5), we are apparently to
understand that he refers to that shared hope of the
resurrection; and the same will be true in Acts 28:20,
where he tells the Roman Jews, this time without mentioning his Pharisaic origins, that he is there "on
account of the hope of Israel." This is to say that,
while Paul's language in Acts 26:6 and 28:20 does
not specifically include reference to the resurrection
and might, in fact, be taken in a broader sense,[20]
nevertheless the connection with the resurrection
has already been made in 23:6, and the reader will
presumably not have forgotten that.[21]

---

[19]This is not, however, why they are "the very best
party" among the Jews, as e.g. K. Löning, Die Saulustradition in der Apostelgeschichte (NTAbh; Münster:
Aschendorff, 1973) 169, states; cf. further below
in this essay.
    [20]It is certainly not above Luke to produce such an
ambiguity deliberately, as in the case of his many
subjectless verbs in the Passion Narrative. More
precisely, while Luke probably intends to have Paul
say in Acts 26:6 and 28:20, in the first instance,
that it is because of his (Jewish) belief in the resurrection that he has been imprisoned, Luke would not
mind if his readers also thought something more general,
e.g., that Paul was imprisoned simply because he was
a religious Jew.
    [21]So also P. Vielhauer, "On the 'Paulinism' of Acts,"
in Studies in Luke-Acts, 41. Of course, Luke has
quite overstated his case here, since it is obvious
that Christians and Pharisees do not really have the
same belief in the resurrection, inasmuch as Christians
believe that Jesus has risen from the dead (also Vielhauer, ibid.). One might even wonder if Luke actually
expected his readers to fall for this platitude.
The motif of Christianity as the true and authentic
Judaism, however, has doubtless overwhelmed all other
considerations on this point. So also R. Maddox,

Of course, it is not the case that the Pharisees
are as consistently friendly with Jesus and his followers
in Luke-Acts as in the episodes just recalled here;
there are occasions of conflict. Even the conflict,
however, is contained within certain limits. As we
have already noted, the Pharisees are kept entirely
out of the Lucan Passion Narrative, and they have
nothing whatsoever to do with the Christian martyrdoms
in Acts. This is in spite of one appearance of Pharisees
in the Marcan Passion Narrative (Mark 12:13), where
the Pharisees are baiting Jesus. Furthermore, Pharisees
do not plot against Jesus in Luke as they do in Mark
and Matthew. Thus, whereas Mark says plainly at the
conclusion of the Narrative of Jesus' healing the
man with the withered hand (Mark 3:1-6) that "the
Pharisees immediately took counsel with the Herodians
against him about how they could destroy him" (v 6;
similarly Matt 12:14), Luke moves the Pharisees to
the first of the narrative where they become the subject
of Mark's subjectless verb, "kept an eye on" (Mark
3:1 // Luke 6:7), and he does not mention them again
at the end of the narrative (as does Mark), where
he writes that "they were quite disoriented and discussed
among themselves what they might do to Jesus" (Luke
6:11).[22] To be sure, "they" here are certainly still
the "Scribes and Pharisees" from v 7, but Luke has
reduced their presence at the end of the episode by
mentioning them earlier instead of later and by writing
only "they (αὐτοί)" at the end; and he has, furthermore,
turned a clear plot against Jesus into something rather
more vague. Luke does not want the charge of plotting
Jesus' arrest laid to the Pharisees, and Luke-Acts

The Purpose of Luke-Acts (FRLANT; Göttingen: Vandenhoeck
& Ruprecht, 1982) 41, emphatically; similarly Haenchen,
The Acts of the Apostles. A Commentary (Philadelphia:
Westminster, 1971) 102. J. Roloff, Die Apostelgeschichte
(NTD; Göttingen: Vandenhoeck & Ruprecht, 1981) 328,
says that Luke is "simplifying" here in representing
"Christians as true Pharisees." Haenchen, "Source
Material," 278, refers the simplification, probably
correctly, to Luke's apologetic interest.

[22]K. L. Schmidt, Der Rahmen der Geschichte Jesu (reprint
ed.; Darmstadt: Wissenschaftliche Buchgesellschaft,
1964) 92, considers the change irrelevant; J. A. Fitzmyer, The Gospel According to Luke (I-IX) (AB; Garden
City, N.Y.: Doubleday, 1981) 608, notes it but offers
no explanation.

contains no such plot on their part.[23]   In what ways, then, is the Pharisaic hostility toward Jesus and his followers portrayed in Luke-Acts?

If we leave aside for the moment what Jesus says to or about the Pharisees and confine our attention to their behavior in the narrative, we see that, quite strangely, Luke has omitted nearly all the instances of Pharisaic hostility toward Jesus that appear in Mark and Matthew and has substituted his own. Thus, in addition to what he has done in Luke 6:7,11, he has only "some" claim that Jesus is in league with Beelzebul (Luke 11:15), whereas Mark 3:22 had attributed the charge to the Scribes and Matt 12:24 to the Pharisees; and the introduction to the saying about divorce (Matt 19:3-8 // Mark 10:2-10)[24]--which is in Matthew, in any case, a Streitgespräch with the Pharisees "trying" him--simply does not appear in Luke, which includes only the saying minus the introduction (Luke 16:18 // Mark 10:11-12; Matt 19:9). As we have also noted already, Luke has it that Scribes and Priests--not Pharisees, as in Mark (Luke 20:20; Mark 12:13)--bait Jesus in the Passion Narrative on the issue of tribute to Caesar. We also need to note, in addition to these instances of Lucan omission of Pharisaic hostility, one reduction; in Luke 6:2 it is only "some of the Pharisees" who inquire about the Sabbath behavior of Jesus' disciples, not, as in Mark and Matthew, "the Pharisees."[25]

---

[23]Löning (Saulustradition, 170, and "Paulinismus in der Apostelgeschichte," in Paulus in den neutestament-lichen Spätschriften, ed. K. Kertelge [Quaestiones disputatae; Freiburg, Basel, Wien: Herder, 1981] 213) and G. Klein (Die zwölf Apostel. Ursprung und Gehalt einer Idee [FRLANT; Göttingen: Vandenhoeck & Ruprecht, 1961] 124-125) are thus wrong to imply that the pre-Christian Paul persecuted the church as a Pharisee. When Paul's persecuting activity is mentioned nothing is said of his being a Pharisee, and when Paul emphasizes that he is a Pharisee it is to underscore his Torah fidelity and belief in the resurrection; cf. Acts 22:3-4 and 23:6.

[24]Part of the "Little Omission," to use Fitzmyer's term.

[25]George, "Israël," 497, thinks that removing the Pharisees from these several conflict scenes is part of Luke's way of showing that "an important part of Israel . . . now refuses Jesus." Why only "an important part"?

SANDERS

In spite of these reductions of evidences of
Pharisaic hostility,[26] however, Luke has introduced
five instances of their opposition that do not appear
in Mark or Matthew.[27] In Luke 5:21 it is Pharisees
who suggest (cf. Mark 2:7; Matt 9:3) that Jesus may
be blaspheming by forgiving the sins of the paralytic;
and Luke introduces his parable chap. 15 by noting
that Pharisees and Scribes are "grumbling" because
Jesus "receives sinners and eats with them" (Luke
15:2). After the invective against the Pharisees
and "legists" in chap. 11 (// Matthew 23), Luke includes
the conclusion, which does not appear in Matthew,
that "the Scribes and the Pharisees began to have
a terrible grudge and to ask him about all kinds of
things, lurking to catch him in something that he
would say" (Luke 11:53); and in 16:14 he writes that
"the Pharisees, being lovers of money, . . . derided"
Jesus. Finally, in 19:39, he writes that "some of
the Pharisees" wanted Jesus to "scold" his disciples
because of their hailing Jesus at the Triumphal Entry.
In addition to these cases, furthermore, the behavior
of Jesus' Pharisaic hosts in chaps. 7 and 14 is ambiguous, since, although they invite him to dine, his
host in the one case (7:39) questions his prophetic
powers and his association with a sinner, while the
Pharisees in the other case (14:1) "were keeping an
eye on him."[28] Surely Luke, by omitting some references

[26]Ziesler, "Luke and the Pharisees," 152, is willing
to explain the differences between Luke and Mark in
this regard by supposing that Luke may have been lazy!
    [27]Since Luke introduces Pharisees into this Gospel for
a Gentile readership, whereas they were not in his
sources at these points, his writing out of Pharisees
in other cases could not be a matter of sensitivity
to Gentile confusion about Jewish technical terms,
as D. M. Crossan, "Anti-Semitism and the Gospel,"
TS 26 (1965) 192, suggests.
    [28]On the behavior of the Pharisaic host in 11:38, cf. be-
low in this essay.

to Pharisaic hostility and by introducing others,[29] has sought to present the Pharisees in a particular way. Mere references to a "special Lucan source" are inadequate to explain his intent, since we would still, then, have to explain Luke's preference for the material in such a source over that in Mark and Q (or Matthew).[30] Luke's presentation is intentional, not unintentional. If we now add to our evidence the other places where, in agreement with Mark and Matthew, Pharisees figure in Luke's narrative, we shall be able to gain a reasonably good picture of that intent.

In Luke 5:30, Luke agrees with Mark 2:16 that "the Pharisees and their Scribes" (Mark had written, "the Scribes of the Pharisees") raised the question with Jesus' disciples about their eating and drinking with "toll collectors and sinners"; in 5:33 // Mark 2:18, the same questioners as in 5:30 (again somewhat different from Mark, who had "John's disciples and the Pharisees") ask why Jesus does not fast; in 6:2, "some of the Pharisees" (Mark 2:24: "the Pharisees") confront the disciples with their apparent breaking of the Sabbath by working; and in 11:37-38 // Matt 15:1-2 (cf. also Mark 7:1-5), the Pharisee who invites Jesus to dinner (this is, of course, the Lucan touch) is "amazed that he did not first wash before the meal" (similarly Mark 7:5; Matt 15:2). Thus the only conflict scenes between Jesus and the Pharisees that Luke has taken over from Mark and from Q or Matthew are scenes in which the Pharisees are objecting to Jesus' (or his disciples') breaking the Torah--or, perhaps more precisely, to Jesus' and his disciples' peculiar way of following the Torah, to their halakah. A particular instance of this variant "life style" is Jesus' association with "sinners" (Luke 5:30). This theme, then, also governs two of the five conflict scenes that Luke has added. The Pharisaic "grumbling" of Luke

---

[29]The word, "Pharisee," occurs twenty-seven times in Luke; in only nine of those places does the word also appear in the Marcan or Matthaean parallel.

[30]My own suspicion is that the additional references to the pharisees are the product of Luke's "gift of invention" (to use the phrase of H. Köster, Einführung in das Neue Testament [Berlin and New York: de Gruyter, 1980] 753); but the ultimate origin of his extra Pharisees is irrelevant for the discussion at hand.

15:2 repeats the theme of 5:30 // Mark 2:16, where the issue was eating with sinners; and the issue of proper interpretation of Torah also lies behind 11:53, for, if the Pharisees are going "to ask [Jesus] about all kinds of things" in order "to catch him in something that he would say," then it would appear that they have discussions about Torah interpretation in mind. Naturally, of course, the preceding invective against the Pharisees and legists in Luke 11:39-52 has been extremely provocative, so that a motive of revenge is natural, but both the way in which the hope for vengeance is put ("ask . . . about all kinds of things"; "catch him in something that he would say") and the content of the invective lead to the conclusion that the vengeance is to be sought in a discussion about the Law; for Jesus had said in the invective that the Pharisaic manner of cleansing was improper (v 39), that the Pharisees did not lay sufficient weight on almsgiving (v 41), that they tithed improperly (v 42), and that the scriptural interpretation of the legists was such as to keep people away from God's salvation rather than to bring them to it (v 52). Thus, even if the rest of the invective is cast in more general terms (e.g., the Pharisees "love the first seats in synagogues," v 43), it has indicated disagreement over halakah sufficiently to make the orientation of the Pharisees' hope for vengeance clear. When they hope "to catch him in something that he would say," then they wish to best him in a discussion of Torah.[31] Luke has therefore, so it would appear, gone to considerable lengths to define the Pharisaic opposition to Jesus, over against Mark and Matthew, as being limited to questions of halakah or Torah interpretation.[32] That he dines with sinners is men-

---

[31]This is thus the nearest that Luke gets to the notion of a Pharisaic plot against Jesus.
[32]So also Ziesler, "Luke and the Pharisees," 151. J. B. Tyson, "The Opposition to Jesus in the Gospel of Luke," Perspectives in Religious Studies 5 (1978) 148-49, and "Conflict as a Literary Theme in the Gospel of Luke," in New Synoptic Studies, ed. W. R. Farmer (Macon, GA: Mercer University Press, 1983) 318-19, has also seen this point. He writes ("Conflict," 326), "Luke associates the early and less malevolent conflicts with Pharisees and with issues of Torah observance [but] the very bitter conflicts, which resulted in Jesus' death, with priests, Jerusalem, and the temple."

tioned twice (and both times the Pharisees are said to γογγύζειν).

S. G. Wilson thinks that he sees in Jesus' discussions with the Pharisees about Sabbath observance an example of the way in which Luke presented the issue of Christian obligation to the Torah ambiguously in the Gospel. [33] According to Wilson (he refers specifically to Luke 6:1-5), one cannot tell whether Luke meant to show that Jesus and his followers "remain[ed] under obligation to Sabbath law," or whether he intended to show that "the law . . . is subordinate to Jesus." He thinks that Luke's interest is primarily "christological" and that "Luke nowhere makes the distinction between law and tradition." Aside from the fact that Wilson has here and elsewhere mistaken practice for tradition, his general point is mistaken; for Luke certainly does want to distinguish between Torah and halakah, between divine intent and practice. The argument with the Pharisees about the Sabbath is not about the holiness of the Sabbath but about the way in which one must keep the Sabbath holy. The thirty-nine classes of work are not in the Torah.

All of the instances of Pharisaic opposition to Jesus in Luke fall into this category of Torah interpretation except three, all uniquely Lucan. In Luke 5:21, as we recall, Pharisees accuse Jesus of blasphemy when he pronounces someone's sins forgiven, and in 19:39 they encourage him to scold his disciples after the disciples have acclaimed him on the occasion of the Triumphal Entry into Jerusalem. One possible explanation of both these instances is that Jesus is represented as divine in both, and that Luke shows that Pharisees react against such a notion. Inasmuch as the forgiveness of sins is properly reserved to God, the Pharisees' claim in Luke 5:21 that Jesus is blaspheming would then be understandable. [34] Further,

---

It is unfortunate that Tyson seems to think ("Conflict," 318) that the Pharisees can be Jesus' opponents in Luke only to the degree that they are "leaders."

[33]S. G. Wilson, Luke and the Law (SNTSMS; Cambridge, et al.: Cambridge University Press, 1983) 35; cf. also 35-39.

[34]Loisy, Evangiles synoptiques, 1.471, who thinks that Luke is just "enlarging the audience" by introducing Pharisees here, while at the same time anticipating

only Luke among the Synoptic Evangelists puts the
term, "the King," into the quotation of Ps 118:26
on the occasion of Jesus' Triumphal Entry into Jerusalem
(Luke 19:38), thus perhaps making understandable the
Pharisaic reaction that the disciples who voiced such
blasphemy are in need of correction. Still, while
such an explanation of these two occasions of Pharisaic
opposition to Jesus seems reasonable, other possibilities
also suggest themselves. For example, we note that,
in the account of the healing of the paralytic, the
forgiving of whose sins had provoked the Pharisaic
charge of blasphemy, there is a shift in audience
attitude at the end of the story. Here the "amazement
[that] took hold of everyone" and the "fear [with
which] they were filled" (Luke 5:26) must have taken
hold of and filled the Pharisees along with everyone
else, and the Pharisees must have joined in the common
statement, "We have seen something contrary to reason."
But if that is so, if we are to think of the Pharisees
as making this statement along with everyone else,
then Luke has shown them to have a certain change
of mind; for, whereas earlier they did not hesitate
to say that Jesus was "speaking blasphemies," after
the healing they are uncertain. Perhaps Luke intended,
in a sense, for the reader to see both themes: 1)
the Pharisees consider Jesus' proposal to forgive
sins blasphemy, since such a proposal assumes divine
prerogatives, but 2) the ensuing miracle is so impressive
that everyone (including the Pharisees) has to wonder
about the earlier premise and, in fact, simply does
not know what to think.

   There is also another possibility for understanding
the Pharisees' call for a rebuke of the disciples
who have just called Jesus King (Luke 19:38-39), and
that is that they are encouraging caution.[35] If in
13:31 they warned Jesus away from Jerusalem out of

---

the conflict coming up at the beginning of Mark 3,
and W. Schmithals, Das Evangelium nach Lukas (Zürcher
Bibelkommentare; Zürich: Theologischer Verlag, 1980)
71, who proposes that Luke is representing Jesus here
as a great teacher who draws other teachers from all
over to his audience, have missed the theological
implications.
[35]So Grundmann, Lukas, 367.

fear for his safety, then the same motive might prompt
them to encourage Jesus to quiet those who would make
such claims for him as to get him in difficulty with
the authorities.[36] It seems unwise to make a hard
choice among these alternatives, however, inasmuch
as Luke's clues in both episodes are a bit soft.
If the former uniform explanation is correct, then
Luke portrays the Pharisees as hostile to Jesus on
two points, his loose interpretation and following
of Torah (the major bone of contention) and his implied
claims to divinity (not as important as the previous
issue).[37] Alternatively, however, it is possible
to understand Luke 5:17-26 and 19:38-39 in such ways
that Pharisaic hostility seems not to be the real
issue in the two passages, in which case we are left
only with opposition in the matter of Torah and halakah.
Certainty here does not seem possible. Finally, the
Pharisaic "deriding" of Jesus in Luke 16:14 lacks
a meaningful context and appears groundless. Jesus'
preceding saying (v 13) about human inability to serve
two masters could hardly have been objectionable to
either real or Lucan Pharisees. Furthermore, Luke's
slander that they are φιλάργυροι is without basis

---

[36]F. Keck, Die öffentliche Abschiedsrede Jesu in Lk
20, 45-21, 36 (Forschung zur Bibel; Stuttgart: Katholisches Bibelwerk, 1976) 26-27, is quite certain that
this is the proper understanding; similarly also
E. Schweizer, Das Evangelium nach Lukas (NTD; Göttingen:
Vandenhoeck & Ruprecht, 1982) 199, and J. Ernst, Das
Evangelium nach Lukas (RNT; Regensburg: Pustet, 1977)
527.
[37]Loisy, L'Evangile selon Luc (Paris: Nourry, 1924)
470, thinks that the Pharisaic scolding of the disciples
in 19:39 is an expression of "la jalousie et l'impuis-
sance du judaïsme devant le succès chrétien"; similarly
A. Valensin and J. Huby, L'Evangile selon Saint Luc
(Verbum Salutis; Paris: Beauchesne, 1952) 368. Schmidt,
Rahmen, 278-279, sees Luke as playing up the hostility
to Jesus of his opponents versus the "prais of the
people." The most unique explanation of the Pharisaic
rebuke is that of E. E. Ellis, The Gospel of Luke
(The Century Bible, New Edition; Greenwood, SC: Attic
Press, 1966) 225, who finds here a rejection of Jesus'
ministry at its conclusion, parallel to that in Luke
9:51 at its beginning.

in the Gospel or the Acts.[38] We learn from this brief
statement, therefore, that Luke has a profound dislike
for Pharisees and that he thinks of them as making
light of Jesus, but the grounds for both escape us.

Before we return to the Acts, one other aspect
of Luke's portrayal of the Pharisees in the Gospel
that has been alluded to before needs to be emphasized,
and that is that Luke contradicts Mark and Matthew
by distinguishing Pharisee from Pharisee. The singular,
"Pharisee," never appears in Mark and occurs in Matthew
only in 23:26, where the meaning is not, nevertheless,
that an individual is intended. In this case, at
the conclusion of the Matthaean version of the invective
against the Scribes and Pharisees, Jesus employs the
vocative singular, "blind Pharisee (Φαρισαῖε τυφλέ),"
when he challenges the Pharisees to "cleanse first
the inside of the cup." Thus the singular here is
merely a form of address to Pharisees in general;

---

[38]Schneider, Lukas, 336, explains that the Pharisees
"laugh at Jesus" because, being lovers of money, they
reject Jesus' explanation that one cannot "serve Mammon"
and God at the same time. While this connection with
v 13 is doubtless correct, it still adds little to
our understanding of Luke's opinion of the Pharisees,
for Luke will have thought in this way: "I want to
introduce Pharisees here again criticizing Jesus;
since I just included the saying about not serving
'Mammon,' I'll make them criticize him for that and
explain their critical attitude by pointing out that
they are   φιλάργυροι . " For us to see that, however,
does not help us to understand what it is about the
Pharisees that Luke does not like. When Schneider
further (ibid.) tries to connect the slander of v
14 to Jesus' sayings about the Pharisees in vs. 15--and
also in 11:39, 42, 43--he is in one sense correct,
since, as we shall see, those sayings present Luke's
opinion of the Pharisees clearly enough; nevertheless,
Jesus does not, in those sayings, refer to a Pharisaic
greed. V 14 is merely a Lucan slander.

In the opinion of L. Schottroff and W. Stegemann,
Jesus von Nazareth--Hoffnung der Armen (Stuttgart,
et.al.: Kohlhammer, 1978) 123, the Lucan Jesus here
addresses not real Pharisees, but rich people in the
church, and that explanation "does not even need to
be justified here again." How can German "scholars"
get away with such blatant dodges?

it does not single out an individual Pharisee. Luke, however, early shows that he is willing to make distinctions among the Pharisees when in 6:2 he changes Mark's "the Pharisees" to "some of the Pharisees," who inquire about the propriety of the disciples' Sabbath behavior. Also, Luke's introduction to the invective against the Pharisees and legists in chap. 11 is quite different from Mark and Matthew just in this respect; for, whereas Mark 7:1; Matt 15:1 had indicated that Scribes and Pharisees from Jerusalem were Jesus' interlocutors when the handwashing question came up (the episode that in Luke forms the introduction to the invective against the Pharisees and legists), Luke puts only one Pharisee--who had, incidentally, invited Jesus to dinner--into the picture and lets him ask the leading question (Luke 11:37-38). Furthermore, two of the Lucan additions to the Synoptic corpus of Pharisaic material also make this distinction. In Luke 7:37-39 it is the Pharisee who has invited Jesus to dinner who wonders about Jesus' prophetic ability; and, in Luke 19:39, it is "some of the Pharisees" who encourage Jesus to "scold" his disciples. Thus, in all these scenes of conflict between Jesus and Pharisees, [39] Luke has seen to it that his readers know that it is only "some of the Pharisees" or "a Pharisee" who questions the propriety of Jesus' behavior. The conclusion seems unavoidable that Luke wants to make it clear that not all Pharisees opposed Jesus, even on the more narrowly defined ground of opposition that Luke presents. This drawing of distinctions regarding Pharisaic opposition is thus the counterpoint to the friendliness of the Pharisees toward Jesus and the church in Luke-Acts, which in the Gospel finds its positive expressions in the Pharisaic invitations to dinner and the warning about Herod's plans. If we now return to the Acts, other parts of the portrait will come into view.

In Acts, the distinction that Luke makes between Pharisee and Pharisee is different from the distinctions that he made in the Gospel. The distinctions in the Gospel have to do with opposition to Jesus' behavior; often it is only "some" Pharisees or "a" Pharisee who questions his behavior. The point there seems to be that, while some Pharisees opposed Jesus' halakah, not all did, and some were friendly to him. In the

---

[39]If that is in fact what 19:39 is, as we were just discussing.

Acts, while a distinction is made, it is not the same distinction, so that one may not think that Luke reproduced in the Acts the distinctions between Pharisee and Pharisee found in the Gospel. What the Gospel and the Acts have in common is that some Pharisees are friendly to Jesus and to the church and that distinctions are to be made among Pharisees; in the Acts, however, the Pharisees who are friendly to the church are non-Christians, and the Pharisees who cause the problems are the Christian Pharisees! Thus all appearances of Pharisees in Acts are friendly except for that of the Christian Pharisees in Acts 15:5 who propose the following solution to the problem created by the success of the Gentile mission: "It is necessary to circumcise [the Gentile Christians] and to admonish them to keep the Law of Moses."[40] Now, surely every reader of this essay recognizes such a proposal as one that Luke, himself, would find unacceptable and even abhorrent.[41] It flies in the face of all that his hero Paul sought to accomplish; and the conclusion of the Apostolic Council (Acts 15:6-29), which is convened to deal with the proposal made by the Christian Pharisees, sets their proposal aside. Luke clearly

---

[40]When A. Wikenhauser, Die Apostelgeschichte (RNT; Regensburg: Pustet, 1956) 170, then calls them "former Pharisees," he has not clearly analyzed their attitude; similarly I. H. Marshall, The Acts of the Apostles (Grand Rapids: Eerdmans, 1980) 249. These Christians in Acts 15:5 who want Gentile Christians to be circumcised are "Pharisees." Cf. Lampe, "Acts," 908: "The legalist party at Jerusalem consists of converted Pharisees." F. F. Bruce, Commentary on the Book of the Acts (NICNT; Grand Rapids: Eerdmans, 1954) 305, also gets it right.

[41]We need recall only the well-known statement of Haenchen, Die Apostelgeschichte (MeyerK: 7th [16th] ed.; Göttingen: Vandenhoeck & Ruprecht, 1977) 110-111 (cf. Acts, 100), that "the historian Luke contends from the first to the last page with the problem of the Gentile mission that is free from the Law" (emphasis his). Ziesler, "Luke and the Pharisees," 148, asserts that the Pharisees of Acts 15:5 are not to be contrasted to Pharisees elsewhere in Acts. That he actually dimly glimpses Luke's meaning, however, is seen when he then qualifies that proposal by writing that the Pharisees in Acts are consistently "'political,' if not always the theological, friends of the Church."

favors that conclusion.[42] Thus the position of the Christian Pharisees of Acts 15:5, that Gentile converts to Christianity must be at the same time full converts to Judaism, is rendered null and void in the Acts of the Apostles.

We thus see that the one appearance of Pharisees in Acts as obstructionist is an appearance of __Christian__ Pharisees who disagree with what we might call Luke's __halakah__, i.e., Luke's interpretation of how Gentile Christians ought to live in fidelity or in harmony with the Mosaic Torah. Stated in other terms, the obstructionist Pharisees of Acts 15:5 disagree with Luke on the criteria for Gentiles' being church members. This brief appearance, therefore, provides the clue for understanding the variegated portrait of the Pharisees in the Gospel, for those Pharisees in the Gospel who correspond to the Christian Pharisees in the Acts are not the ones who are __friendly__ to Jesus but those who __oppose__ him because of what they consider his misinterpretation of Torah and his improper associations. This must then be why Luke reduces the Pharisaic opposition in the Gospel almost entirely to this one issue; the Pharisees in the Gospel who oppose Jesus are, for Luke, prototypes of traditionally Jewish Christians (like the Pharisees in Acts 15:5). They "grumble" because Jesus "receives sinners and eats with them" (Luke 15:2) or because he eats and drinks with "toll collectors and sinners" (5:30); they ask why he does not fast (5:33); they question whether some Sabbath behavior is proper (6:2), and they raise their eyebrows over the fact that he does not wash his hands before dining (15:1-2). These are halachic issues. In fact, therefore, inasmuch as Luke identifies as Pharisees those Jewish Christians in Acts who uphold the strictly (as some people put it today) "Torathic" Jewish position, we might even go so far as to say that Jesus' Pharisaic opponents in the Gospel __stand for__ traditionally Jewish Christians. It thus would appear that, in Luke's opinion, there were those in the early Jewish church

---

[42]In order not to extend this study beyond a reasonable length, we must neglect an analysis of the Lucan version of the Apostolic Council here, which narrative is, of course, not unrelated to Luke's portrayal of the Pharisees.

who opposed accepting Gentiles who did not become at the same time full proselytes to Judaism, who also opposed other aspects of Jesus' practice and insisted rather on maintaining Pharisaic halakah, and who, perhaps, opposed the claims of Jesus' divinity made by at least some of their fellow Christians. Whether such a "party" actually existed within early Jewish Christianity and whether, if it did, it was a "Pharisaic party" it is not our purpose to determine here. Its existence is not improbable, and there is certainly evidence from other early Christian literature that at least some of the positions that Luke attributes to his Christian Pharisees did, in fact, exist in early Jewish Christianity. We have taken a significant step on the way to understanding Luke's portrayal of the Jews when we realize that he makes use of the Pharisees in the Gospel tradition to characterize some Jewish Christians of his own day.[43]

---

[43]There is, of course, a certain propriety in Luke's identifying such a group as "Pharisaic," inasmuch as it was the Pharisees who were primarily interested in halakah. Nevertheless, there is good reason for preferring the more general term, "traditional Jews," here as a better description than "Pharisees" of the group that Luke wishes to characterize by the role that he alots to the Pharisees. While on the one hand, in Luke's day (i.e., after the destruction of Jerusalem), the Pharisees were the only one of the earlier parties or groups within Judaism that still had any significant role among the Jewish people, the Sadducees and Essenes having gone into eclipse as a result of the Roman destructions, still, however, when Luke has his Christian Pharisees, in Acts 15:5, call for circumcision and obedience to Torah, he attributes to them a position that might well have been upheld by many religious Jews other than Pharisees. (One could hardly, for example, imagine Christians who had come out of Qumran requiring anything less for Gentile converts.) Thus it seems that Luke uses "Pharisees" to stand for Christian Jews who are religious in the traditional sense of giving strict allegiance to the Law of Moses, and for this reason it seems better to refer to those characterized as being "Christian Pharisees" as traditionally Jewish Christians. Cf. the remark of H. J. Schoeps, Theologie und Geschichte des Judenchristentums (Tübingen: Mohr [Siebeck], 1949) 259, that the Christian Pharisees of Acts 15:5

We have noted that, both in the Gospel and in the Acts, Luke has two groups of Pharisees. The distinction is clearer in the Acts--where Christian Pharisees who have wrong ideas about Torah observance are distinguished from non-Christian Pharisees, who are quite friendly and helpful to the church--than it is in the Gospel, but the distinction is nevertheless there; and the unfriendly Pharisees in both volumes are identical. They are the traditionally Jewish Christians whom Luke does not like. What, however, is the function of the other Pharisees, the friendly but non-Christian ones? Again it is Acts that is clearer. The friendliness demonstrated by the behavior of the non-Christian Pharisees in Acts, by the fact that Paul was a Pharisee, and by the common belief in the resurrection points, it would seem, to an important moment in Lucan theology, namely that Christianity is the true and authentic Judaism. The friendly, non-Christian Pharisees in Acts underscore the linkage between Christianity and the ancestral Israelite religion.[44] While they do

---

represent the "extreme Jewish Christian group" in early Christianity, and that they are the true "ancestors of the later Ebionites."

[44]That this is the function of Luke's friendly Pharisees has been exactly seen by F. Keck, _Abschiedsrede_, 26-28. "The Pharisees," he writes, "are . . . in Acts demonstrably an element by which Luke exhibits the continuity that exists between church and Judaism" (ibid., 28). Unfortunately, however, Keck has overlooked the role of the Christian Pharisees in Acts 15:5 and of Jesus' frequent rebukes of the Pharisees in the Gospel and thus thinks that Luke presents all Pharisees in the friendly mode. Haenchen, also, who gave some attention to the Pharisees in his commentary, failed to take sufficiently into account the Lucan hostility toward the Pharisees and so also understood them as Luke's way of demonstrating that Christianity shares the true belief in the resurrection with Judaism (_Acts_, 101-102). Haenchen then (ibid., 444, n. 6) brought the Christian Pharisees of Acts 15:5 into connection with Paul's statement in 26:5 that they are the "very best party" in Judaism--that is, the very best Jews support circumcision and Torah observance. Incidentally, one can thus see here how mistaken interpretations can come from considering only Luke or Acts to the exclusion of the other. It is therefore more surprising when Fitzmyer, _Luke_, 1.581, who otherwise goes to

not, themselves, become Christians, they and Paul
repeatedly score Luke's point that Christianity is
not something radically different from the older Israelite religion but is rather just one small step removed
from the religion of the "very best party" in Judaism.[45]

Are these friendly non-Christian Pharisees in
Acts, then, identical with those in the Gospel who
invite Jesus to dinner and who warn him of Herod's
plans (the positive side of the Pharisaic friendliness
in the Gospel)? That is not so clear. "Identical"
would, in any case, hardly be the word; "derivative"
perhaps. But it is also possible that the Pharisaic
friendliness in the Gospel is related at least as
much to Luke's using the Pharisees to represent traditionally Jewish Christians as it is to the issue of
continuity. The continuity is not expressed in connection with the friendly Pharisees in the Gospel,
as it is in the Acts, and it is precisely the friendly
Pharisees in the Gospel who receive Jesus' attacks
on them (which we are just about to take up in detail).
These observations might incline one rather toward
the view that all the Pharisees in the Gospel represent,
in one way or another, the traditionally Jewish Christianity that Luke does not like. On the one hand, they
are overtly friendly toward Jesus and certainly have
nothing whatsoever to do with his martyrdom (anticipating
their eventual conversion), while, on the other hand,
Pharisees in the Gospel oppose Jesus' stance with
regard to the Torah (anticipating the eventual opposition
of traditionally Jewish Christians to Luke's kind
of Gentile Christianity). In Acts, while the obstructionist Pharisees continue to represent the traditional

---

such great lengths to consider the two works together,
follows the opinion just described and asserts that
Acts 26:5 gives "Luke's evaluation of" the Pharisees.
[45]Cf. Loisy, Actes, 284: Gamaliel is "un vrai juif,
and one whose opinion counts more than that of all
the Sadducees combined," inasmuch as Gamaliel is "docteur
de la Loi . . . . Authentic Judaism comes from his
mouth." Loisy does not, then, make the mistake of
trying to bring the position of the Christian Pharisees
in Acts 15:5 into harmony with that of the friendly
Pharisees; cf. ibid., 570-71.

Jewish Christianity, the friendly Pharisees are employed
in another way than in the Gospel, i.e., to help to
make Luke's point about Christianity as the authentic
Judaism.[46]

There is one other facet of the friendly-Pharisee
complex in Acts that still has not received adequate
explanation, and that is Paul's Pharisaism. Isn't
Paul's Pharisaism, which Luke emphasizes, a third
type of Pharisaism, a friendly but Christian type?
Perhaps it is, but there are some problems with such
an opinion. Especially we note that Paul's Pharisaism
is always mentioned only in his defense.[47] The first

---

[46]No one makes clearer than Loisy how much the friendliness
toward Christianity of these "authentic Jews" is the
product of Luke's "narrative skill" (i.e., in Loisy's
terms, of the redactor's skill in writing fiction).
Loisy, ruminating on Gamaliel's advice in Acts 5:34
(Actes, 290-291), observes that it is one thing to
discuss the "abstract principle" of letting things
work out according to divine plan but something quite
different than to make a "rule" of the principle. The
thinking behind Gamaliel's reasoning, Loisy concludes,
is that such a rule makes perfect sense to Luke, since
in his day the Christian preaching was already successful! When R. B. Rackham, The Acts of the Apostles.
An Exposition (London: Methuen, 1901) 73-74, explains
Gamaliel's ploy as being "opportunist" in order to
keep the rival Sadducees from doing away with an ally
(Christianity), he quite misses the point. Roloff,
Apostelgeschichte, 101, thinks that the Pharisees
supported Christianity as long as the Christians kept
the Law, and he thus explains the proposal of the
Pharisees in Acts 15:5 as a reaction to a change in
Christian policy. In this, he has failed adequately
to distinguish Christian from non-Christian Pharisees,
for the non-Christian Pharisees are still friendly
after Acts 15:5.

[47]Thus used, it has nothing to do with his having persecuted the church in his pre-Christian days, as Löning
states and as Klein strongly implies (cf. Löning,
"Paulinismus," 213; Klein, Zwölf Apostel, 122-124;
cf. further Löning, "Paulinismus," 217, and Saulustradition, 166, 170, 175-176). When Paul first perse-
cutes the church (Acts 9) nothing is said about his
being a Pharisee, and later, when he recalls that
he earlier persecuted the church (Acts 22:4), he does

time that the Lucan Paul uses the defense (Acts 23:6-9)
he does so in connection with belief in the resurrection;
he is a Pharisee and believes in the resurrection.
As we have already had occasion to note, this theme
recurs. To the degree that Luke brings out that Pharisees believe in the resurrection, he shows the straight-
line development of Christianity from "biblical Israel"
--that is, Christianity does not represent a break
with the tradition, since even non-Christian Pharisees
believe, as do Christians, in the resurrection. In
this sense, Luke presents a gradation of groups in
the development from "biblical Israel," with the Christians being in direct continuity;[48] the Pharisees,
while wrong in not becoming Christians, still partly
right in believing in the resurrection; and other
Jews being altogether wrong or "off the track." That
Paul's Pharisaism and his belief in the resurrection
are mentioned together is thus a particular case in
Luke's theology of the Israelite-Christian continuum.

But we must inquire somewhat more closely into
the function of Paul's Pharisaic defense in Acts 23.
Luke states that Paul brought up this point in his
defense (v 6) after he "recognized that one faction
[in the Sanhedrin] was Sadducee and the other Pharisaic,"
and that the result of this ploy was an argument between
the factions that quite disrupted the hearing (vv 9-10).
In other words, the function of Paul's Pharisaic defense

---

not mention his Pharisaism, and vice-versa (Acts 23:6).
Even when the two motifs are juxtaposed (Acts 26:4-12),
no connection is made between them, but they are rather
two points in his defense: 1) I have been an exemplary
Jew, a Pharisee; 2) don't think that I was some kind
of "Christian-lover," for I even persecuted them.
His persecution of the church is thus not "typically"
Pharisaic, as Löning and Klein seem to think.
   [48]So Loisy, Actes, 830, understands Paul's appeal to
the Pharisees for help; cf. also ibid., 858, on Acts
24:14-16; 892, on Acts 26:6; and 932-933, on Acts
28:17-22. Cf. also A. J. Mattill, Jr., "The Jesus-Paul
Parallels and the Purpose of Luke-Acts: H. H. Evans
Reconsidered," NovT 17 (1975) 22-23. Roloff, Apostelgeschichte, 328, thinks that "Luke simplifies here
and gives an image of Christians as true Pharisees."
Cf. further ibid., 337-338.

in Acts 23:6 is not so much to impress upon the reader that Paul believes in the resurrection <u>as Pharisee</u> as to show what a disharmonious and confused bunch the Jews are, how easily they can be thrown off the track by Luke's intelligent hero, and how, of course, they are unable to convict Paul of anything. To be sure, the ploy makes sense only if Pharisees believe in the resurrection, and Luke explains that fact in v 8, but Paul is not affirming in any serious way his Pharisaic beliefs, he is just playing a trick on his audience. One might say that, as in Acts 9:22, Paul "was confusing" his Jewish audience.

The one other time that Paul's Pharisaism is mentioned is again in a defense, this time before Herod (Acts 26:4-5). Here the defense is serious, i.e., not of the nature of a trick, and what Paul emphasizes is the righteousness of his life--that is, that he has been an exemplary Jew, even a Pharisee (v 5). How ironic (thus the implication) that so blameless a Jew should be charged with crimes against the state precisely by his fellow Jews! And for what? For nothing more than his Jewish belief in the resurrection (v 6). The readers are surely not expected to have forgotten the point earlier made that Pharisees believe in the resurrection, but Luke's way of putting together Paul's Pharisaism and his belief in "the hope of the promise to the [Israelite] fathers" is not such as to emphasize that his belief in the resurrection is something that he holds <u>as a Pharisee</u>. Indeed, Luke specifically adds that this hope is one for which <u>all Israelites</u> (τὸ δωδεκάφυλον ἡμῶν) yearn; and he has Paul make the same point in his defense before Felix, Acts 24:15. The motifs of being a Pharisee and of believing in the resurrection belong together, rather, in the "Why are they accusing me? I'm such a good Jew" defense. When Paul then adds that he used to persecute Christians (vv 10-12), the orientation is the same. All these things--his Pharisaism, his belief in the resurrection, and his persecution of the church-are aspects of his defense; they prove that he is a blameless Jew.[49] Thus Paul's Pharisaism

---

[49]G. Stählin, <u>Die Apostelgeschichte</u> (NTD; Göttingen: Vandenhoeck & Ruprecht, 1962) 296, writes of Paul's defense in Acts 24, "The accenting of what causes him to be recognized as a good Jew, what therefore connects him with his opponents, moves through the

is, indeed, different from that of the Pharisaic Christians of Acts 15:5 as well as from that of the non-Christian friendly Pharisees; for Paul is a Pharisee mutatis mutandis--that is, he is a Christianized Pharisee, not a Pharisaic Christian.

Let us bring together what we have seen of Pharisaic behavior in Luke-Acts. In the Acts there are, aside from Paul, two groups, the friendly non-Christian Pharisees, who share with Christians the belief in the resurrection and who try to help the Christians out of difficulties with the authorities, and the obstructionist Christian Pharisees, who promote the (for Luke) ridiculous idea that Gentile Christians ought to be circumcised and ought to follow the Law of Moses. It is probably better to say that, in the Gospel, the Pharisees are viewed under a dual aspect than that they are divided into two groups. On the one hand they are like the friendly non-Christian Pharisees in Acts and thus invite Jesus to dinner and try to keep him out of difficulty with the authorities, but on the other hand they have serious disagreements with him over matters of Torah interpretation, thus appearing in this respect like the obstructionist Christian Pharisees of Acts. It seems that Luke has portrayed the Pharisees in this strange way in order to let them represent the position within Christianity of traditional Jews, with the added nuance that the friendly Pharisees in Acts help him to demonstrate the continuity between ancient Judaism and Christianity.

Now we must examine what Jesus says to and about the Pharisees in the Gospel of Luke. While the Pharisees

---

entire speech from vs. 11 to vs. 21." Stählin further observes (ibid.), however, what the difference is, i.e., Paul believes the same scripture, but in the Christian way; he believes in the same resurrection, but the Christian version; he takes pains to be scrupulously religious, but from a Christian perspective. If Luke finds opportunity to emphasize, in different places, now one, now the other side of that coin, in Acts 24:14-16 he manages to show both at once. Cf. further the remarks of Haenchen, Acts, 729 (on Paul's final encounter with Jews in Rome), regarding how, for Luke, Christianity must be both Jewish and opposed by Jews.

may appear in different guises in the narrative of
Luke-Acts, what Jesus says of the Pharisees in the
Gospel does not display this variation, and it lets
us see exactly what Luke thinks of Pharisees.

The invective against "Scribes and Pharisees,
hypocrites" in Matthew 23 is certainly among the better
known parts of the New Testament, and we may conveniently
begin our examination of the Pharisees as they appear
in speech in Luke by taking note of what Luke does
with this invective.[50] Whether or not Luke has the
more original form of this invective is of no moment
for the present investigation, since our purpose is
to understand Luke's own presentation,[51] but we need
to remind ourselves that a great deal of the invective
that appears in Matthew does not appear in Luke:[52]
Matt 23:2-3, "The Scribes and the Pharisees sit on
Moses' seat," but you are to do what they say, not
what they do;[53] Matt 23:5, "They do all their deeds

---

[50]This statement should not be taken to mean that I
intend to take a position on the issue of whether
Luke had Matthew or Q for a source. If he used Q,
then he either followed it more or less accurately
or he changed it around considerably, but in either
case he used it to say what he wanted it to say.
If he used Matthew, then he changed it around considerably, using it to say what he wanted to say. As
C. H. Talbert has recently warned, it "is necessary
[to give] a negative answer" to the question, "Can
one simply assume the two-source theory today?" (review
of Kreuzweg und Kreuzigung Jesu by F. G. Untergassmair,
JBL 102 [1983] 343).
    [51]Cf. again the preceding note. There are surely, of
course, signs in Matthew of embellishment, since Matthew
everywhere betrays a vicious hatred of the Pharisees.
Ziesler, "Luke and the Pharisees," 153-154, also refers
to this problem. One may wish to consult R. Bultmann,
The History of the Synoptic Tradition (Oxford: Black-
well, 1968) 113-114, on the issue of Luke's and Matthew's
alterations of their common source.
    [52]Cf. also Ziesler, "Luke and the Pharisees," 154.
    [53]If this saying was in Luke's source, his omission
of it would be entirely understandable, since he would
hardly have wanted to allow it said that Pharisees
actually occupied a place of authority in the interpretation of the Torah, inasmuch as that is precisely
what is at issue for Luke; for Luke, it is Christianity

SANDERS

to be seen by people, for they broaden their phylacteries and make their fringes bigger"; Matt 23:8, "Don't you be called rabbi" (as well as the following advice to the disciples, vv 8-12); Matt 23:15, about their seeking proselytes; Matt 23:16b-22, which has to do with the relation between oath taking and the Temple and its furnishings; Matt 23:33, the Pharisees are venomous snakes; and Matt 23:38, "Thus on the outside you appear righteous to people, but on the inside you are full of hypocrisy and iniquity."[54] Because of these differences, we need to exercise due caution when approaching Luke and not let ourselves unwittingly be influenced, while we are reading Luke, by what Matthew says against the Pharisees. To repeat, much of the Matthaean version of the invective does not appear in Luke; Luke has less to say against the Pharisees than does Matthew.[55] In the second place, what Luke does have of the invective of Matthew 23 is not all together in one place,[56] and part of it refers

that properly "sits in Moses' seat."

[54]While Luke would probably not have been interested in some of these sayings--if they were, in fact, in his source--e.g., the liturgically related admonishments in Matt. 23:16b-22, I can see no reason why he would have gone out of his way to avoid Matt. 23:5, about the superficial character of Pharisaic righteousness, since he elsewhere includes this theme, e.g., Luke 11:42. Such an observation might lead one to the assumption that Luke and Matthew had a sayings source in common for this invective, and that each embellished or reduced it according to the dictates of his own interests. But I digress.

[55]Luke also (11:37-38), as does Matthew, omits the explanation about Pharisaic handwashing that appears in Mark 7:2-5. I am unable to perceive any particular animus in this omission. M. S. Enslin, "The Samaritan Ministry and Mission," HUCA 51 (1980) 31, also notes the milder form of the invective in Luke, but he seems to overstate the case when he has the Lucan Jesus display "an attitude of regretful sorrow" toward the Pharisees in response to their failure to accept his message.

[56]It is often, of course, noted (correctly) that Matthew gathers sayings material into several more or less unified discourses. In this instance, however, such an observation should not be used to help solve the Synoptic problem in favor of the existence of Q, since

168

to other persons, not to Pharisees. As far as the
location of the sayings goes, the charge of Matt 23:16
that the Scribes and Pharisees are "blind guides"
appears in Luke rather as a general word of advice
(not directed to any specific group) in Luke 6:39;
and, of course, as we have already noted, Luke places
the bulk of the invective that corresponds to Matthew
23 earlier in his gospel than does Matthew in his,
so that Luke does not connect the invective against
the Pharisees with the invective against the Scribes
of Mark 12:27-40. Luke 20:45-47 simply follows Mark
12:27-40, whereas Matthew combines the invective that
appears in Luke 11 with the invective against the
Scribes in Mark 12:27-40 and makes it all refer to
Pharisees as well, thus producing the long invective
of Matthew 23. Furthermore, in Luke 11, only vv 39-44
are designated as being against the Pharisees, the
rest of the invective (vv 46-52) being directed only
against the "legists."[57] Now, whether the Matthaean
pattern, according to which all the invective is directed
against Scribes <u>and</u> Pharisees, or the Lucan pattern,
in which a brief invective against the Pharisees is
followed by a longer one against the legists, is the
more original pattern is immaterial for our discussion.[58]
Either Luke reproduced from his source the pattern

Luke would have a very good reason for putting the
bulk of the invective into the Travel Narrative and
not into the Passion Narrative, where it would be
if he were following Matthew, since, as we have already
seen, he keeps the Pharisees out of the Passion Narrative. (Matthew 23 agrees with Luke 20 in order.)
   [57]Translating νομικοί as "lawyers" is ill-advised, since
that term implies to Americans people who deal with
the law professionally--those who are called in England
"barristers" or "solicitors." Luke, however, has
in mind those who are sticklers for the Torah (   );
cf. P. Parker, "Lawyer," <u>IDB</u> (1962) 3.102.
   [58]By applying all the invective after v 44 to the legists,
Luke avoids charging the Pharisees with complicity
in the murder of the prophets (vv 47-51; cf. Matt
23:29-32, 34-36), and he avoids saying that they have
the "keys" (v 52; cf. Matt 23:13). Inasmuch as the
Lucan versions of these sayings therefore reflect
Lucan interest, one should avoid assuming that Luke
necessarily has the more original form of the invective,
as does L. Gaston, <u>No Stone on Another</u> (NovTSup; Leiden:
Brill, 1970) 320-321.

that we find in the Gospel of Luke because he liked
it the way it was or he altered the pattern that he
found in Matthew or Q to its present form because
that was the way that he wanted it. In either case,
the polemic against the Pharisees in Luke 11 comprises
only six verses and deals mainly with Pharisaic halakah
(dishwashing, almsgiving, tithing), an aspect of the
invective that has been especially well seen by S. G.
Wilson,[59] who has observed that it is not "Pharisaic
scrupulosity" as such that is criticized here, but
rather "the neglect of essentials alone." Thus Luke
does not portray the conflict between Jesus and the
Pharisees as being over Torah, but as being about
halakah. Wilson writes, "Luke apparently saw nothing
objectionable in a Pharisaic lifestyle per se . . . ;
he objects only to the neglect of central commands."
Wilson's choice of expression is rather unfortunate,
since it is the Pharisaic "neglect of central commands"
that effectively determines the "Pharisaic lifestyle";
what he means is that Luke objects not to the Pharisaic
attempt to do the will of God, expressed in the Torah,
but to the Pharisaic way of doing that. The invective
of Luke 11 concludes with two broadsides (vv 43-44),[60]
that the Pharisees like public acclaim and position
and that they are "like blank gravestones."[61]

---

[59]Wilson, Luke and the Law, 18-19.

[60]F. Keck, Abschiedsrede, 94-95, sees only these slanderous
denunciations in the invective, not the halachic argument, and therefore takes the intention of the invective
to be a warning against "greed."

[61]Ellis, Luke, consistently reinterprets the Pharisees
as problem "church members"--that is, he gives a homi-
letical interpretation to the Pharisees in Luke:
"The churchmen observe only the forms of religion"
(ibid., 69; cf. also G. Bouwman, Das dritte Evangelium.
Einübung in die formgeschichtliche Methode [Düsseldorf:
Patmos, 1968] 147, 151-161; A. Hastings, Prophet and
Witness in Jerusalem [London, New York, Toronto:
Longmans, Green, 1958] 109). While this approach
has the value of shifting the interest of the reader
away from those bad Jews to Christian self-criticism,
it is historically misleading and has the effect of
leaving Luke's antisemitism lying there like an unde-
tonated bomb waiting to be tripped over by a less
generous interpreter.

We also note that the Matthaean form of the invective includes the oft-repeated refrain, "Woe to you, Scribes and Pharisees, hypocrites," which does not appear in Luke. This represents only a formal difference, however,[62] since Luke writes, "Woe to you," three times for the Pharisees (vv 42, 43, 44) and three times for the legists (vv 46, 47, 52), and since he places at the close of the invective the saying, which Matthew and Mark have elsewhere (Mark 8:15 // Matt 16:6), about how one should "be on guard against the leaven of the Pharisees," to which he then adds, "Which is hypocrisy" (Luke 12:1).[63] Thus the only meaningful difference between Matthew and Luke on this point is that Luke reserves the charge of hypocrisy for the Pharisees alone.[64] That such is deliberately Lucan is seen in the parallels, for Mark and Matthew agree in placing this saying earlier in their respective Gospels, and neither includes the word, "hypocrisy." Luke has, therefore, clearly appropriated the saying from another context to make it the conclusion of his invective against the Pharisees and legists, and he has added the word, "hypocrisy."[65] The bad leaven

---

[62]Also Schweizer, Lukas, 132-133.

[63]Cf. also Tyson, "Opposition," 149. Luke does not "avoid" (Grundmann, Lukas, 246) calling the Pharisees hypocrites.

[64]M.-R. J. Lagrange, Evangile selon Saint Luc (EBib; 7th ed.; Paris: Gabalda, 1927) 352, sees that the "hypocrisy" of Luke 12:1 is a summary of the several references to that trait in Matthew. Schmid, Lukas, 214, explains that the saying represents an "ethical value judgment about" the leaven, not a "designation of [its] content," and that it does not warn the disciples "to be on guard . . . against the Pharisees," but rather "not to imitate them." Thus he leans toward the position also taken by Ellis and Bouwman (cf. n. 61).

[65]Cf. H. L. Egelkraut, Jesus' Mission to Jerusalem. A Redaction Critical Study of the Travel Narrative in the Gospel of Luke (Europäische Hochschulschriften Reihe 23, Theologie; Frankfurt: Peter Lang; Bern: Herbert Lang, 1976) 103. This realization inclines one naturally toward the view that at least that aspect of the Matthaean form of the invective that includes "hypocrites" with the repeated "woes" is the more original form, and that Luke has taken the hypocrisy out of the repeated woes to place it in his concluding statement, which he applies only to Pharisees. (So

of the Pharisees, which works hidden within the dough
to spoil the whole, is their hypocrisy.[66]

Inasmuch as Luke separates the invective against
the Scribes from that against the Pharisees and calls
the Scribes not Scribes but "legists," we need to
give some attention at this point to this Lucan peculiarity. To begin with, we can be certain that Luke
uses "legist" as another word for "Scribe" and does
not think of the legists as a separate group. This
becomes obvious at the conclusion of the invective,
where (v 53) it is Scribes and Pharisees, not legists
and Pharisees, who "began to have a terrible grudge"
against Jesus, although the invective had referred
to legists, not to Scribes. Thus, in two of the three
places in Luke, outside the invective of chap. 11,
where legists appear (7:30 and 14:3), they are merely
the associates of Pharisees, as are the Scribes elsewhere. Furthermore, Luke seems to have got the term
from Matthew or Q and to have understood it as a variant
of "Scribe," as we can see from the way in which the
three Synoptic Gospels introduce the Great Commandment.
Mark had written that "one of the Scribes" asked Jesus
about the commandment (Mark 12:28); but Matthew, shifting
the apothegm to a Streitgespräch, first mentions Pharisees and then reports that "one of them, a legist"
put the question to Jesus (Matt 22:35, the only occurrence of the word νομικός in the Gospels outside of
Luke). Luke seems to have looked at Mark and Matthew
(or Q) together and to have concluded that "legist"
was another term for scribe," insofar as Scribes are
associated with Pharisees and not with priests (as
is sometimes the case in the Gospels); and thus he
has a "legist" put the question (Luke 10:25, the remain-
ing occurence of the term outside chap. 11). Luke
seems to have liked this term as an alternate for
"Scribe" either as a more understandable term for
his Gentile readership or because he thought that
it conveyed something that he wanted to convey.[67]

Ernst, Lukas, 393; U. Wilckens " ὑποκρίνομαι , κτλ .,"
TWNT 8 [1969] 566). Ziesler, "Luke and the Pharisees,"
152, cannot tell if Luke intends to be more or less
critical of the Pharisees here than his sources are.
[66]The Lucan Pharisees should, therefore, not be called
"leaders" (e.g. Schmithals, Lukas, 141), inasmuch
as the role of leaven is not that of leadership.
[67]Parker, "Lawyer," 102, opts for the former alternative.

Inasmuch as the term, "Scribe," predominates in Luke, the former possibility can be ruled out.

What was it, then, that Luke wanted to convey by his occasional use of "legist" instead of "Scribe"? In part, the term itself answers the question, for its use allows us to see that Luke wants his readers to think of those people associated with Pharisees as being particularly involved with the νόμος , i.e., the Torah. To this degree Luke is abetting his portrayal of the Pharisees as "Torah maniacs." Beyond the mere use of the term, however, we have only the invective of chap. 11.

Luke lays three charges on the legists: They "load people with loads that can hardly be borne" but don't lift a "finger" to help (11:46). They "build the tombs of the prophets" (v 47), which act ties them to the ancestral killing of the prophets (v 48) and justifies the "requiring" of "the blood of all the prophets . . . from this generation" (vv 50-51). And they "withhold the keys of knowledge" (v 52). The first and third charges seem to refer to (first) the unbearable requirements of the Torah according to its Pharisaic interpretation and to (second) the way in which this interpretation locks people out from the true interpretation (i.e., Jesus' interpretation a la Luke). Thus, even though the word, βυστάζω , is common enough, it seems difficult to avoid the conclusion that Luke wants to make a connection between the legists' loading up people with loads "that can hardly be borne (δυσβάστακτα)" and Peter's explaining in the Apostolic Council (Acts 15:10) that requiring Gentile converts to Christianity to keep the Torah is "to put a yoke on the neck of the disciples that neither our fathers nor we have been able to bear (βαστάσαι)." [68] Since this interpretation of the Torah-- that is, Pharisaic halakah--is the going one--or, to be more precise, is the prime competitor with the Gentile Christian interpretation--it prevents proper knowledge of the Torah, it "locks up the keys of knowledge."

These two charges Luke could have laid to the Pharisees, but the middle one, that the legists share complicity in the death of the prophets, he could

---

[68]Schweizer, Lukas, 132, also makes this connection.

not. Thus he seems to have employed the legists here,
in the one place where he gives them any definition,
to accuse the associates of the Pharisees (logically
enough) in terms that would have been appropriate
for the Pharisees themselves, but also to lay a charge
against "legalistic Judaism" that he would not, under
any circumstance, have laid against the Pharisees:
killing the prophets. In this way Luke reminds his
readers that, while the Pharisees themselves do not
share the guilt of "the Jews," they nevertheless parti-
cipate with the rest of Judaism in the wrong interpretation of the Torah, which wrong interpretation
is tied to the Jewish guilt (cf. Stephen's speech;
Paul's statement in Acts 13:27). Put otherwise, if
the Jews could have understood their own scripture
they would not always have rejected the purposes of
God and killed the prophets, including Jesus. But
the Pharisees, who are never said to be guilty, nevertheless do not disassociate themselves from that wrong
interpretation of scripture. So where does that leave
them?

Luke has made the occasion of the invective in
chap. 11 one of Jesus' frequent dinners at a Pharisee's
house, and this pattern is also followed on the two
other such occasions (Luke 7:36-50; 14:1-6)--that
is, every time a Pharisee invites Jesus to dinner
Jesus accepts and then takes the opportunity to scold
the Pharisees for their incorrect lifestyle.[69]   That
is the case not only in Luke 11:37-44, as we have
just discussed, but also in 7:36-50. Here also a
Pharisee has invited Jesus to dinner;[70] and here also
Luke takes the opportunity to have Jesus point out

---

[69]Cf. Gilmour, "Luke," 142. Ziesler, "Luke and the
Pharisees," 150, has noted this odd juxtaposition
but admits that he cannot explain it. J. C. O'Neill,
The Theology of Acts in Its Historical Setting (2d
ed.; London: S. P. C. K., 1970) 71, finds in the
three dinners with Pharisees "a development in the
relationship between Jesus and the Pharisees   of
increasing antagonism." Why there is more antagonism
in 14:1-6 than in 11:37-44 + 12:1 is not, however,
clear.
    [70]Mark 14:3-9 and Matt. 26:6-13 include what is more
or less the same story, but without designating Jesus'
host a Pharisee and without the scolding of the host.
These are Lucan elements.

to the Pharisee what is wrong with Pharisaism, for in Luke the sinful woman who anoints Jesus' feet becomes the foil for Jesus' critical dialog with the Pharisee.[71] The Pharisee thinks, "If he were a prophet he would have known" the wicked truth about the woman, "for she is a sinner" (v 39). The implication seems fairly clear that Jesus is accepting into his company someone whom the Pharisee finds unacceptable. Jesus' response to these thoughts is twofold; first he puts an example (or a parable) to the Pharisee about two debtors whose debts were forgiven, in the one case a large debt and in the other a small, and about their correspondingly large and small gratitude (vv 40-43), and then he explains in detail how what the woman did for him far surpasses the Pharisee's actions (vv 44-46).[72]
If we draw back a bit from the details of this episode so as to focus on the themes, then we see that Jesus accepts into his company someone whom the Pharisee, who also wishes to be in Jesus' company--he did, after all, invite him to dinner--finds unacceptable because of her sins. Jesus, on the other hand, indicates that the sinner's acts of contrition more than make up for any absence of traditional righteousness. Thus the issue here is who is an acceptable member of Jesus' company, with Jesus emphasizing the qualifications of repentance and contrition while the Pharisee emphasizes the qualifications of proper behavior. We shall therefore do best to understand the contrast that Jesus then draws between the Pharisee and the sinner in vv 44-46 not as referring to their respective behavior with regard to the person of Jesus--as if Christology were the issue[73]--but as referring still

---

[71]Wilckens, "Vergebung für die Sünderin (Lk 7,36-50)," in Orientierung an Jesus. Für Josef Schmid, ed. P. Hoffmann (Freiburg, Basel, Wien: Herder, 1973) 418, sees it the other way round: The Pharisee is the foil for the Christian lesson.

[72]B. Weiss (with J. Weiss), Die Evangelien des Markus und Lukas (MeyerK; 9th ed.; Göttingen: Vandenhoeck & Ruprecht, 1901) 395, notes that the contrast does not mean that Jesus' Pharisaic host has neglected normal politeness, only that the woman's behavior is of a different order from his. That appears to be correct.

[73]Ziesler, "Luke and the Pharisees," 151, thinks that the narrative "concerns both attitudes to the Law, and Christology."

to this issue of the proper qualifications for being
accepted into Jesus' company. If this interpretation
of this episode has anything to commend it, then we
see that the Pharisee here is a prototype of those
Christian Pharisees in Acts 15:5 who want Gentile
Christians to be circumcised and to follow the Law
of Moses. The Pharisee Simon, in Luke 7:36-50, also
wants only righteous people in Jesus' entourage, not
those "sinners" who get in only on the basis of repentance, contrition . . . and belief; for Jesus concludes
this episode extremely pointedly by proclaiming to
the sinner that her "faith has saved" her. It is
the criteria for church membership that are under
discussion here, not Christology.[74]

In Luke 14:1-6 the issue is again halakah. A
Pharisee--this time one "of the rulers of the Pharisees"
(v 1)[75]--invites Jesus to dinner on the Sabbath, and
Jesus is confronted with a person in need of healing. There follows, then, the halachic discussion:
to heal or not to heal on the Sabbath. Jesus bests
his Pharisaic opponents (thus the one Pharisee has
become in v 3; legists, too), as we see from the conclusion, "They were unable to rebut him on these points"
(v 6), and then he carries on with the healing. Thus
the opposition has to do again with proper behavior
in view of the Torah.

---

[74]The term, "church membership," is chosen advisedly
in order to do justice to the fact that Luke does
not draw a heavy line between becoming a Christian
and being a Christian (as, for example, Paul does).
Thus Wilson, Luke and the Law, 72, in discussing the
Apostolic Decree, observes correctly that "the issue
. . . is . . . not merely post-conversion behavior
but what constitutes true conversion in the first
place."
[75]It is possible to translate the phrase as, "one
of the Pharisees who was a ruler," especially if, as
in a few important manuscripts, the article before
φαρισαίων is missing. So T. Zahn, Das Evangelium
des Lucas (Kommentar zum NT; 4th ed.; Leipzig and
Erlangen: Deichert, 1920) 544, prefers to read.
In view of the way, however, in which Luke otherwise
keeps the Pharisees neatly separate from the religious
authorities, I would regard such a translation as
impossible, even if the article is not original.
Cf. the discussion in Schneider, Lukas, 312.

The brief interchange between Jesus and the Pharisees in Luke 16:14-15 is, as we have already had occasion to note, without sufficient context, so that Luke's description of the Pharisees here (they are "lovers of money" and "derid[e]" Jesus) appears as slander.[76] Jesus' response to the Pharisees, however, is quite in line with the theme that has been dominating, as we have been observing, all Jesus' statements to and about the Pharisees--that is, opposition to the insistence of traditionally Jewish Christians that Gentile converts to Christianity must also convert to Judaism; for here Jesus again addresses briefly the same issue that he had addressed at considerably greater length when he was at the house of the Pharisee Simon (Luke 7:36-50), i.e., the issue of the criteria for church membership. The Pharisees, Jesus says, are "those who make themselves righteous before people,[77] but God knows [their] hearts." One might quite justifiably call this saying a capsule summary of the point of Luke 7:36-50. The point of the saying is so obvious that the corollary--that repentance and contrition are, in Jesus' view, the proper path to take in order to be made righteous--does not even need to be expressed.

Luke also uses several parables to make his point about the Pharisees. Especially noteworthy is the trilogy in Luke 15,[78] which follows the note that the Pharisees and Scribes are "grumbling" because of Jesus' association with "sinners" (Luke 15:2). Jesus replies with three parables. In the first (vv 4-7) a shepherd rejoices greatly over a lost sheep that he is able to recover, not over ninety-nine sheep that stayed in the fold. In the second (vv 8-10) a woman gives a party because she finds a lost drachma, not because of the nine that she did not lose. And in the third (vv 11-24) a man makes a major social

---

[76]Löning, Saulustradition, 168, mistakenly thinks that "greed" is Luke's primary criticism of the Pharisees. Ernst, Lukas, 470, thinks that the reference to greed brings in the issue of idolatry.

[77]An attitude which is then labeled, "abomination," as Egelkraut, Jesus' Mission, 132, emphasizes.

[78]Cf. esp. the discussion by J. Lambrecht, Once More Astonished. The Parables of Jesus (New York: Crossroad, 1981) 33-52, who proposes--almost correctly--that Luke intended to relate these parables to the issue of "rigorous" and "tepid" Christians in his own day.

event out of the return home of his prodigal son,
not out of the fact (vv 25-32) that he had another
son who never left. The point seems inescapable that
the Lucan Jesus is contrasting here God's attitude
toward repentant sinners and toward all those--symbolized
by the Pharisees--who stay in the fold, who don't
get lost, who pursue the prescribed righteousness.

This last point is particularly obvious in the
Prodigal Son, for here the elder son, who had "never
transgressed [his father's] commandment" (15:29),
is by virtue of both aspects-temporally prior and
commandment-observing--the representative of the obser-
vant Jew, whereas the other son is more recent, dwells
in "a distant region" (v 13), and feeds pigs (v 15),
and is therefore the stand-in for the Gentiles.[79]
While in the Lost Sheep and the Lost Coin there is
not the slightest intimation that there is anything
wrong with what was never lost in the first place,
do we not begin to get a whiff of such in the Prodigal
Son? Is the portrayal of the elder son simply neutral?
Or do we not detect in him a certain ungracious and

---

[79]Cf. my article, "Tradition and Redaction in Luke XV
11-32," NTS 15 (1969) 433-438. Loisy, who in Evangiles
synoptiques, 2.155, stated that the parable did not
contain a Jew-Gentile allegory, reversed himself in
Luc, 37, 402-403 and proposed that the second part
of the parable was added in order to turn the parable
into an allegory of saved Gentile and self-rejecting
Jew. While a few scholars, e.g., E. Klostermann,
Das Lukasevangelium (HNT, 2nd ed.; Tübingen: Mohr
[Siebeck], 1929) 157, incline toward Loisy's later
view, most consider the parable integral, and a great
many reject the notion of any allegorizing. Yet cf. S.
Sandmel, Anti-Semitism in the New Testament? (Philadelphia: Fortress, 1978) 79, n. 13. Since publishing
my aforementioned article, I have inclined toward
the later view of L. Schottroff, "Das Gleichnis vom
verlorenen Sohn," ZTK 68 (1971) 27-52, that Luke composed
the entire parable; cf. also J. van Goudoever, "The
Place of Israel in Luke's Gospel," NovT 8 (1966) 121,
who takes the position that Luke composed the parable
out of the raw material of the parable of the Two
Sons in Matt 21:28-32. Although the main points are
different, such use seems possible. In any case,
numerous commentators see that the parable refers
to the Pharisees.

resentful air, brought on by his father's royal treatment of one who has no right to claim anything (as he admits)? When the elder son affirms that he "never transgressed [the father's] commandment" (v 29), he seem to ally himself with the Christian Pharisees of Acts 15:5, who are resentful over the admission of Gentiles into the church without any obligation to keep Torah.

To propose, therefore, that the parable is not "stamped by the Lucan theology or, as the case may be, soteriology" is simply to turn aside from the obvious.[80] Whatever the parable may have meant in its pre-Lucan form (if there was one), in Luke it must be viewed in the overall context of Luke-Acts. It is fully in keeping with that context to disparage those who keep the commandments and who are not sinners in any traditional sense (Pharisees) while approving repentant sinners who "come home."

The most effective device, however, that Luke found to make the point that the proper criteria for church membership are repentance and contrition, not following Pharisaic halakah, was the parable of the Pharisee and the Toll Collector.[81] The vivid imagery of this parable has conveyed to millions over nineteen centuries a tableau of the starkly contrasting self-righteous Pharisee and the contrite and humble repentant sinner.[82] It is a contrast in black and white, with

---

[80]F. Schnider, Die verlorenen Söhne (Orbis biblicus et orientalis; Freiburg, Schweiz: Universitätsverlag; Gottingen: Vandenhoeck & Ruprecht, 1977) 87.

[81]This is Fitzmyer's translation (Luke, 1.140) of τελώνης. While it may make one think mistakenly of someone in a booth on one of our nation's highways, it is more suitable than the less wieldy "customs tax collector."

[82]That the Pharisee in the parable is supposed to appear "odious" (C. G. Montefiore, The Synoptic Gospels [2nd ed.; London: Macmillan, 1927] 2.557) and the toll collector winsome is, of course, universally recognized. And, of course, it is precisely the Pharisee's Jewish halachic righteousness that makes him so objectionable to Luke (Schmid, Lukas, 281). It is my assumption that Luke is the author of the parable, but who first told it is irrelevant for our considertion here. The points are, in any case, all Lucan.

SANDERS

no gray area between. How perfectly, how terribly
righteous the Pharisee of the parable is! He is not
a thief, not unjust, not an adulterer, and certainly,
thank God! not a toll collector (Luke 18:11); his
fasting and tithing, further, leave nothing to be
desired (v 12). The sinner, on the other hand, offers
nothing in his own behalf. His only prayer is, "Bring
redemption to me the sinner." Luke's conclusion to
the parable, then, that "the latter was justified
(δεδικαιωμένος)" not "the former," provides the counterpoint to the saying in 16:15, that it is the Pharisees
who "make themselves righteous (οἱ δικαιοῦντες ἑαυτούς)
before people." [83] The Pharisee of the parable, like
the Pharisees of Luke 16:15, follows a certain halakah
and thus manages to appear righteous before people.
The Lucan Jesus, however, contends that what is important
is rather being righteous in God's sight, for which
Pharisaic halakah is not effective, but for which
true repentance and contrition suffice. The moral
that Luke appends to the parable, then, "Everyone
who exalts himself will be humbled, and the one who
humbles himself will be exalted" (v 14), simply strengthens the conclusion about the sinner's being made
righteous. This Pharisee of the parable is therefore
hardly to be distinguished from Jesus' Pharisaic host
in Luke 7:36-50.[84] Both think that they know the

_____

[83]While Paul is likely the originator of the Christian
use of the verb δικαιοῦμαι to mean something more
or less synonymous with "to be saved" (an examination of the concordance alone will confirm that likelihood), and while Luke to that degree also uses the
word in the same way, still Luke attaches his own
meaning to the verb, inasmuch as he lays emphasis
on the righteousness that comes through contrition
and repentance as opposed to that which comes through
"behaving righteously." J. Jeremias, The Parables
of Jesus (revised ed.; New York: Scribner's, 1963)
141, of course thinks that "our passage shows . . . that
the Pauline doctrine of justification has its roots
in the teaching of Jesus." Via Luke's Gospel?
[84]So also Lampe, "Luke," in Peake's Commentary on the
Bible, 831. J. Koenig, Jews and Christians in Dialogue
(Philadelphia: Westminster, 1979) 115, is overcome
by the occasional friendliness of the Lucan Pharisees
and thus thinks that the Pharisee of the parable does
not represent all Pharisees. Cf. also Ziesler, "Luke
and the Pharisees," 151.

proper way to righteousness: Pharisaic halakah; both
think that sinner who neglects that halakah and offer
only their repentance and contrition, however sincere,
are defective in their righteousness. Thus these
Pharisees in the Gospel are the prototypes of the
Christian Pharisees in Acts 15:5 who likewise advise
that those desiring admission to the church should
strictly follow the Law of Moses and not rely merely
on their "belief" (Luke 7:50) to get in. [85]

It is against this background, apparently, that
we have to understand the summary that Luke has thrown
into the midst of Jesus' sayings about John the Baptist
(Luke 7:29-30), according to which "all the people,
when they heard [what Jesus had been saying about
John], and the toll collectors justified God,[86] since
they were baptized in John's baptism; but the Pharisees
and the legists set aside the plan of God for themselves,
since they were not baptized by him."[87] The end result

---

[85]The parable, of course, is intended to have a wider
application--that is, to refer to the argument with
Jewish Christians over criteria for church membership.
To see the Pharisee, however, as "represent[ing] unbe-
lieving Jews" (Loisy, Luc, 444) is to miss the point.
[86]What, exactly, Luke meant by "justifying God" is less
than clear. Fitzmyer, Luke, 1.676, seems correctly
to understand it to mean that they "acknowledged God
as righteous," but the reason, then for translating,
"Acknowledged . . . God's claims on them" (ibid.,
670,676), seems to be more interpretation than strict
meaning. It will surely not fail to strike the reader
that the key terms in this little summary are "toll
collectors," Pharisees," and "justify," in other
words the same key terms that appear in the parable
of the Pharisee and the Toll Collector. Fitzmyer,
ibid., 673, 675-676, has overlooked that connection
and is thus puzzled by the summary statement. C. H. Talbert, Reading Luke. A . . . Commentary (New York:
Crossroad, 1982) 85, is probably correct in proposing
that "to justify God was to acknowledge the rightness
of his call in John and Jesus and to repent and be
forgiven."
[87]The absence of the Pharisees from Luke 3:7, whereas
they appear in the parallel, Matt. 3:7, is therefore
possibly a deliberate Lucan device; Luke may remove
the Pharisees from John's audience in anticipation
of the statement in Luke 7:30. In this case, however,

of Pharisaic thinking is thus announced. Reliance
on the Law of Moses for salvation rather than on contrition and repentance (which are implied in submitting
to John's baptism)--such, as we have seen, is the
contrast that Luke consistently draws--spells ultimate
doom for the Pharisees.[88] "Since the will of God
set forth in John's ministry was summed up in his
'baptism of repentance for the forgiveness of sins'
(3:3), for the evangelist to say the Pharisees rejected
God's purpose for them is to say they did not repent
and did not receive God's forgiveness."[89] Does this
judgment of doom apply even to those who, a la Acts
15:5, are Christians?

     We have now arrived at the most difficult question
of all; for can it be that Luke intends for his readers
to understand that even those Pharisees who became
Christians are without hope of salvation? Or does
he rather understand that, whereas the Pharisaic menta-
lity and lifestyle (halakah) are contradictory to
the (Lucan) Christian understanding of salvation,
nevertheless, inasmuch as salvation is open to all,
some Pharisees were able to bridge the chasm and to
"believe"--for, in Acts 15:5, Luke does, after all,
refer to "Pharisees who have believed"? Perhaps if,
with this question in mind, we rethink the evidence
that we have examined, we shall be able to reach a
satisfactory answer.

     The evidence of what Jesus says to and about
Pharisees would appear to be uniformly clear; their
Torah-strict halakah has taken a wrong turn, so that,
compared even with toll collectors who repent with
true contrition, their situation appears hopeless.[90]

---

it must be considered equally likely that Matthew
could be responsible for the presence of the Pharisees
and Sadducees in his version (Matt. 3:7).
     [88]The Pharisees are not here representatives of "official
Judaism" (Lampe, "Luke," 831) or "authorities in Israel"
(Fitzmyer, Luke, 1.673). The Pharisees are never
that in Luke-Acts.
     [89]Talbert, Reading Luke, 85.
     [90]Thus under no circumstances do the Pharisees in Luke,
as H. Flender, St. Luke. Theologian of Redemptive
History (Philadelphia: Fortress, 1967) 108, thinks,
"represent that group among the Jewish leaders which
is receptive to the Christian message."

They are not "justified" (Luke 18:14) however often
they may invite Jesus to dinner, and even though they
had nothing at all to do with the execution of Jesus.
Furthermore, when the Lucan Jesus admonishes his followers (i.e., the church) to beware the Pharisaic
leaven of hypocrisy (Luke 12:1), he must have in mind
the Christian Pharisees, not the non-Christian ones,
for what else can this warning mean to the Lucan church?
We have seen that the way in which the warning is
put is distinctively Lucan. What situation can Luke
have in mind in the early Christian church that would
justify this warning against the leaven of Pharisaic
hypocrisy, if it is not the problem of the traditionally
Jewish Christians within the church? Leaven works
within the dough, not outside it. The hypocrisy of
the Pharisees is within the church, not outside it.
Thus Luke does not have Jesus rail against the hypocrisy
of Pharisaic behavior in individual cases, as does
Matthew; rather, he reserves the charge of hypocrisy
for a general statement, one that emphasizes their
spoiling activity within the church.

The portrait of the Pharisees in the Acts supports
this understanding and, indeed, renders it unavoidable;
for it is clear that a charge of hypocrisy could scarcely
be leveled at the non-Christian Pharisees in Acts,
who could hardly behave better toward Christians if
they were the church's fairy god-mother. No, it is
not the non-Christian Pharisees in Acts on whom the
label, "hypocrites," is to be attached; it is the
Christian Pharisees. Thus now we know exactly wherein
the hypocrisy lies. The leaven of hypocrisy is the
attempt of traditionally Jewish Christians to get
Gentile Christians to follow the Torah. It is the
Christian Pharisees who are obstructionist; it is
they who want to be in Jesus' company (thus the dinner
invitations) but who want to keep others out who do
not follow their pattern of being in that company,
their way (halakah); it is they who object especially
to the inclusion of such sinners as prostitutes (Luke
7:36-50) and toll collectors (Luke 18:9-14) on the
basis of their repentant contrition alone and who
press (Acts 15:5) for all in the church to adhere
to the Torah;[91] and it is they on whom falls Jesus'

---

[91]Tyson, "Opposition," 149, correctly sees that the
"demand" of the Christian Pharisees of Acts 15:5 "for
the circumcision of Gentile converts is consistent

summary judgment (Luke 18:14), "Everyone who exalts himself will be humbled, and the one who humbles himself will be exalted." In that judgment we have it all. That is the statement that makes clear to us exactly why Luke sketched the Pharisees as he did; for he is contending with the traditionally Jewish Christians over the criteria for Gentiles' membership in the church. The way of his opponents he regards as an attempt to exalt themselves, to justify themselves; for they have a prescription, a teaching, a way, and that way is called, "Moses." In Luke's opinion, however, Jesus had proposed another way into the church, another way into the Kingdom of God, another halakah of salvation, if you will; and that way, the way of repentance and true contrition alone, was a much more suitable way for Gentiles to follow in entering into the Kingdom of God than was the halachic way of the traditionally Jewish Christians.[92] Conzelmann proposed that Pharisees in Acts are "inconsistent" if they do not convert, inasmuch as they share the Christian belief in resurrection;[93] but they are, in fact, inconsistent if they do convert, because they bring with them the "baggage" of Torah fidelity, which is the "bad yeast" that spoils the dough of the church. Only Paul escapes this double jeopardy by giving up the characteristically Pharisaic insistence that Gentile Christians follow the Law of Moses.

Everything in Luke's portrait of the Pharisees in the Gospel conforms to this pattern, and nothing contradicts it. Only in Acts does a different picture emerge, where there are non-Christian Pharisees who help the church when they can. These Pharisees, however--along with Paul's Pharisaism--help Luke to show the bridge, the link, the continuity between the religion of the "Old Testament" and Christianity.[94] These

---

with the role [the Pharisees] play in the Gospel"; but Tyson fails to find the opposition here and thinks that Luke views these Pharisees as friendly, "though of a more conservative stripe than Luke's heroes."

[92]Thus Jervell, People of God, 138-139, misses the point when he emphasizes that Jesus, in Luke, never criticizes the Torah.

[93]Conzelmann, Theology, 148.

[94]F. Keck, Abschiedsrede, 27-28, has seen this side of Luke's portrait of the Pharisees, but to the exclusion of the other side of the portrait.

non-Christian Pharisees in Acts are, so to speak, the other side of the coin; for, if Luke uses the Pharisees in the Gospel and the Christian Pharisees in the Acts to show that traditional Torah observance, even in the church, leads into a cul de sac of condemnation on the basis of self-exaltation, he uses the non-Christian Pharisees in the Acts to help remind his readers that there is more than one road that leads from pre-Christian Judaism into the present time, and that Christianity is surely the right one.

Luke's normal term for "Christian" is "believer," and "to believe" means to become a Christian (cf., e.g., Acts 2:41; 21:20). Yet Luke understands this belief to be further defined in two ways. On the one hand, belief involves true contrition and repentance, as in Luke 7:36-50 or in Acts 2:38. On the other hand, however, this belief is not to be encumbered by irrelevant or extraneous additional requirements such as, specifically, requirements from the Mosaic Torah normally applied to Gentiles who converted to Judaism; and that means especially, to be even more precise, circumcision. Where does this leave the Christian Pharisees of Acts 15:5? Of course they have believed, since it is "believers" that Luke calls them, thereby indicating that they are Christians; but have they believed in true contrition and repentance?[95] That is not so clear. Luke does not discuss the quality of the belief of the Christian Pharisees in Acts 15:5; nevertheless, everything said to and about them in the Gospel argues that Luke thinks of them there, in any case, as not being truly contrite. Pharisaic Torah fidelity and true contrition seem to be mutually exclusive, as Luke regards the matter, since to adhere to the requirements of the Mosaic Torah in addition to belief is to seek to "justify" oneself or to "exalt" oneself (Luke 18:14), and to promote such notions in the church is to be, in Luke's thinking, in the precise sense of the term, a "hypocrite" (Luke 12:1)--that is, one who pretends to be something that one is not. The Christian Pharisees of Acts 15:5 stand, in the view of the author of Luke-Acts, under the charge of hypocrisy (Luke 12:1) because,

---

[95]We do not need to ask whether they have sought to add Mosaic requirements to the criterion of belief, because that, of course, is what Luke says about them and is precisely the point in contention.

while seeming to be "believers," they are in reality
promoting self-justification and self-exaltation.
Thus the truly contrite sinner "goes down to his house
justified instead of" the Pharisee--yes, instead of
even the Christian Pharisee.

It is against the background of this insight
that we can understand why it is the Pharisees to
whom Jesus addresses his much discussed saying in
Luke 17:21, "The Kingdom of God is among you"; 96 for
we again have here, apparently, a contrast between
a truly repentant and contrite sinner and the Pharisees.
In this case the sinner is not a Judahite religious
outcast like a prostitute or a toll collector; he
is a Samaritan (Luke 17:16); and his response to Jesus
cannot properly be labelled contrition or repentance,
since what he did was to "fall on his face at [Jesus']
feet and thank him" (v 16). Luke, however, seems
willing to consider this pure and unblemished expression
of gratitude as more or less equivalent to the repentance
and contrition that he elsewhere demands, and thus
he has Jesus say to the thankful Samaritan exactly
what he had said earlier to the contrite prostitute,
"Your faith has saved you" (v 19). With what unmiti-
gated gall do the Pharisees then dare to question

96Some authors, of course, have not seen the presence
of Pharisees in this scene as being of any importance.
Thus F. Hauck, Das Evangelium des Lukas (THKNT; Leipzig:
Deichert, 1934) 215, sees them as representatives
of the Jews and, indeed, of the human race; and
Schweizer, Lukas, 181, also thinks of humanity generally. Similar interpretations are given by several
commentators. Others emphasize suddenness or unex-
pectedness of the Kingdom's appearance; cf., e.g.,
H.-W. Bartsch, Wachet aber zu jeder Zeit (Hamburg-Berg-
stedt: Herbert Reich--Evanglischer Verlag, 1963)
114, and Schmid, Lukas, 274; and, of course, the text
is the backbone of "realized eschatology," as in,
e.g., C. H. Dodd, The Parables of the Kingdom (revised
ed.; New York: Scribner's, 1961) 84, n. 1, and W. E.
Bundy, Jesus and the First Three Gospels (Cambridge,
MA: Harvard University Press, 1955) 388. Yet the
saying, in Luke, is addressed to Pharisees, as, e.g.,
Lagrange, Luc, 460, and Montefiore, Synoptic Gospels,
2.546-550, have seen. Our interest here is not what
ἐντὸς ὑμῶν is supposed to mean, but what it means
that the saying is addressed to Pharisees.

"when the Kingdom of God is coming" (v 20)! Jesus
has just demonstrated amazing spiritual power (he
has healed ten lepers), he has provided an object
lesson on the nature of true faith, and then the Pharisees ask when the Kingdom is coming. If they had
any sensitivity to the issue at all they would have
drawn the obvious implication from the preceding episode: It is there among them.[97] They do not see
that any more than those who, one page earlier, could
not understand the point about eternal refreshment
and punishment even though "they have Moses and the
Prophets" (Luke 16:29). Indeed, these Pharisees in
Luke 17:20 cannot be distinguised clearly from those
Jews in 16:29 who have the Bible. There is something
wrong in their perceptual orientation, and we know
what it is. It is the way in which they understand
the Bible. The cloud of doom that hangs over those
who, in the parable of the Rich Man and Lazarus, cannot
understand the Torah thus appears also to darken the
future of the Christian Pharisees in Acts 15:5. "Having
believed" could have worked for their "salvation";
but they remained hardened in their tradtitional interpretation of Scripture. They thus become "hypocrites,"
not true members of the Christian community.[98]

---

[97]J. Zmijewski, Die Eschatologiereden des Lukas-Evangeliums
(BBB; Bonn: Hanstein, 1972) 394, and W. Bruners,
Die Reinigung der zehn Aussätzigen und die Heilung
des Samariters Lk 17,11-19 (Forschung zur Bibel; Stuttgart: Katholisches Bibelwerk, 1977) 327, think that
the Pharisees represent Christians contemporary with
Luke who misunderstand the Kingdom; and Bruners adds,
further, that they likewise misunderstand Jesus.
But there is no direct reference to Christology here.
Thus I do not quite see why the Pharisees, with their
question, are put into the same position as that of
the nine who did not offer thanks (Bruners, ibid.,
335). Bruners later (ibid., 353) presents what seems
a more balanced statement. On the presence of the
Kingdom in Jesus' ministry cf. Conzelmann, Theology,
122-123.
[98]It should also be stated that, much as Luke dislikes
the Christian Pharisees, i.e., the traditionally Jewish
Christians, even to the point of slandering them (Luke
16:14), he does not attribute ulterior motives to
those who (Acts 15:5) prompt the Apostolic Council,
as does E. Jacquier, Les Actes des Apôtres (EBib;
2nd ed.; Paris: Gabalda, 1926) 445, who claims that

Understanding how Luke presented the Pharisees in his two-volume work has allowed us at the same time to see why he portrayed them as he did. Primarily, his dislike of a Jewish Christianity that sought to keep Christianity Jewish led him to characterize the Pharisees as he did; and, secondarily, his desire to show Christianity, and not continuing Judaism, as the true descendant of "biblical" Israel also colored his portrait. A number of questions remain. Does Luke's opinion of the Jewish Christianity of his own day provide an accurate picture of what it was really like? Were all Jewish Christians like Luke's Pharisees? What does Luke's account of the Apostolic Council have to do with the argument between Jewish Christianity and Gentile Christianity? To what degree does Luke continue Paul's position on the issue, and how is he different from Paul? How should Christians today respond to Luke's characterization of the Pharisees? These questions and others, however, will have to be addressed in another setting.

"the Pharisees"--not distinguished as Christian and non-Christian--"wished by means of Christianity to make Gentiles Jews."

CHAPTER ELEVEN

PURSUING THE PARADOXES OF JOHANNINE THOUGHT:
CONCEPTUAL TENSIONS IN JOHN 6.
A REDACTION-CRITICAL PROPOSAL

Robert Kysar

Ernest W. Saunders has suggested that the work
of the fourth evangelist "reflects the mental and
artistic qualities of a theological poet . . . He
delights in the use of antitheses . . ."[1] Indeed,
the paradoxical nature of much of the thought of the
Gospel of John is well known and widely recognized.
One may call it poetry, contradiction, paradox, or
dialectic, in accord with how generous you would like
to be; but its presence is hardly deniable. Many
of the motifs of the gospel are presented in a perplex-
ingly paradoxical manner which is puzzling at best.
It is this feature of the gospel which led C. K. Barrett
to label johannine thought "dialectical."[2] To be
sure, this recognition that the evangelist thought
in such a dialectical fashion helps one deal with
the contradictions of the thought of his work. But
perhaps there is more involved.

The question is whether or not redaction criticism
of the gospel casts any light on the dialectical method
of the evangelist. That is, is it possible to find
in the poles of that dialectical thought the distinction
between tradition and redaction? If such a discovery
were possible, it would enable us to understand better
the paradoxes of the thought of the gospel and to
deepen the nature of the evangelist's dialectical
method --deepen it by providing historical and communal
dimensions within which that method was developed
and employed.

---

[1]Ernest W. Saunders, John Celebrates the Gospel (Nash-
ville/New York: Abingdon, 1968) 20.
[2]C. H. Dodd, New Testament Essays (London: SPCK, 1974)
54, 55, 68.

The thesis of this article is that such a discovery is possible in a provisional way. It is feasible to say that the dialectical manner of thought and expression which we attribute to the evangelist arose out of the dialogue between his own views, as well as those of his contemporary community, and traditional positions. Hence, the dialectical method of the fourth evangelist is really the theological method of his community, as it dealt with its own experience in the light of the thought which was passed on to it from earlier times.[3]

Is it possible to demonstrate this to be the case? I propose that one can understand the gospel in this manner when equipped with two essential tools and procedures. The first is the ideological or content criteria for source and redaction distinction. Contradictions of thought in the text may be indications of the collision of tradition and redaction.[4] Therefore, one must attend to the ideological tensions, expose them, and explicate them as fully as possible. These tensions must be allowed to stand for what they are;

------

[3]This is to view the theology of the gospel as "community theology" (_Gemeindetheologie_), to borrow the expression of Ulrich Müller, _Die Geschichte der Christologie in der johanneischen Gemeinde_ (Stuttgarter Bibelstudien 77; Stuttgart: Katholisches Bibelwerk, 1975) esp. 69-72. Examples of this approach are to be found in Jürgen Becker's study of johannine dualism ("Beobachtungen zum Dualismus in Johannesevangelium," _ZNW_ 65 [1974] 71-87) and Joseph Coppens' thesis regarding the Son of Man motif in John's gospel ("Le Fils de l'homme dans l'evangile johannique," _ETL_ 52 [1976] 28-81).

[4]For a brief survey of this and other methods of distinguishing tradition and redaction employed in contemporary scholarship, cf. Robert Kysar, _The Fourth Evangelist and His Gospel_ (Minneapolis: Augsburg, 1975) 15-24. The use of the "content criterion" or of "ideological tension" is best seen at work in Barnabas Lindars, _Behind the Fourth Gospel_ (London: SPCK, 1971) and _The Gospel of John_ (New Century Bible Commentary; Grand Rapids, Michigan: Eerdmans, 1972), Rudolf Schnackenburg, _The Gospel According to St. John_ (3 vols.; New York: Seabury, 1968-1982), and Ernst Haenchen, _The Gospel of John_ (Hermeneia, 2 vols.; Philadelphia: Fortress, 1984).

and all tendencies to harmonize them must for the moment be suspended.

The second tool required for exploring the paradoxes is simply the findings of other tradition-redaction studies and related constructions of the history of the johannine community. I refer here specifically to the findings of Robert Fortna in his quest for the isolation of the "Signs Gospel" and the fourth evangelist's redaction of it[5] and the proposals of J. Louis Martyn along with Raymond E. Brown and others regarding the history of the johannine community.[6]

---

[5]Robert T. Fortna, The Gospel of Signs (SNTS 11; Cambridge: University, 1970). Cf. Kysar, The Fourth Evangelist, 13-82. In the literature discussing Fortna's enterprise three contributions are especially worthy of note: Edwin D. Freed and Russell B. Hunt, "Fortna's Signs-Source in John," JBL 94 (1975) 563-579. D. Moody Smith, "The Setting and Shape of a Johannine Narrative Source," JBL 95 (1976) 231-241. D. A. Carson, "Current Source Criticism of the Fourth Gospel," JBL 97 (1978) 411-429.

[6]J. Louis Martyn, History and Theology in the Fourth Gospel (2nd ed.; Nashville: Abingdon, 1979). Raymond E. Brown, The Gospel According to John (AB, vols. 29 and 29a; New York: Doubleday, 1966, 1970) and The Community of the Beloved Disciple (New York: Paulist, 1979). For other support of Martyn's general thesis, cf. the surveys in Kysar, The Fourth Evangelist, 149-156; "Community and Gospel: Vectors in Fourth Gospel Criticism," Interpreting the Gospels (ed. James Luther Mays; Philadelphia: Fortress, 1981) 273-274; "The Gospel of John in Current Research," RSR 9 (1983) 316-318. Serious questions and challenges are appropriately being raised to Martyn's insistence that the expulsion of the johannine community from the synagogue was a result of the formal propagation of the Birkath ha-Minim. Cf. esp. Rueven Kimmelman, "Birkat ha-Minim and the lack of Evidence for an Anti-Christian Jewish Prayer in Late Antiquity," Jewish and Christian Self Definition (ed. E. P. Sanders, 3 vols; Philadelphia: Fortress, 1981), 2. 226-244, and Steven T. Katz, "Issues in the Separation of Judaism and Christianity After 70 C.E.: A Reconsideration," JBL 103 (1984) 43-76. It is much more likely that the experience of expulsion for John's church occurred as a result of a localized and informal decision on the part of a single synagogue and that it took place much earlier than Martyn has

With some modifications I suggest that we can use
the work of scholars in these two areas to help us
understand the emergence of the contradictions in
johannine thought. After one has isolated and clarified
the tensions in a given passage, the poles of that
paradox are to be viewed in the light of what we can
know of the tradition of the community and its history.[7]
When we do so, the possibilities of a tradition-redaction distinction may be seen. That is, in some cases
we will find that one pole or the other would seem
to have been more compatible with the Sitz im Leben
of the earlier johannine community as Fortna, Martyn
or others have described it. This is not, of course,
to say that we can prove certain passages or ideas
to have been part of the evangelist's tradition in
distinction from others. At best what we are able
to do is to find certain passages or ideas which would
seem to have been more at home in the pre-gospel tradition than in that setting in which we understand the
gospel to have been written. I suggest that what
we are trying to do here is to define the contours,
the general shape of the tradition as it appears in
the gospel. What is attempted is the description
of a feasible view of tradition and redaction. It
is necessary to understand that we can do no more
than this--no more than a general description (a silhou-
ette, if you will) of the tradition which seems coherent,
albeit speculative.

---

proposed (perhaps as early as 70-80). That expulsion,
as I image it, was part of an "intra-family" argument
reflective of conditions in John's city and not necessarily of the general Jewish-Christian relationship
in the second half of the first century. An earlier
dating of the expulsion also allows one to see it
as a result, in part, of the reaction of Judaism to
the destruction of the Temple. Still, Martyn's thesis
has proven helpful in elucidating the setting of the
gospel.
    [7]We leave to one side for now those cases in which
we find not simply one pair of contradictory concepts
in a passage but a myriad of countervailing ideas,
such as I think are present in the christologies of
the gospel. I am content for now to show how this
proposed method might handle a simple pair of opposing
ideas.

With this general description of the proposal before us, I will suggest the way it might work in the analysis of two themes in chapter 6: the themes of faith and eschatology.

I

Human and Divine Responsibility
in the Act of Faith

We are confronted in chapter 6 with certain passages which seem to presuppose an act of will for which one is responsible in believing or not believing in Christ, on the one hand, and certain other passages which seem to suggest that a divine act alone is responsible for faith. We want to be careful not to impose upon the text the modern issue of free will and determinism. Still, in the text there seems to be present a tension between human and divine responsibility for faith, and it is that tension we want to examine and reflect upon.[8]

The most striking of the passages which appear to stress the divine cause of belief in humans is v 44. There Jesus is made to say, "No one can come to me unless the Father who sent me draws (ἐλκύσῃ) him . . ." (cf. 12:32). The point is made equally clear in those occasions in which Jesus refers to believers as those whom the Father has given him (δίδω-μι); there are three such passages in the chapter--vv 37, 39, and 65. In v 64 we learn that Jesus knew who would not believe, as if the matter had been determined by divine choice. If this emphasis on the divine role in the faith act is a kind of election of some sort, the fact that Jesus claims that he chose the twelve may be another bit of evidence (v 70).

The evidence in the chapter for an emphasis on the human responsibility in the act of faith is less dramatic but nonetheless real. In v 29 the "work" (ἔργον) God wants of persons is that they believe. The use of "he who comes to me" (ὁ ἐρχόμενος πρὸς

---

[8]The major work on this theological theme has been done by D. A. Carson, Divine Sovereignty and Human Responsibility (Atlanta: John Knox, 1981) and Roland Bergmeier, Glauben als Gabe nach Johannes (Beiträge zur Wissenschaft vom Alten und Neuen Testament; Stuttgart: Kohlhammer, 1980).

ἐμὲ) in v 35 and its variant in v 37b would by themselves seem to imply human volition. In v 36 we are
told that some see but do not believe, which presupposes that believing is an act of the will after having
"seen" the Son. For v 40 claims that all who see
and believe are given eternal life. The most interesting
assertion of the human role in believing and failing
to believe is found, however, in the closing verses
of the chapter. Some disciples (μαθηταί , i.e., those
who had believed) find Jesus' words too difficult
and leave him. They will not follow him further (v
66). And then Jesus asks the twelve (δώδεκα) if they
too will leave him, implying that they are free to
do so (v 67). This powerful conclusion of the chapter
makes little sense if we do not suppose that one is
responsible, to some degree at least, for his/her
own belief and unbelief.[9] Verse 30 likewise may presuppose the willful act of believing as a response to
a sign. Verses 40 and 45b may also be evidence of
the importance of human action in faith.[10]

In this chapter, then, we find the evangelist
caught between two conflicting points of view with

---

[9]Fortna says of this narrative, "The source may have
continued here (after verse 25) with material which
is now buried in the rest of chap. 6, notably in the
episode with Peter in 6:67ff" (Signs Gospel, 238).
   [10]Commentators tend, for the most part, to minimize
the conflict among these passages and to harmonize
them with hasty generalizations. Typical of such
are the following: Brown, The Gospel According to
John 1, 277; Schnackenburg, 2, 50; Lindars, The Gospel
of John, 263; and Barrett, The Gospel According to
St. John (2nd ed.; Philadelphia: Westminster, 1978)
295. Notable, however, are comments by two very different scholars. Rudolf Bultmann writes of v 44, ". . .
faith has no support outside itself." The Gospel of
John: A Commentary (Philadelphia: Westminster, 1971)
232. F. F. Bruce comments on the same verse, ". . . The
divine initiative in the salvation of believers is
emphasized. The responsibility of men and women in
the matter of coming to Christ is not overlooked (cf.
John 5:40); but none at all would come unless divinely
persuaded and enabled to do so" (The Gospel of John
[Grand Rapids, MI: Eerdmans, 1983] 156). Cf. Kysar,
John, the Maverick Gospel (Atlanta: John Knox, 1976)
58-62.

regard to responsibility for faith. The tension is
tightened by the fact that the two poles of the paradox
appear side by side (cf. the chart below). While
v 36 seems to make the most sense if we suppose some
importance attributed to the human will in believing,
v 37 clearly asserts that those who believe are those
whom the Father has given the Son. Likewise, the
Father gives some the possibility of coming to Jesus
(v 65), but those who believe are free to cease believing
and turn away from Jesus (v 66). While John seems
to want his readers to know that there is a human
dimension to the act of faith, he seems to want to
stress equally that faith is possible only among those
whom the Father has "drawn" or "given" to the Son.
John appears to intend the paradoxical truth of these
two positions; hence he affirms both views side by
side.11

It may be enough to say that the fourth evangelist
thought dialectically about the responsibility for
the faith-act (and that would indeed put him in some
good company). That he was convinced that faith was
a dual responsibility may be all that we can say.
But is it possible to view this paradoxical tension
as a result of tradition and redaction? Is it possible
that John is a dialectical thinker on this issue pre-

11It is interesting to note that the tension we are
here documenting does not evidence itself in vv 51-59.
These verses are by almost common agreement a second
form of the bread of life discourse and one in which
the eucharistic interpretation of the discourse is
to be found, according to some interpreters. The
fact that it is devoid of the ideological tension
with regard to the issue of faith may be a further
suggestion of its separation from the discourse form
in vv 25-50 and the narrative in vv 60-71. However,
it will be seen that vv 51-59 do contain the tension
between future and present eschatology (cf. chart
above). If the section is a somewhat later eucharistic
interpretation of the words of Jesus, as I believe
it is, then it becomes clear that the redactor has
dropped any interest in the question of the responsibility for the faith-act in favor of the sacramental
motif. The continued presence of the eschatological
tension is to be explained by the fact that the eucharist
was an experiential expression of the "now and not-yet"
quality of God's presence.

cisely because of a dialogue he and his contemporaries
were having with their tradition? There is no way
to demonstrate that this is the case. We can, however,
suggest a feasible way in which this dialectic grew
out of the relationship between John and his tradition.

Fortna proposed that the evangelist utilized
a simple "Signs Gospel" in constructing his work,
and that gospel was a missionary tract designed to
win converts.[12] Its view was a rather simplistic
one: if you could read a straight-forward account
of the wonders done by this man, Jesus, you would
soon come to believe in him as messiah. The wonders
are narrated in order to arouse faith. The conclusion
of the Signs Gospel, Fortna suggests, is found now
at 20:31 and reflects the original purpose of the
source: "These are written that you may believe that
Jesus is the Christ, the Son of God."[13]

It appears that the basic tradition passed on
to the evangelist emphasized the human responsibility
for faith and unbelief. We could perhaps reconstruct
one thread of the johannine community along these
lines: The community early in its history held to
a simple voluntaristic point of view when it came
to the question of responsibility for faith. In their
missionary efforts, they maintained that the individual
was free to respond in faith to the story of Jesus.
But with the passage of time and with increasing difficulties in winning converts to their faith (especially,
I think, from the synagogue), the position of the

---

[12]Fortna, Signs Gospel, 225. Althoughhisunderstanding
of the signs source is considerably different from
Fortna's, W. Nicol shares the view that the source
was designed primarily as a missionary document.
The Semeia in the Fourth Gospel (NovTSup 32; Leiden:
Brill, 1972) 44.
[13]Fortna, Signs Gospel, 197-199. Fortna's proposed
source was, of course, a collection of narratives,
and we are discussing discourse materials (for the
most part). I am supposing that the point of view
found in the signs source pervaded the whole of the
johannine tradition, discourse as well as narrative.
As we have seen, the presumption of human responsibility
for faith is represented in the discourse materials
of the chapter, as well as in the narrative piece
in vv 60-71.

community began to shift. They were again and again confronted with the unwillingness of persons to be persuaded that Jesus was the messiah; indeed, there was mounting hostility among their Jewish colleagues in the synagogue to their missionary efforts.[14] The idealism which characterized the earlier period of their history became tempered with a hard realism: some people are not going to embrace the gospel message when they encounter it. With this experience, they had to begin to rethink their earlier optimistic and rather naïve point of view, namely, that humans are totally responsible for belief and unbelief.

By the time John wrote there was a sober recognition that people did not so readily respond in faith to the kerygma. It was in the context of this realization that he introduced into his gospel a second layer or stratum of material.[15] In that layer faith is understood as more than the simple, free response of persons to the narration of Jesus' wonders. There is a sense in which faith is the Father's gift to some and not to others. That motif which credits divine action as responsible for faith was the effort to explain the reality of unbelief--to account for the failure of the gospel to evoke faith from so many persons. John could not simply repeat the point of view of his tradition, because the experience of the community proved that point of view inadequate by itself.[16]

---

[14]Cf. J. Louis Martyn, The Gospel of John in Christian History (New York: Paulist, 1978) 102-103.

[15]It is equally feasible that the proposed second layer of material was introduced before it was incorporated into the gospel, in which case the evangelist inherited the tension between the two views and preserved it as he found it in the tradition. It seems clear, however, that the second layer arose in the community after the experience of the expulsion from the synagogue. It is more likely that this second stratum comes from the mind of the evangelist and reflects his own critique of the tradition and/or that of his community at the time of the composition of the gospel.

[16]Martyn offers a proposal which supports the argument developed here. Behind 1:35-49, he suggests, lies an early sermon adapted by John from his tradition. That sermon stressed the "passivity" of Jesus expressed in the invitations "to come" and "to find." That emphasis on human initiative is in contrast ". . .with

But the experience of the johannine community
probably involved more than the simple frustration
of their evangelistic enterprise. Rather than succeeding
in winning many of the residents of the city to their
faith, as they had hoped to do, there were those in
their city who had turned on them and were persecuting them for their faith (e.g., 16:1-4). The johannine
community was in the throes of a heated and even violent
battle with its brothers and sisters of the local
synagogue. Out of this environment of disillusionment
and struggle arose the view that belief and unbelief
are the results of God's activity (and, incidentally,
that the cosmos was divided dualistically along the
lines of "light" and "darkness"). The earlier view
which stressed human responsibility for faith was
now set in opposition to a newer emphasis on the divine
responsibility for faith. The paradoxical understanding
of this matter which we find in chapter 6 (as well
as elsewhere in the gospel, e.g., 17:6 and 20:27b)
is the result of a dialectical tension arising from
the relationship of tradition and redaction.

II
Realized and Futuristc Eschatology

If we grant the possibility that the conceptual
tension regarding the responsibility for faith arose
in the relationship between tradition and redaction,
we can view another such tension as further evidence
of that relationship: the commonly recognized polarity
of realized and futuristic eschatology in the gospel.
My thesis is that we can see the likelihood that the
future eschatology of the gospel is rooted in the
johannine tradition, while the present or realized
eschatological view is the theological reflection
of the community in dialogue with that tradition. [17]

---

key passages in the Fourth Gospel in which the initiative
of Jesus (or of God) is polemically affirmed," and
Martyn cites 6:44, 65 and 15:16, 19 in particular.
The latter reflects most likely the redactional work
of John (The Gospel of John in Christian History,
93 and 95).
    [17]On the eschatology of John, cf. Kysar, The Fourth
Evangelist, 207-214.

The futuristic emphasis is visible in chapter
6 in the refrain, "that I should raise him on the
last day," or some form of that statement. It is
found in vv 39b, 40b, 44b, and 54b.[18] Over against
this promise of the future work of Christ is the affirmation of the presence of an eschatological blessing.
In some form or another, the assertion that the believer
already has eternal life is to be found in vv 40a,
47, 51, 54a, 58b, and 50b. (The latter contains the
promise that those who eat the heavenly bread will
not die). So here we are suspended again on the poles
of the johannine dialectic, again made worse by the
close proximity of the affirmations. Notice their
back to back setting in v 40 and again in v 54. The
intentionally contradictory relationship here is inescapable, as it is elsewhere in the gospel (e.g., 5:24-
29).

Elsewhere I have argued against Bultmann's thesis
that the future eschatology is the addition of the
ecclesiastical redactor.[19] It seems more feasible
that the fourth evangelist is intentionally revising
(demythologizing, if you like) futuristic eschatology
with his own realized eschatology. Now I would like
to press that argument one step further by suggesting
that the tension between those two modes of eschatological thought is the result of changes in the conditions
of the community and hence in its theological reflection. It is not hard to imagine that the futuristic
eschatology was part of the tradition John inherited
and that the earliest community embraced such a view.
Indeed, it may have been an only slightly Christianized
form of an apocalyptic view embraced by the synagogue,
of which the johannine community had been a part.
Can we, then, conceive of the present eschatology
emerging out of the experiences of the community in

---

[18]The view that this refrain betrays the hand of a later
redactor (e.g., Bultmann, The Gospel of John, 219-220)
is widely and correctly rejected among commentators
today: e.g., Barrett, The Gospel According to St. John
294; Schnackenburg, The Gospel According to St. John,
2, 48; Bruce, The Gospel of John, 154; Lindars, The
Gospel of John, 261; and Brown, The Gospel According
to John, 1, 276.
[19]"The Eschatology of the Fourth Gospel: A Corrective
of Bultmann's Redactional Hypothesis," Perspective
13 (1972) 23-33. Cf. John, the Maverick Gospel 84-110.

the time between its comfortable life in the synagogue
and its troubled existence expelled from its religious
home?

If it is the case that the johannine Christians
were locked in controversy with the Jews of their
former synagogue, we may imagine that it was natural
for johannine theology to begin to move away from
a futuristic eschatology which was only an adaptation
of a Jewish view. Granted that the synagogue had
come under the influence of Jewish apocalyptic thought,
the members of the synagogue in John's city may have
embraced an eschatology very much like those of the
johannine church. As a result of the dialogue with
the Jews, the Christians may have sought a more distinctive view of eschatology, and their search may
have led them naturally to an eschatology which stressed
more the present than the future. The search involved
a quest for a peculiar self-identity by which the
community could understand itself apart from its roots
in the synagogue. There can be little doubt that
some realized eschatological themes were already present
in tradition, for those themes were a part of the
earliest Christian thought. It was left to the evangelist only to revive, strengthen, and elaborate them.[20]
Furthermore, if the trauma of the expulsion from the
synagogue was as severe as it seems to have been,
and if the life of the johannine Christian was threatened
in a violent controversy with their former colleagues,
realized eschatology may have been an attempt to respond
to a need for a more meaningful present for the believers. What I am suggesting is that the trauma of expulsion and persecution was answered in johannine thought
with a view that affirmed the immediate blessings
of God in spite of the difficulty of the present.
The need of the present was addressed in johannine
theological thought, not by a further emphasis upon
a future hope, but by a new emphasis upon the present

---

[20]That such a tension between the present and future
was early represented in Christian tradition is illustrated in Paul's thought (Rom 10:9-10). The Christian
is already justified (Rom 3:24) and yet looks forward
in hope for salvation (Rom 8:24). Such a tension
may have its roots in Jesus' own proclamation that
the kingdom of God is both present and yet to come
to power.

reality--the believer already has eternal life.[21] If this proposal is at all feasible, combine it with a suggestion that johannine Christians, not unlike their brothers and sisters of other churches, were in need of a revision of eschatology in light of the delay of the parousia, and you have a reasonable view of the emergence of the present eschatology of the fourth gospel (cf. 14:1ff and 16:18-19).[22]

---

[21]A strict "trajectory" view of the johannine community would suggest, if this thesis is correct, that we would find only a present eschatology emphasized in the later johannine epistles. This is, of course, not the case. Instead, we find that a futuristic eschatology is strongly attested in 1 John (e.g., 2:18-20), although the remnants of the present eschatology of the gospel are most clear (e.g., 3:14 and 5:11). A number of factors account for the preservation and even revitalization of the older eschatology in the later stages of the history of the community. First, closer associations with other Christian churches after the writing of the gospel brought the community to a renewed affirmation of the future promises of God. Second, this was natural after the intense dialogue with the synagogue had subsided and the necessity of Christian self-definition overagainst Judaism had passed. Third, the occasion of the internal division within the community which precipitated the writing of the epistles stirred nearly apocalyptic expectations (e.g., the "antichrist"). In search of a defense against those who had separated themselves from the community, the author of 1 John sought an eschatological context for understanding the experience. Cf. Brown, The Epistles of John (AB 38; New York: Doubleday, 1982).

[22]The importance of social experience for early Christian thought, especially eschatology and christology, is shown by David E. Aune, The Cultic Setting of Realized Eschatology (Leiden: Brill, 1972). Cf. the seminal work by Wayne A. Meeks, "The Man From Heaven in Johannine Sectarianism," JBL 91 (1972) 44-72. Other possible causes for the emergence of John's realized eschatology are discussed in Schnackenburg, 2, 435-437.

III
A Further Complication

The attempt here is to sketch a picture of the development of johannine theology which is consistent with our knowledge of the tradition and the history of the community, and which adds historical and communal depth to our view of the paradoxical thought of the gospel. There is, however, one further and complicating note on these themes in chapter 6 which must be added. I have suggested above that the close proximity of the poles of the paradox is a result of the deliberate effort of the evangelist to related tradition and redaction in a dialogical manner. That point is further highlighted by the additional juxtapositioning of futuristic eschatology and the view that faith is the responsibility of the Father's action. At vv 39 and 44 we find the proposed later view of responsibility for faith linked with the proposed earlier view of eschatology. And in v 40 both types of eschatology are yoked with an emphasis on the proposed traditional view of the human responsibility for faith (cf. the chart below).

What are we to make of this? It appears that the further we probe the paradoxes of the fourth gospel the more aware we become of the deliberate tension the evangelist wanted to create between the theology of his tradition and his own views. He apparently wanted to affirm the views of his tradition, while at the same time claiming the necessity of rethinking those views. The result is his position, that truth is always multisided. To understand faith, one must see both the divine and human dimensions. To articulate the way in which God has made the realities of the last days available to the Christian, one must speak both of the fulfilled and the unfulfilled, yet promised, sides of the issue. To understand those two themes in relationship with one another one could only think of the two interlaced with each other. Hearing the theological message of the fourth evangelist, then, is like listening to stereophonic music--countervailing sounds come at you from both the right and the left simultaneously, so closely related that to separate one from the other deprives you of the full impact of the music. This was all part of the "theological poetry" he wrote.

The dialectical method of John is, therefore, the result of the way in which he preserved and affirmed the theological positions of his tradition, while at the same time offering revisions and correctives out of his own thought (and that of his contemporary church). John is affirming, again and again, throughout much of the thought of his gospel, that theological reflection proceeds within the fiery dialogue between traditional and contemporary positions. We hear him saying through his paradoxes that religious thought always emerges in a context shaped at once by historical tradition and the contemporary experience of the community of faith. For the evangelist, his tradition was a "living text" to be re-read, under the guidance of the Spirit-Paraclete, in the light of the needs of his church. In this way, the dialectical thought of the evangelist is more than the brilliance of a single mind. It is the continuous conversation of a community with its own past and its own present experience. [23]

IV
Conclusions

We are left now only with the task of briefly assessing the perils and promises of the proposal here sketched. There are at least three dangers which need to be mentioned. First, the method for seeking tradition and redaction distinctions employed may be perilous because it is dependent on our own logic of contradiction. That is, what we view as ideological tension, paradox, or contradiction is necessarily defined by our own concept of what is opposite in thought. Are we safe in assuming the evangelist embraced a similar concept of logical opposition, or is the problem of paradox in the gospel our problem and not his? We must assume, I think, that John was as sensitive to logical contradiction as we are, until we can know otherwise.

But another peril of this enterprise lurks in the dependence upon the recent work of source criticism and reconstructions of the history of the johannine

---

[23]This view has much in common with that of Klaus Wengst, Bedrängte Gemeinde und verherrlichter Christus (Biblisch Theologische Studien 5; Neukirchen-Vluyn: Neukirchener, 1981).

community. If they are wrong, so are we![24] Still,
I wonder if our understanding of the gospel is going
to grow if we sit cautiously by, awaiting the day
when we have a proven thesis upon which to proceed.

Still another peril that must be faced is the
fact that our approach presupposed that religious
thought emerges out of historical conditions and reflects
those conditions. The redactional views we propose
to find in the gospel are accountable on the basis
of the concrete social and historical setting of the
community, which we suppose to have been the case.
However, to say that religious thought is a reflection
of historical and social conditions is not necessarily
a reductionism; it is but a suggestion of one of the
several influences which may account for religious
thought.[25] Such a view as this does not minimize
the creativity of the evangelist or his community;
it only recognizes the context within which that creativity took place.

On the other hand, the proposal here outlined
promises several things: first, it promises to provide
a way of sketching the broad perimeters of tradition
and redaction in the thought of the fourth evangelist--a
method greatly needed in contemporary theological
interpretation of the gospel. At least in a general
and provisional way, then, we may be able to outline
the shape of the history of johannine religious thought.
However general and tentative the results may be,
at least it affords us an opportunity to grasp some
sense of the flow of ideas in the history of the johannine community.

---

[24]For instance, Bruce Woll has proposed a rather different
setting for chapters 13 and 14. While intriguing,
his thesis is not entirely convincing, although it
should be taken seriously as an indication that the
proposed setting for the gospel employed in this article
is not the whole picture, nor necessarily a true one:
Johannine Christianity in Conflict (SBLDS 60; Chico,
California: Scholars, 1981).
[25]Even Martyn demurs before a radical statement of the
social roots of johannine Christology. Of conclusions
drawn by David Aune (110) he writes, "One can easily
imagine the fourth evangelist shuddering at such statements" (The Gospel of John in Christian History, 105,
n. 168).

Second, our proposal may provide us a glance into the theological method of one of the most perplexing writers of first century Christianity. As a result of this hazardous and speculative experiment, we may be able more clearly to see how the poetic mind of the fourth evangelist worked--indeed, how he and his community conceived of the theological task itself. That, in turn, has implications for the way in which theological reflection in the church of the twentieth century might be done. This promise is surely worth the perils of the proposal!

Human and Divine Responsibility for Faith

Divine Responsibility	Human Responsibility
	v 29 The work of persons is to believe (ἔργον... πιστεύω)
v 37 Those who come to Son are those given by God (δίδωμι)	v 30 A sign occasions faith (σήμειον)
v 39 * Son should not lose those given him by God (δίδωμι)	v 36 Persons see but do not believe
	v 40 + God wants all who see and believe to have eternal life (πᾶς)
v 44 * No one comes to Son unless drawn by the Father (ἕλκω)	
v 64b Son knew from the beginning who would not believe (ἐξ ἀρχῆς)	v 64a Some do not believe even though Son has spoken words of spirit and life (cf 63b: πνεῦμα ἐστιν καὶ ζωή ἐστιν)
v 65 Those who have possibility of coming to Son are those God has given (δίδωμι)	v 66 Disciples left Jesus because of his words
	v 67 The 12 are asked if they will leave Jesus
(cf v 70)	(cf vv 35,37b,40,45b)

Future and Present Eschatology

Present Eschatology	Future Eschatology
"The believer has eternal life" (e.g. v 40a: ἔχῃ ζωὴν αἰώνιον)	Son will raise believers on the last day (e.g. v 39b: ἀναστήσω αὐτὸ [ἐν] τῇ ἐσχάτῃ ἡμέρᾳ))
	v 39b *
v 40a +	v 40b +
v 47	v 44b
v 51	*
v 54a	v 54b
v 58	
(cf v 50b)	

*Proximity with future eschatology
+Proximity with human responsibility and both present and future eschatology

CHAPTER TWELVE

THE SON OF MAN: A RECONSIDERATION

Reginald H. Fuller

It is notorious that there are almost as many opinions about the Son of man as there are scholars who deal with it. Everyone who tackles the subject has his or her own views about it which no one else exactly shares. Moreover, as is the case now-a-days with the synoptic problem, people are much better at arguing against the positions of others than they are in defending their own position.

The most notable instance of this deficiency is the way in which German scholars continue blithely to assume without question that pre-Christian Judaism was familiar with an apocalyptic Son of man with clearly defined judgmental and salvific functions. The most recent example of this which has come to my notice is a work by Helmut Merklein, a German Catholic.[1] Merklein discusses Jesus' self-understanding and its relation to the proclamation of the Kingdom of God, and without any compunction, he goes straight to the Similitudes of Enoch as evidence for early Judaism before Jesus. He is simply oblivious of the dating of the Similitudes of Enoch, which is now generally accepted to be late in the first century, and therefore useless as evidence for Judaism in Jesus' time. Merklein does not even bother to argue, as Colpe did in his Wörterbuch article on the Son of man, that Enoch and the Gospels were dependent upon an earlier, now lost source. In addition, Merklein even assumes that Daniel's "one like a Son of man" is a reference to the same firmly established figure.

It is for this reason that many English speaking scholars prefer Norman Perrin's alternative explanation,

---

[1]Helmut Merklein, Jesu Botschaft von der Gottesherrschaft: Eine Skizze (Stuttgart: Katholisches Bibelwerk, 1983) 152-164.

viz., that the apocalyptic Son of man entered into a post-Easter Christian usage and late first century Jewish apocalyptic as the result of independent pesher interpretations of Daniel 7:13.[2] Correctly, Perrin saw the difficulty of making this pesher development the origin of the present Son of man sayings, and so fell back upon David Daube's explanation of these, as given in his well-known appendix to the third edition of Matthew Black's An Aramaic Approach to the Gospels and Acts.[3] Jesus could have used bar nasha as an equivalent for first person singular in speaking of his present activity. Later, under the influence of the pesher sayings, the present Son of man acquired the force of a christological title.

Perrin's thesis about the pesher origin of the future sayings is for the most part convincing. The only difficulty about it is the remarkable coincidence that a similar development should have taken place simultaneously and independently within non-Christian Jewish apocalyptic. It is this difficulty that gives plausibility to the postulation of a common source for the Christian and Jewish development, as C. Colpe has done.[4]

A further difficulty with Perrin's thesis is that the future Son of man sayings are not all of one type. While we may agree that such sayings as Mark 13:26, 14:62, and the future sayings in Luke 17 (par. Matthew 24 Q) are pesher products, this is much more difficult to argue for Luke 12:8 Q. Here the salient features of Daniel 7:13 are conspicuously lacking--viz., the Son of man's coming, the clouds of heaven, the gathering of the elect. The only possible echo of the Daniel text might be the mention of the angels. A further difficulty in Perrin's assignment of this text to the post-Easter community is the distinction that it makes between the earthly figure of Jesus and the Son of man in heaven. Since Perrin's

---

[2]N. Perrin, "Mark xiv. 62: The End Product of a Christian Pesher Tradition?" NTS 12 (1965-66) 150-55; reprinted with a postscript in A Modern Pilgrimage in New Testament Christology (Philadelphia: Fortress, 1974) 1-22.

[3]Matthew Black, An Aramaic Approach to the Gospels and Acts (3rd edition; Oxford: University Press, 1967).

[4]C. Colpe, TDNT 8. 403-481.

pesher theory postulates an identification of Jesus with the heavenly Son of man at the beginning of the tradition-process after Easter, it is unclear how such a saying could have arisen at a later stage of that process.

Perhaps however the chief problem with the Perrin-Walker reconstruction of the tradition history is their assumption of the wholesale creativity on the part of the early post-Easter community. It has become almost a game which NT scholars play: If you want to prove you are really good as a NT critic, you deny the authenticity of sayings which have been previously accepted by Bultmann! David Hill has however questioned the assumption that early Christian prophets created logia of the risen Jesus and that these were then transferred wholesale to the historical Jesus.[5] Perhaps Hill went too far in denying all creativity on the part of the church. A reasonable position would be to admit that the early church did add new applications and extensions to the authentic sayings of Jesus but that it did not create them wholesale. Above all, there is no evidence in the history of the tradition for the transference of prophetic sayings of the exalted Lord to the earthly Jesus, and it is time such theories were abandoned. At the very minimum we must now work on the assumption that there was a basis in the original authentic Jesus tradition for all three types of Son of man sayings, present, suffering, and future, however much they were added to and adapted in the post-Easter tradition.

The difficulty about the present sayings, which if authentic must be non-titular, is the lack of evidence in Aramaic usage at the time of Jesus of the use of bar nasha as a self-reference.[6] But do we have to have such evidence? Jesus could have had characteristic ways of speaking which were peculiar to him. In fact, one might also argue the authenticity of such sayings from the criterion (or index) of dissimilarity! The problem is not so much Jesus' use of bar nasha as

---

[5]D. Hill, "On the Evidence for the Creative Role of Christian Prophets," NTS 18 (1973-74) 262-274.
[6]See the criticisms of Vermes's theory of the Son of man as a self-reference in J. Fitzmyer, A Wandering Aramean: Collected Aramaic Essays (Missoula: Scholars Press, 1979) 152-153.

a self-referent but how his hearers would have taken
it. Could they possibly have heard it as the equivalent
of an imprecise pronoun like the French "on" or the
German "man"? It would mean literally "a man," "a
fellow," or "a guy," as we might say "Can't a guy
do what he likes?" when we mean "Can't I do what
I like?" The objection might be made that ὁ υἱὸς
τοῦ ἀνθρώπου has a definite article, the Son of man.
But the presence of the article ὁ before σπείρων in
Mark 4:3 does not prevent the RSV from translating
the phrase as "a sower" rather than "the sower."
If this is possible, there would seem to be no reason
why we should not contemplate the authenticity (e.g. of
the present Son of man saying in Mark 2:10) which
could be translated "But that you may know that there
is a fellow who has authority on earth to forgive
sins." The same explanation might be offered for
Mark 2:28, except that that saying is suspect on other
grounds, and may be simply an expansion of the saying
in the previous verse.7 Yet if it is a later construction, it is modeled on the use in Mark 2:10 and not
derived from the apocalyptic Son of man, since there
is no influence of Daniel 7:13 here. It is therefore
part of the Wirkungsgeschichte of Jesus' use of Son
of man as a self-referent. Two of the present Son
of man sayings in Q would be susceptible of a similar
translation:
> A fellow (ὁ υἱὸς τοῦ ἀνθρώπου) has nowhere to
> lay his head (Matt 8:20 par Q)
> A fellow (ὁ υἱὸς τοῦ ἀνθρώπου) has come eating
> and drinking (Matt 11:19 par Q)

The last of these sayings indicates clearly the context
in which Jesus used this self-effacing self-referent.
It was precisely when speaking of his vocation as
eschatological prophet. Hence the expression, though
never in itself a christological title, had the poten-
tiality for acquiring christological associations
after Easter.

Most recently, Merklein has stigmatized the suffering Son of man sayings on two familiar grounds. First,
they are absent from Q, and secondly they are suspected

7See the commentaries ad. loc.

of post-Easter origin as <u>vaticinia ex eventu</u>.[8] It
has often been pointed out that their absence from
Q is not decisive, for the suffering sayings are associated with the passion narrative; and there is no passion
narrative in Q.[9] As regards their being <u>vaticinia
ex eventu</u>, greater discrimination is called for, and
in particular, we need to fulfill Perrin's sound advice
that with every saying we treat we should offer a
thorough reconstruction of the history of the tradition.
We may in fact detect three strata in the Marcan Passion
predictions (Mark 8:31; 9:12; 9:31, 10:33-34; 10:45;
14:21; and 14:41). The most obvious stratum consists
of words and phrases which recall the Marcan passion
narrative itself. These include:

....by the elders and the chief priests and the
scribes (Mark 8:31)

...to the chief priests and the scribes, and
they will condemn him to death...they will mock
him and spit upon him, and scourge him (Mark
10:33-34).

These materials will belong to the latest stratum,
having entered the tradition either from the Marcan
redaction itself, or (if we follow Pesch) from the
pre-Marcan redaction of the pre-Marcan passion narrative.

This leaves us with another stratum, one that
recalls the kerygma of the post-Easter church (cf. 1
Cor 15:3-8 and the kerygmatic speeches in Acts).
These include reference to the "killing" of Jesus,
his dying and rising or being raised on the third
day or even after three days. As well as these kerygmatic elements, there are also scriptural echoes from
testimonia, as well as statements that these things
happened "according to the scriptures," e.g.,

-suffer many things and be rejected...be killed
and after three days rise again (Mark 8:31)
-suffer many things and be treated with contempt

---

[8]Merklein, <u>Botschaft</u>, 153, following L. Oberlinner,
<u>Todeserwartung und Todesgewissheit Jesu: Zum Problem
einer historischen Begründung</u> (SBB 10; Stuttgart:
Katholisches Bibelwerk, 1980) 140-146.

[9]I pointed this out long ago in my first work, <u>The
Mission and Achievement of Jesus</u> (SBT 12; London:
SCM, 1954), but the argument continues to be repeated,
most recently by Merklein (<u>Botschaft</u>, 153) who objects
that in Q the group of suffering sayings "noch nicht
bekannt ist."

FULLER

(Mark 9:12).
-and they will kill him; when he is killed, after
three days he will rise (Mark 9:31).
-everything written of him by the prophets will
be accomplished...and kill him; after three days
he will rise (Mark 10:32-34).
-...as it is written of him (Mark 14:21).
In addition, we note one element in the Son of man
passion predictions which appears to reflect the language
of liturgical catechesis:
-give his life a ransom for many (Mark 10:45;
cf. Mark 14:24).

This leaves us with the following elements which
are immune from the contaminations of knowledge of
the passion narrative, and of the kerygma and liturgical
catechesis:
-the Son of man will be delivered into the hands
of men (Mark 9:31).
-the Son of man goes his way; but woe to that
man by whom the Son of man is handed over (Mark
14:21)
-the Son of man is handed over into the hands
of (sinners) (Mark 14:41)

The surviving portions of Mark 9:31 and Mark
14:41 point to a basic saying, "the Son of man (a
fellow) is handed over to the hands of men." Since
this saying preserves an Aramaic word-play, Son of
man/men, it must be at least as old as the earliest
post-Easter Aramaic church.[10] The concept of "handing
over" is certainly found in pre-Pauline tradition
(cf. Rom 4:25) and is arguably post-Easter and kerygmatic. However, the term is deeply rooted in the martyrological language of Judaism, and there would seem
to be no conclusive reason why it should not have
been used by Jesus.[11]

The second type of suffering saying is "the Son
of man goes his way" (ὑπάγει). The verb is used frequently in reference to Jesus' death in the Fourth
Gospel (John 7:33 etc.). Unfortunately, the Johannine

_____

[10]Ferdinand Hahn, The Titles of Jesus in Christology
(London: Lutterworth, 1969) 37-38.
[11]The martyrological associations of παραδίδοναι are
noted by F. Büchsel, TDNT 2. 172.

212

instances are never in Son of man sayings. So the parallel is only partial, not complete. Further, Jesus speaks of his death as a "going" in Luke 13:33 (SpL), though there a different word is used (πορεύεσθαι) and the subject is the first person singular instead of the Son of man. We cannot therefore claim that this type of Son of man saying has full multiple attestation, though it does perhaps have some confirmation in the Johannine tradition and Special Luke.

A third surviving type of suffering Son of man saying is the logion about service (Mark 10:45a). This is often included among the present sayings; and indeed it is similar to the present Son of man sayings, Matthew 11:19 Q (see above). However, the service tradition occurs in the context of the Last Supper in both the Lucan and johannine traditions (Luke 22:27; John 13:1-17, esp. δοῦλος , v 16). If Jesus did actually speak of his service at the Last Supper, it is arguable that he interpreted his death specifically as his climactic act of service. The Marcan version supports the possibility that he did so in the self-effacing self-reference, Son of man: "One has come not to be served but to serve."

We have rejected Mark 10:45b as unauthentic on the ground that it reflects the language of liturgical catechesis. There is however another possibility. While the liturgical catechesis appended to the Marcan cup word (ὑπὲρ πολλῶν , Mark 14:24) is clearly a post--Easter formulation, lacking as it does multiple attestation, the whole phrase "give his life" is not found there. Is it possible that there was an original suffering "Son of man" saying which read "and to give his life"? Such a saying might be reflected in the familiar Johannine expression, "lay down his life" (John 10:11 etc.). Was there originally an authentic Jesus saying, "The Son of man came to lay down his life"?

We turn now to the one future Son of man saying for whose authenticity we have argued, namely Luke 12:8f par. Q. In a paper read at the New Testament Congress at Oxford in 1961, I reconstructed the following as the original form of the tradition:
Everyone who acknowledges me before men,
The Son of man will acknowledge before the angels of God;
But he who disowns me before men,

213

> The Son of man will disown before the angels
> of God. [12]

At the time, I assumed that there was a pre-Christian
apocalyptic Son of man. I also considered the present
and suffering sayings to be unauthentic. We are now
faced with a two-fold problem. Having argued that
Jesus probably used bar nasha as a self-effacing self-
referent, how could he have used it here with reference
to a figure other than himself (the heavenly Son of
man)? And secondly, if there was no pre-Christian
apocalyptic Son of man, what kind of figure had Jesus
in mind? In answer to the first question, I would
suggest that the term bar nasha, as a self-effacing
self-referent rather than as a messianic title, could
precisely for that reason be used of another figure
than Jesus himself. A French person who uses "on"
or a German who used "man" of himself can equally
use those terms of others. Hence Jesus could have
said "one will deny before the angels of God." Who
is the "one?" Is Jesus assuming here his own vindication, and therefore speaking of himself after all?
That is unlikely, for Jesus never in authentic sayings
speaks of his own personal vindication or exaltation
but only of the coming of the Kingdom of God and of
the general resurrection. Or is it possible that
"the Son of man will acknowledge/disown" is equivalent
(as "on" or "man" would be) to a passive, "will be
acknowledged/disowned," leaving quite unspecified
who will do the acknowledging or disowning. We must
admit we are not very satisfied with this solution
and are only putting it forward very tentatively. [13]
But the alternatives are even more problematical:
either Jesus used Son of man in two quite different
senses, as self-referent and as a title for the eschatological judge and savior, quite distinct from himself;
or alternatively, following Norman Perrin and taking
verse 9 as the clue to the original tradition, to

---

[12] R. H. Fuller, "The Clue to Jesus' Self-Understanding,"
in Studia Evangelica (TU 88; Berlin: Akademie, 1964)
3. 58-66.

[13] A new possibility has been opened up for Luke 12:8
Q by Barnabas Lindars (see postscript). The imprecise
"Son of man" may refer to the archangel Michael, who
acts as advocate for the people of God in the heavenly
court. This would explain why the genitive "of God"
is used with "angels." There is no reverential periphrasis intended here.

postulate an original divine passive "be acknowledged,"
a synonymous parallelism. But the latter suggestion,
as we have observed already, is open to the objection
of supposing that the post-Easter church, familiar
as it was with Jesus' use of Son of man as a self-referent, would have introduced a saying which appeared
to distinguish between Jesus and the Son of man.
Also to sustain his argument for the divine passive,
Perrin should have excluded the phrase "of God" ("angels
of God") from the original text, leaving "before the
angels" as part of the reverential periphrasis.

A special problem is constituted by the future
Son of man sayings in Q (Luke 11:30 par.; 12:40 par.;
17:24 par.; 17:30 par.). Here the influence of the
pesher texts, especially Daniel 7:13, is minimal.
Perhaps such influence is discernible in "coming"
(Luke 12:40 par.) and "revealed" (Luke 17:30). At
the same time other features of these sayings are
coherent with the general message of Jesus. The End,
for instance, is portrayed in them as sudden and incal-
culable. Also the allusive reference to OT figures
like Jonah (Luke 11:30), Noah (Luke 17:26-27), and
Lot (Luke 17: 29-33) is characteristic of Jesus.
There are similar allusions to Jonah and to Solomon
in Luke 11:32 par. Q and Luke 11:31, sayings generally
accepted as authentic. Now these last sayings refer
to the present aspect of Jesus' proclamation: something
greater than Jonah or Solomon is here, whereas the
sayings we are concerned with refer to its future
aspect. I would like therefore to hazard the suggestion
that the Q future Son of man sayings cited above originally referred to the futurity of the eschatological
salvation, in short to the kingdom of God, and that
in the post-Easter church "kingdom of God" was replaced
by "Son of man." They would therefore have read:
  -The kingdom of God is coming at an unexpected
  hour (Luke 12:40)
  -So will it be when the kingdom of God comes
  (Luke 17:26)
  -so will it be when the kingdom of God is revealed
  (comes?) (Luke 17:30).
It is worth noting that Matthew has redacted a Marcan
kingdom saying by adding a reference to the parousia
of the Son of man (Matt 16:28; cf. Mark 9:1). Two
future Son of man sayings still need to be accounted
for--viz. Luke 11:30 par. Q and Luke 17:22. Luke

215

11:30 occurs in a context in which the <u>presence</u> rather than the futurity of eschatological salvation is being discussed. This would suggest that "Son of man" in this saying is really a present use—i.e., "so will a man turn out to be a sign for this generation." As for Luke 17:22, the idea of the "days of the Son of man" appears to be a peculiarly Lucan concept and will therefore be redactional.

In the post-Easter Church the quantity of Son of man sayings was expanded. The early church was so familiar with the Son of man as a self-referent of Jesus that it developed other present Son of man sayings (e.g., Mark 2:28) and substituted Son of man for "I" with reference to Jesus in some places (e.g., Luke 20:6, [Q or Lucan redaction]). But when it evolved the pesher Son of man saying based on Daniel 7:13, this need not imply that it now regarded the Son of man as a christological <u>title</u> for Jesus. It remained a non-titular self-referent. Jesus is now made to speak of himself as one who would be exalted to the right hand of God, who would come on the clouds of heaven, and act as judge and Savior at the End. This perhaps answers the problem created by the fact that the Son of man was developed independently in Jewish apocalyptic. There it is actually a title for the eschatological judge and savior. It is thus not really a case of a parallel and independent development of the same title, but represents a completely different development. In Jewish apocalyptic it is a title rather than a self-referent.

Conclusion

The Son of man is so controverted a problem that no one can expect that his or her arguments will carry the day. The problem remains insoluble and we can only suggest possibilities for its solution. Every solution proposed to date has some weaknesses, and we claim no finality for our proposals. All we hope to do is to put some new suggestions into the hopper.

Postscript

Since the above essay was drafted a new work by Barnabas Lindars has come to hand.[14] Arguing with

---

[14]<u>Jesus Son of Man</u> (London: SPCK, 1983).

a profounder knowledge of the Hebrew, Aramaic, and Jewish background than I possess, Lindars proposes a development of the Son of man tradition which is in many respects quite close to my own here. In particular, he agrees that Jesus used the term Son of man as a self-effacing self-referent, though, unlike me, he stresses that this was not intended to be exclusive to Jesus himself. It meant: "a person like me." Lindars also argues for the authenticity of a basic quantum of suffering Son of man sayings, and goes further than I do in arguing for the authenticity of Mark 10:45b, though minus the word λύτρον . Mark 10:45b thus comes out very close to John 15:13, which he sees as a variant of the same saying. Like me, Lindars also argues for the authenticity for Luke 12:8 par. Q and takes it in the same unspecified sense. As regards the growth of the other future sayings, he does not buy into Perrin's later work, as I have done; nor does he call them specifically pesher developments.

We welcome Lindars' new work, and are pleased that his thinking is developing along the same lines as our own.

CHAPTER THIRTEEN

THE TEXT OF 1 THESSALONIANS

Helmut Koester

In the new Novum Testamentum Graece (Nestle-Aland, 26th edition)[1] the text of 1 Thessalonians has been changed from its predecessor, the 25th edition of Nestle-Aland,[2] in thirteen instances. To be sure, a comprehensive review of the text of the entire Corpus Paulinum is required in order to evaluate this new text of one of the Pauline Epistles.[3] But it may be permitted to raise some questions with regard to 1 Thessalonians, not voiced by a specialist in textual criticism, but by an exegete who would like to settle the textual problems of this Pauline letter in order to complete a commentary on this writing.

---

[1]Kurt Aland, et al., eds., post Eberhard and Erwin Nestle, Novum Testamentum Graece (26th ed.; Stuttgart: Deutsche Bibelstiftung, 1979 and reprints; I am using the 4th reprint of 1981).
[2]Eberhard Nestle, Erwin Nestle, Kurt Aland, eds., Novum Testamentum Graece (25th ed.; Stuttgart: Privilegierte Württembergische Bibelanstalt, 1963).
[3]No comprehensive study of these changes has yet appeared to my knowledge, although there are a number of brief reviews: e.g., F. Neirynck, "The New Nestle-Aland: The Text of Mark in N26," ETL 55 (1979) 331-56; J. Duplacy, "Une nouvelle edition du Nouveau Testament grec," RTL 11 (1980) 229-32; Johannes Karavidopoulos, "Nestle-Aland, Novum Testamentum Graece, 26th ed., 1979," Deltion Biblikon Meleton 9 (1980) 82-87; J. K. Elliot, "An Examination of the Twenty-sixth Edition of Nestle-Aland Novum Testamentum Graece," JTS 32 (1981) 19-49; Hans-Werner Bartsch, "Ein neuer Textus Receptus für das griechische Neue Testament?" NTS 27 (1981) 585-92; H. J. de Jonge, "De nieuwe Nestle: N26," NedTTs 34 (1980) 307-22.

The most striking feature in the changes introduced by Aland is the increase in the use of brackets.[4] In the 25th edition of Nestle, brackets were used three times: 1 Thess 1:4; 4:10; and 5:25. Aland's 26th edition uses brackets in these three instances, adds brackets in three other cases (1:5; 1:10; 4:8), and adds words in brackets in five more passages (1:5; 1:8; 3:13; 4:11; 5:15). Apart from this increased use of brackets, the text has been changed in five other instances (2:7, 8, 13; 5:10, 13). I shall first discuss the cases in which words in brackets have been added.

1 Thess 1:5 Nestle-Aland 26th ed.: ἐν δυνάμει καὶ ἐν πνεύματι ἁγίῳ καὶ [ἐν] πληροφορίᾳ πολλῇ = A C D F G Ψ 𝕸 r vgmss. The bracketed ἐν is missing in B ℵ 33 lat. Tischendorf, Westcott-Hort, and Nestle did not admit ἐν into their text. It is easily understood why scribes would have added the preposition here: both preceding nouns have the same preposition.[5] On the other hand, its omission is not motivated. That in is also missing in most of the Latin tradition confirms the age of this reading. It is **lectio difficilior** and should be preferred.

1 Thess 1:8 Nestle-Aland 26th ed.: ἐν τῇ Μακεδονίᾳ καὶ [ἐν τῇ] Ἀχαίᾳ = C D F G Ψ lat. The bracketed words are missing in B K 6. 33. 365. 614. 629. 630. 17-39. (1881) al r vgmss. Only Tischendorf admitted ἐν τῇ into his text, revealing his well-known preference for ℵ ; von Soden bracketed the words; but Westcott-Hort and all other editors (including Nestle) reject them. This secondary addition is motivated by 1:7: ἐν τῇ Μακεδονίᾳ καὶ ἐν τῇ Ἀχαίᾳ .[6] The tradition that does not contain these words is old; though ℵ does not support the reading, B is backed by 1739,

---

[4]The extensive use of brackets had already been criticized with respect to the United Bible Societies' Greek text by J. K. Elliot, "The Use of Brackets in the Text of the United Bible Societies' Greek New Testament," Bib 60 (1979) 575-77.

[5]B. Rigaux, Saint Paul: Les Epitres aux Thessaloniciens (EBib; Paris: Gabalda, 1956) ad loc.

[6]For similar instances of the secondary addition of ἐν, cf. Rom 13:9; Col 2:7.

the important companion of P46.[7]

1 Thess 3:13 Nestle-Aland 26th ed.: μετὰ πάντων τῶν ἁγίων αὐτοῦ, [ἀμήν] = א *2 A D* 81. 629 pc a m vg bo. The bracketed word is missing in 1 B D2 F G Ψ 𝔐 it sy sa bomss. Editors are almost unanimous in rejecting this later liturgical addition.[8] Examples for the secondary addition of "Amen" are numerous (especially at the end of letters and after liturgical formulae). The textual basis for the omission is very good. It includes all older translations (it sy sa), whereas only the later translations (vg bo) are witnesses of this secondary expansion.

4:11 Nestle-Aland 26th ed.: ταῖς [ἰδίαις] χερσὶν ὑμῶν = א* A D1 𝔐 . The word ἰδίαις is missing in א2 B D* F G 6. 104. 365. 1175. 1739. 1881 pc syh. Tischendorf, Westcott-Hort, Merk, Bover, and Nestle do not include the word in their editions. ἰδίαις is a redundant addition that wants to harmonize this passage with 1 Cor 4:12 and Eph 4:8 (ταῖς ἰδίαις χερσίν). In those two passages there is no following possessive pronoun, whereas ἰδίαις in 1 Thess 4:11 conflicts with the following ὑμῶν.[9] As in the case of 1 Thess 1:5, the minuscule 1739, frequent companion of P46, supports B, whereas א joins the secondary "Majority Text."

5:15 Nestle-Aland 26th ed.: το ἀγαθὸν διώκετε [καὶ] εἰς ἀλλήλους καὶ εἰς πάντας = P30 2 B Ψ vgst syh. καί is missing in * A D F G 6. 33. 1739. 1881. 2426 pc it vgcl syp; Ambst Spec. Tischendorf, Westcott-Hort, Merk, and Nestle do not include καί in their text, though Westcott-Hort lists it as a marginal reading. Von Soden includes καί in brackets. The evidence for the inclusion of καί is not very strong, whereas 1739 (thus probably also P46) together with א and the Western witnesses strongly support

---

[7]The text of P46 is not extant in any instance discussed in this paper. But its text or Vorlage survives in 1739; cf. G. Zuntz, The Text of the Epistles (London: Oxford University Press, 1953), 68-84.

[8]Only Von Soden adds the word in brackets. Tischendorf, again follows the original reading of א .

[9]The word ἴδιος is frequently used as a possessive pronoun; cf. BAG s.v. 2. See also Rigaux, Thessaloniciens, ad loc.

a text without καί. Zuntz has investigated the instances of "the interpolation of καί to correspond with a second καί later on"[10] and observes with respect to 1 Thess 5:15 that the addition of καί is "so evidently spurious as to require no discussion."[11] It is hard to understand the addition of καί in the 26th ed. of Nestle-Aland (even in brackets).[12]

In three instances Nestle-Aland 26th ed. brackets words of the text of the 25th ed. of Nestle.

---

[10]Text of the Epistles, 199-200.

[11]Zuntz, Text of the Epistles, 199. Zuntz (200-201) has made some very important observations with regard to the value of the preservation of original asyndeta in P46, "almost always joined by one, or a few, members of the 'Alexandrian' group; most often B and/or 1739; while the larger part of this group . . . is in opposition and wrong" (201).

[12]While in this new edition a superfluous connecting particle was added to the text, no attempt has been made to eliminate other secondary particles from the text; e.g., the second δέ in 1 Cor 12:10 (missing in P46 B 1739); δέ after ἄλλος in 1 Cor 3:10 (missing in P46 D and others -- the variant is not listed in Nestle-Aland 26th ed.); δέ after οὐ πολύ in Heb 12:9 (not in Nestle 25th ed., but added in brackets in Nestle-Aland 26th ed.); οὖν in 1 Cor 6:7 (missing in P46 ℵ D 1739 and others; cf. Zuntz, Text of the Epistles, 188-93. A most striking case is 1 Cor 7:34: The reading of P46 A D P 33. (629). 1175. 2495. pc a t vgcl syp; Epiph is τῷ σώματι καὶ τῷ πνεύματι. Nestle-Aland 26th ed. with all other previous editions adds καί before τῷ σώματι (Westcott-Hort is uncertain). But Zuntz (Text of the Epistles, 199) rightly argues that this καί is an intrusion from an old variant without articles, καὶ σώματι καὶ πνεύματι (P15 F G and others -- not listed in Nestle-Aland 26th ed.), thus creating the reading καὶ τῷ σώματι καὶ τῷ πνεύματι that "is bad from every point of view. It is overlong and rhythmically clumsy; the twofold καί gives undue weight to the plain phrase 'in body and soul,' and the evidence for this reading is small and narrowly confined" (Zuntz, Text of the Epistles, 199). Nestle-Aland 26th ed. is here still so much under the spell of ℵ and B (both have the additional καί) that P46 is not permitted to outweigh their combined witness.

TEXT OF FIRST THESSALONIANS

1 Thess 1:5 Nestle-Aland 26th ed.: [ἐν] ὑμῖν
δι᾽ ὑμᾶς . The bracketed word appears in B D F G Ψ
it sy(p), and all editors include it in their text.
It is missing in ℵ A C P 048. 33. 81. 104. 326*. 945.
1739. pc vgst. The cause for this omission is an
obvious haplography after ἐγενήθημεν . ἐν before ὑμῖν
is required by the context: "among you" (not: "through
you" or "for you"). It is difficult to understand
why brackets were introduced here.

1 Thess 1:10 Nestle-Aland 26th ed.: ἐκ [τῶν]
νεκρῶν . The evidence for the omission of the article
is very narrow: A C K 323. 629. 945. 2464. 2495 al,
whereas the article is well attested: ℵ B D F G I
Ψ 𝕸 Eus. Only Westcott-Hort put the word in brackets;
all other editors judge it to be an original part
of the text. In all other instances Paul does not
use the article before νεκρῶν when speaking of Christ's
resurrection.13 This explains why a scribe would
delete the article here. Moreover, Paul seems to
quote a formula in 1 Thess 1:10.14 There is no reason
to doubt that the article is part of the original
text.

1 Thess 4:8 Nestle-Aland 26th ed.: τὸν θεὸν
τὸν [καὶ] διδόντα τὸ πνεῦμα αὐτοῦ . The καί is missing
in A B D1 I 33. 365. 614. 1739*. 2464 al b syp bo;
Ambst Spec. Witnesses for the text are ℵ D*.2 F
G Ψ 𝕸 lat syh samss; Cl. Of the editors only Westcott-Hort does not admit καί into the text. The evidence
for the omission is indeed strong. But bracketing
the word is no solution because this variant is closely
related to the following: διδόντα (ℵ * B D F G I
365. 2464 pc) and δόντα (ℵ 2 A Ψ sy co; Cl).
Bernhard Weiss15 has shown that ΔΙΔΟΝΤΑ is the result
of a faulty copying of ΚΑΙΔΟΝΤΑ, because of the similarity of AI and ΔI. The aorist δόντα is also required
by the context: "God has called you" (ἐκάλεσεν , 4:7)

_____

13Rom 4:24; 6:4, 9; 7:4; 8:11; 10:9; 1 Cor 15:12, 20;
Gal 1:1.
14Cf. πρωτότοκος ἐκ τῶν νεκρῶν in the hymn quoted
in Col 1:10.
15Textkritik der paulinischen Briefe (TU 14,3; Leipzig:
Hinrichs, 1896) 112. See also Rigaux, Thessaloniciens,
ad loc.

223

-- "who **gave** you his holy spirit."[16] Thus καί should stay in the text (without brackets), but δόντα (not διδόντα) must be read following the καί . In this case, only the "Majority Text" has preserved the original reading. [17]

Of the five other changes in Nestle-Aland 26th ed., two are certainly correct.

5:10: τοῦ ἀποθανόντος ὑπερ ἡμῶν (P30 ℵ 2 A D F G Ψ 𝕸) for περι ἡμῶν (ℵ * B 33 = Tischendorf, Merk, Nestle). Although ὑπερ and περί are used synonymously in Hellenistic Greek, ὑπερ ἡμῶν / ὑμῶν is overwhelmingly attested in Pauline usage. [18]

5:13: ὑπερεκπερισσοῦ (ℵ A D2 Ψ 𝕸) for ὑπερεκπερισσῶς (B D* F G pc = Tischendorf, Nestle). Both adverbs are possible, but Paul uses the form ὑπερεκπερισσοῦ also in 1 Thess 3:10.

Doubts can be raised in 1 Thess 2:13 with respect to the word order ἐστιν ἀληθῶς (1 A D F G H Ψ 0208vid 𝕸 lat sy), changed from ἀληθῶς ἐστιν (B 33. 326. 1739. 1881. pc = Westcott-Hort, Nestle). ℵ must be added to the latter, because the **Vorlage** of ℵ certainly read ἀληθῶς ἐστιν : the scribe omitted ἀληθῶς because of homoioteleuton with the preceding καθῶς , the first corrector of ℵ then added the omitted word after ἐστιν . [19] Thus, the evidence for the word order ἀληθῶς ἐστιν is stronger than it appears at first glance, especially in view of the support of 1739 which may indicate that also P46 would support this reading if its text were preserved here. [20]

In the problematic passage 1 Thess 2:7-8, Aland has changed the traditional text of Nestle in two instances. In 2:7 the 26th edition reads νήπιοι (P65

---

[16]Cf. Rigaux, **Thessaloniciens**, ad loc.; see the use of the aorist δόντα in Gal 1:4.

[17]Of the modern editors, only von Soden reads καὶ δόντα .

[18]Zuntz, **Text of the Epistles**, 87. Westcott-Hort, von Soden, and Vogels read ὑπέρ. Cf. also Rigaux, **Thessaloniciens**, ad loc.

[19]Rigaux, **Thessaloniciens**, ad loc.

[20]Rigaux, **Thessaloniciens**, ad loc., prefers the reading now printed in Nestle-Aland 26th ed.

$\aleph$* B C* D* F G I Ψ* 104*. 326c. 2495 pc it vgww sams bo; Cl = Westcott-Hort) for ἤπιοι of the earlier editions ($\aleph$ c   A C2 D2 Ψc $\mathfrak{M}$ vgst (sy) samss = Tischendorf, von Soden, Vogels, Nestle). On the basis of the manuscript evidence alone, this decision may be justified. But the variant is caused by either haplography or dittography after ἐγενήθημεν -- both mistakes could occur repeatedly even in the same family. Other criteria are therefore needed. Considering context and subject matter, there cannot be the slightest doubt that νήπιοι is wrong. To be sure, this word is used elsewhere in Paul's letters, but always with the meaning "babe," "immature" (Rom 2:20; 1 Cor 3:1; 13:11; Gal 4:1, 3; cf. Eph 4:14). The contrast is always "mature," "perfect." The possible meaning "innocent," contrasted with "learned" (σοφός , συνετός),[21] does not occur in Paul. But even in this latter meaning, νήπιος would be awkward in 1 Thess 2:7, because Paul here emphasizes his loving care for the Thessalonians: "like a mother comforts her children" (2:7), "ready to share . . . our own selves" (2:8).[22] Only the term ἤπιος , "gentle," "kind,"[23] fits this context and contrasts well with the preceding "although we could have wielded authority as apostles of Christ" (2:7a).

In 1 Thess 2:8, Nestle-Aland 26th ed. has correctly changed the Atticistic imperfect ηὐδοκοῦμεν (B = WestcottHort, Nestle) to the customary nonaugmented Koine imperfect εὐδοκοῦμεν .[24] This may be the best possible text, but questions remain. Why would Paul choose the imperfect tense -- which could be misread as a present[25] -- rather than the aorist?[26] The preceding

---

[21]Cf. Matt 11:25; Luke 10:21.

[22]See also below on 2:8.

[23]The term ἤπιος is used in the NT only here and 2 Tim 2:24. In 1 Thess 2, it belongs to the standard concepts that describe the behavior of the Cynic philosopher. Paul's apology of his own ministry in 1 Thessalonians 2 draws on this model; cf. Abraham J. Malherbe, "'Gentle as a Nurse': The Cynic Background to 1 Thess ii," NovT 12 (1970): 201-17.

[24]Cf. J. K. Elliot, "Temporal Augment in Verbs with Initial Diphthong in the New Testament," NovT 22 (1980) 5; BDF {66; Rigaux, Thessaloniciens, ad loc.

[25]In 2 Cor 5:8 εὐδοκοῦμεν is present tense.

[26]The aorist εὐδοκήσομεν is read here by 33. 31 pc f vg -- too narrow a basis for a textual emendation.

and following finite verbs are all aorists: ἐγενήθημεν
(2:7), ἐκηρύξαμεν (2:9), ἐγενήθημεν (2:10). Moreover,
the aorist of εὐδοκεῖν occurs in the next chapter
of 1 Thessalonians (3:1) and frequently elsewhere
in Paul's letters,[27] while there is no instance of
the imperfect of this verb in the NT. One must ask,
therefore, whether εὐδοκοῦμεν in 1 Thess 2:8 is not
actually a present tense, caused by the misreading
of the preceding ὁμειρόμενοι as "to be desirous of,"
"to long for." This is apparently an ancient misunderstanding of this rare word as a synonym of ἱμείρομαι.[28]
If ἱμείρομαι ὑμῶν really meant that Paul "longed for"
the Thessalonians (i.e., in a situation in which he
was absent and not present) the present tense of εὐδοκοῦμεν would be called for: "(Now absent) longing
for you, we are ready to share with you not only the
gospel but our own selves." Such misunderstanding
of ὁμείρομαι at a very early stage of the transmission
of the letter could have caused the change of an original
εὐδοκήσαμεν into εὐδοκοῦμεν (present, not imperfect).
However, in view of the context and in view of the
impossibility of translating ὁμείρομαι with "to long
for," "to be desirous of,"[29] εὐδοκήσαμεν is most likely
the original reading: it was then, when Paul, Timothy,
and Sylvanus were in Thessalonike, that they gave
the Thessalonians their own selves. In this context,
ὁμειρόμενοι -- probably a term from the vernacular
language -- must express a loving behavior among members
of the family, analogous to "gentle" and "as a mother

comforts."[30]

---

[27]Rom 15:26, 27; 1 Cor 1:21; 10:5; Gal 1:15; cf. Col
1:19; Heb 10:6.
    [28]Job 3:21 translates the Hebrew הןﬡ "to wait
for," "to long for" with ὁμείρομαι. Hesychius explains
ὁμείρομαι as ἐπιθυμεῖν.
    [29]There is general agreement now that ὁμείρομαι
cannot be equated with ἱμείρομαι / μείρομαι, cf. BDF {101
s.v.; Rigaux, Thessaloniciens, ad loc. (with extensive
literature, p. 421). The third centure CE inscription
on a tomb from Lycaonia ὁ [μει]ρόμενοι περὶ παιδός (CIG
III 4000) is the only other evidence, and it remains
enigmatic.
    [30]But the term remains untranslatable, though it can
be said with confidence that all extant translations
are either wrong or ambiguous.

Did Nestle-Aland 26th ed. improve the Greek text of 1 Thessalonians? In the five instances where words in brackets were added (1:5; 1:8; 3:13; 4:11; 5:15) it can be said with great certainty that these words are not part of the original text. Of the three instances in which words of the Nestle text were bracketed, two are not justified (1:5; 1:10); in the third case (4:8) the brackets do not solve the textual problem. Of the five other changes, two are a definite improvement (5:10; 5:13); one can be disputed (2:13); one is justified, but does not bring us closer to the original text (2:8); and one is clearly wrong (2:7). Thus, though the text has been improved in three cases, it is still problematic in two cases (2:8; 4:8), and it is inferior to its predecessor in eight instances. Most problematic is the greater degree of uncertainty (addition of brackets), the disregard of Zuntz's insights in his masterwork on The Text of the Epistles, and a failure to consider the context and subject matter (especially evident in 2:7).

CHAPTER FOURTEEN

SOCIAL AND RELIGIOUS ASPECTS
OF THE "WESTERN" TEXT

Richard I. Pervo

As a working scholar I discern, in general, two types of textual criticism: that of the commentators—often quite adventurous, aimed at discovering what the author actually wrote, in what order—and that of the standard editions, whose preparers seem most concerned with establishing the manuscript tradition and giving the earliest extant form thereof. The latter seek to justify the canonical text; for the former, the Canon is often seen as an impediment to understanding. To what extent, for example, do the strong arguments for regarding 1 Thess 2:13-16 and 1 Cor 14:33b-36 as interpolations,[1] or even the widely held view that John 21 is an appendix, belong to the domain of text criticism? They do to at least this degree, that one will always hear the quite reasonable objection that no manuscript evidence supports such contentions. The very wealth of data appears to eliminate the need to give conjectures serious attention. In this brief contribution I shall, not for the first time, try the patience and charity of my esteemed colleague Ernie Saunders,[2] by poaching in the forests

---

[1] Other texts could be cited. The situation is such that if a commentary on 2 Cor failed to discuss the possibility of interpolation in 6:14-7:1, the reader would be shocked; but if a standard edition cited a list of scholars who reject the text, one might be even more surprised.

[2] It is my great pleasure to contribute this all too small offering in grateful tribute to Ernest W. Saunders, whose warm and helpful, but never patronizing, assistance to a very junior professor at a sister institution will not soon be forgotten.

and preserves of textual criticism. One quarry is
the ever-useful reminder that in some cases where
the available materials do not provide data for particular proposals, there may well be analogous information
which will at least enhance the degree of probability
to be assigned to them. The second goal of this expedi-
tion is church history. Text critics must know everything. In most cases their vast knowledge of church
history is a tool for ruling out later readings.
I wish to use textual variants to help write church
history.

The basis of this study is the so-called "western"
text of the NT, especially Luke-Acts. Most of the
evidence derives from Codex Bezae. Whatever eccentri-
cities that MS possesses, it does appear to represent
a particular and consistent outlook. The readings
I shall discuss are almost universally regarded as
secondary. The intention of this endeavor is to assemble
a number of observations culled from the labor of
others and look at their significance as a whole.
At the heart of the "western" edition of Luke and
Acts, as well as other NT texts, was a type of Christianity quite similar to orthodox early Catholicism
of the mid-second century. The surviving "western"
readings establish that one technique used by representatives of that movement was the revision of texts through
addition and deletion. I shall now point to three
ways in which the viewpoint of the "western reviser"3
emerges.

3"Western reviser" and "western revision" are shorthand
expressions for the sources of the text now represented
by much later "western" witnesses. Although I seem
to presume one major editorial act and describe it
in part, I am well aware that the material has a complex
history. Groups of readings that cohere are likely
to emanate from a similar time and place, if not an
identical one. My comments omit lists of the particular
support for specific texts and thereby presume that
readers will have reference to critical editions.
All of the variants discussed in this article may
be found in the 26th edition of Nestle-Aland or in
J. H. Ropes, The Text of Acts, The Beginnings of Christianity, vol. 3 (edd. F. Jackson and K. Lake; London:
Macmillan, 1926).

I

A Gentile Movement Shorn of Its Jewish Roots

Eldon J. Epp has painstakingly and convincingly demonstrated that Codex D and various allies operate from a Gentile-Christian perspective which has limited interest in, or patience for, Jews and their institutions.[4] The two groups have clearly gone their separate ways. There is little need to validate Christianity by way of Judaism, and no reason to look for Jewish converts. The Jews are mainly useful as "bad guys" in the drama of redemption. Acts had already made a number of such proposals. The "western reviser" apparently admired them and expanded the list.[5]

The world of Bezae, in which separation from Judaism is no longer regarded with pain, approximates that of the Pastorals, Ignatius, and the Didache. Through these revisions the Book of Acts is drawn toward the world of the Apologists. Those reponsible for the anti-Judaic comments and revisions behind D would be unlikely to take umbrage at the present of the Martyrdom of Polycarp, for instance. Whereas Paul and Luke, in their different generations, wrestled with the problem of Israel's rejection of their message; for the "western reviser" the Jews were simply part of the problem.

In the light of what happens to the Jews in Bezae, it would appear at least a bit improbable that similar improvements might be introduced elsewhere. The callous, Gentile anti-Semitism of 1 Thess 2:13-16[6] has much in common with what emerges in Codex D. The existence of Bezae in no way proves the secondary character of 1 Thess 2:13-16, but it does show that there were people quite willing to attempt such motifications.

---

[4]E. J. Epp, The Theological Tendency of Codex Bezae Cantabrigiensis in Acts (Cambridge: Cambridge University Press, 1966). I am indebted to Prof. Epp not only for his method, but for his kindness in looking for literature on the subject for me.

[5]For Luke's use of the Jews as scapegoats and villains, see my 1979 Harvard dissertation, "The Literary Genre of the Acts of the Apostles," passim.

[6]On the relation of 1 Thess 2:13-16 to Greco-Roman anti-semitism, see B. Pearson, "1 Thess 2:13-16: A Non-Pauline Interpolation?" HTR 64 (1971) 79-94.

II
Church Order and Life

Peter provides the most interesting case for study. The "western reviser" enhanced his position as leader and mouthpiece of the community, heightened his power, and magnified his status.[7] The following examples treat "western" variants in Acts:

1:23-- ἔστησεν. The original plural implies that the community put forward two qualified candidates. The singular makes Peter alone responsible for screening candidates for office. Since lots will decide between the two, the people have lost their power.

2:14-- πρῶτος. This is not an adverb. I would translate, "Peter spoke as chief."

2:37-- λοιποὺς. Through omission of this word Peter is separated from the apostles, who now belong to another group.

5:29-30--More of the same.[8] Peter alone speaks to the Court.

15:7-13--"Western" variants have James "rise and speak" in v 13, thus completing the parallel with Peter, v 7. This similarity, as Epp notes, only serves to heighten the contrasting imputation of inspiration

---

[7]Major discussions of Peter's role in the "western" text of Acts are J. Crehan, "Peter according to the D-Text of the Synoptic Gospels and Acts," TS 18 (1957) 596-603; Epp, Theological Tendency, passim; C. Martini, "La figura di Pietro secondo le varianti del Codice D negli Atti Degli Apostoli," San Pietro (Atti della XIX Settimana Biblica, Brecia: 1967) 279-289; and B. Metzger's extremely useful Textual Commentary on the Greek New Testament (New York/London: United Bible Societies, 1971).

[8]For a discussion of this particular passage see Epp, Theological Tendency, 157.

to Peter (by adding τῷ πνεύματι in v 7).[9] In v 12 the πρεσβύτεροι formally endorse Peter's statement. With such compliant presbyters Ignatius would have been well pleased.

A number of variants glorify Peter by highlighting his personal charisma and endowment with miraculous power.[10] I single out some changes in the story of Cornelius' conversion.

10:24-25--D has Cornelius assemble his family and friends to await Peter's advent. By taking εἰσέλθειν in the political and athletic sense of entry into a city, D makes the whole affair quite public. Cornelius posts a slave at the city gate to give advance warning and, duly informed, rushes outdoors to perform his obeisance in public.[11]

10:33-- ἐνώπιόν σου vs. ἐνώπιον τοῦ θεοῦ, etc. It is the presence of Peter which is now the cause of such excitement. He will be the oracle from whom the message of salvation will come.

11:2--The substantial "western revision" stresses that Peter's return to Jerusalem was not in haste and due to the strident objections of a powerful faction. He returned in his own good time and at his own pleasure, convoking an assembly upon his return.

These changes may appear minor, but their overall significance is not. The Peter of the "western revision" is a leader of a different era. A new ecclesial model

---

[9]Other "western" references to the Spirit in Acts: 15:29,32; 19:1; 20:3-4; 24:10; 26:1. This is not strictly limited to apostles and authorities. The "western" readings like to link the Spirit to baptism, see it as a charisma of officials, and tone down any tendency towards charismatic display. See Metzger, Textual Commentary, 439, and C. Martini, "La Tradition textuelle des Actes des Apôtres es les Tendence de L'Eglise ancienne," Les Actes des Apôtres (ed. J. Kremer; Louvain: University Press, 1979) 21-35, esp. 23-25.
[10]For example: Acts 3:3-5, 3:11, 4:14, 4:24, 5:15, 8:24, 9:34, 9:40, 10:24-25, 10:33, and 11:2. Discussions are as in note 7 above.
[11]Metzger, Textual Commentary, 374, corrects other interpretations of the slave's role.

is coming into being. Peter is the primus, worthy of all honor and source of all wisdom. He has received the Spirit. The other apostles are not his equals. His arrival into town may be described as a παρουσία. By replacing "God's presence" with "your presence," Cornelius appears to subscribe to a sort of ubi episcopus ibi ecclesia theory.

Although the terms are, of course, absent, Peter and the apostles model the rule of congregations by a monarchical bishop and his presbyters. The Church requires strong organization, and the Spirit does not belong to just anyone.

These observations are by no means mitigated when the various passages glorifying and idealizing the apostles, even those intensifying the parallelism of Paul to Peter, are taken into account.[12] Such exaggerations are quite typical of the second century.

The "western revision" also sought to clarify the nature of spiritual gifts and their relationship to Christian initiation. These concerns also occupied the attention of emergent orthodoxy.

8:37,39--In these two famous variants the "western" text includes a creed before initiation, has the Spirit descend upon the eunuch after baptism, and assigns an angel responsibility for Philip's rapture.

11:17--Once again the gift of the Spirit is equated with baptism, through the addition of a phrase.

19:5-6--Baptism is linked to forgiveness of sins, and the gift of the Spirit comes immediately with the imposition of hands. The ecstatic outbursts are not mere glossolalia, for their speech was interpreted. Hanson sees a more fully developed rite of initiation

---

[12]Examples are Acts 4:21, 5:38-39, 8:1, 13:12, 13:42-43, 15:26, and 16:4. R. P. C. Hanson, "The Provenance of the Interpolator in the 'Western' Text of Acts and of Acts Itself," NTS 12 (1965-66) 211-230, was quite stimulating to me. Bishop Hanson discusses the image of apostles on pp. 219-220. See also the index in Epp, Theological Tendency, s.v. "apostles," and note 16 below.

and refers to 1 Tim 5:22 in wondering whether the
imposition of hands was applied to forgiveness.[13]
Despite its frequent, often pedantic references to
the Spirit, the "western revision" was no advocate
for enthusiasm. The Holy Spirit comes in Baptism
and is no source of disorder. The Jews are out and
down. Apostles are up and in charge. The Spirit
is linked to the sacraments conveyed by apostolic
persons. How will women fare amidst all this?

<h1 style="text-align:center">III</h1>
<h2 style="text-align:center">The Status and Function of Women</h2>

Although the presence of a possibly "anti-feminist"
element has been the subject of a number of comments
and observations,[14] there has been little reflection
upon the significance of this bias since William Ramsay
discussed it near the close of the last century.[15]
After reviewing the texts mentioned in this connection,
I hope to advance the discussion of them through a
more systematic analysis.

Bezae et al. wished to obliterate the notion
that Jesus had women disciples and remove them from
the chain of "witnesses." Luke 8:3 identified a group
of women disciples. They appear (at 23:49,55) as
the only witnesses of the crucifixion and burial from
among the followers of Jesus. Luke's term for this
group appears to be αἱ γυναῖκες , "the women." They
last appear as a group in Acts 1:14.

---

[13]Hanson, "Provenance," 218.
[14]Women in Codex Bezae, etc.: Ropes, Text, ccxxxiv;
F. F. Bruce, The Acts of the Apostles (London: Tyndale
Press, 1951) 346, n. 13; P. H. Menoud, "The Western
Text and the Theology of Acts," Bulletin of the S.N.T.S.
2 (1951) 30-32; W. Thiele, "Eine Bemerkung zu Act. 1:14,"
ZNW 53 (1962) 110-111; Martini, "La Tradition," 27,
and the commentaries of Conzelmann, Haenchen, and
Metzger on the various passages listed below. Just
as the research and drafting of this article was completed, B. Witherington's "The Anti-Feminist Tendencies
of the 'Western' Text in Acts," appeared in JBL 103
(1984) 82-84.
[15]W. Ramsay, The Church in the Roman Empire, 5th ed. (London: Hodder & Stoughton, 1897) 160-162, regards Bezae
as a "Catholic recension." His remarks are still
worth reading.

Women disciples, however, do not appear in "western" circles, which want nothing to do with such women:

Luke 23:55 [16]--Whereas B speaks of "The women who had come with him from Galilee. . .," D takes note of "Two women who had come from Galilee." By dropping αὐτῷ, Bezae et al. dissociate these women from Jesus. They were not disciples; indeed, they could be passers-by, pious holiday tourists.

Luke 24:1--The "western reviser" expands the group coming to the tomb, making it more disparate, a hodge-podge of mourning women rather than a small close-knit band of followers.

Luke 24:6--The clear announcement of the resurrection (cf. Mark 16:6) is omitted, the women merely being advised to remember the passion predictions.[17] Of the several possible explanations for such "Western non-interpolations," one deserving consideration here is that the reviser did not wish to portray women as recipients and bearers of the Easter message, a function of the (male) apostles. The preceding and following texts support the "anti-feminist" understanding.

Luke 24:22--By dropping ἐξ ἡμῶν D says "some women," rather than "some of the women members of our group," as B would have it. Again the modification is consistent with established practice.

Acts 1:14--The two added words καὶ τέκνοις transforms Luke's women disciples into mere "wives and

---

[16]G. Rice, "Western Non-Interpolations: A Defense of the Apostolate," Luke-Acts (ed. C. Talbert; New York: Crossroad, 1984) 1-16, called these passages to my attention. Although I am employing them in a different way, it should be noted that the tendency of making excuses for apostles and correcting their failures is typical of the "western revision."

[17]The inconsistency of this message, which in fact presumes that the women had been in Galilee, should remove any doubt about the secondary nature of the reading.

children," that is, into non-entities.[18] Since Luke
is not interested in married apostles (or Christians),[19]
this addition reveals its secondary character and
confirms the secondary nature of those before it.
With remarkable economy the reviser has expunged from
memory a group of women disciples, abolished the role
of these women as witnesses, and transformed such
women as were present into housewives and mothers
only.

Acts 18:2,3,7,18,21,26--D et al. carry out this
program with reference to Prisca and Aquila. He only
is mentioned, or given precedence.[20] She becomes
a spouse, not a missionary nor practitioner of a craft,
just a spouse.

Col 4:5--Witherington notes that D has converted
Nympha into Nymphas by reading "his house" instead
of the original "her." Junia will soon follow, albeit
without need to alter the text (Rom 16:7).

Acts 2:17--It may be intentional that by dropping
the article D appears to imply that only some of their
daughters will prophecy, as opposed to all their sons.

The "western revision" was not fond of women
missionaries or disciples. Not content with that,

---

[18]On this passage see, in particular, Thiele, "Bemerkung."
Note also Conzelmann, Die Apostelgeschichte (HNT 7;
Tübingen: Mohr [Siebeck], 1963) 23, who sees D as
rejecting the role of the women as witnesses, and
E. Haenchen, Die Apostelgeschichte (KEK; Göttingen:
Vandenhoeck & Ruprecht, 1977) 160, n. 2. The link
between Luke 8:3, etc., and Acts 1:14 was made explicit
in the Diatessaron, quoted from the Dura fragment
in Metzger, Textual Commentary, 284. I call "wives
and children" non-entities not because I believe them
to be that, but because of such expression as "the
pioneers moved West, taking their wives and children
with them."
[19]Acts tells of no currently married apostles. Luke
added "wife" to the list of things abandoned for the
Gospel's sake, 18:29 (vs. Mark 10:29). Luke 20:34-35
is remarkably unenthusiastic about Christians entering
into marriage.
[20]The exception in v 18 is presumably linked to the
vow.

"western" readings also play down the prominence of women among early converts.

Acts 17:4--By reading γυναῖκες D et al. speak not of women of prominence in the community, but of the wives of leading citizens. Such converts are quite acceptable, provided that their status comes from their husbands, who will doubtless keep them in line, rather than from their own pedigree or achievements.

17:12--Once more, the attention given to prominent women disappears. Men resume the first place.

17:34--In this difficult passage it is possible to maintain that D has a lacuna.[21] However, εὐσχήμων always applies to women and the reading of e/E mulier honesta / γυνὴ τίμια support the secondary application of this epithet to Damaris and the subsequent deletion of her name. The plural αὐτοῖς in D shows that more than one name had been listed. Those interested in deleting reference to a woman of Athens, among Paul's first converts there, could have drawn support from the awkward "some men ... among whom was a woman."[22] Deletion is thus quite possible.[23] The "western reviser" did not wish to promote the idea that nascent Christianity had a particular appeal to women, including those of high social status. This posture is the mirror image of that found in the Apocryphal Acts, where leading women are the featured converts. One of the most hackneyed plot themes in the Acts-literature begins with the conversion of a prominent woman to Christianity (and celibacy), the subsequent reluctance of the husband to approve such abstinence, invocation of said spouse's legal power (they are often the ruler or governor), and consequent persecution of the apostle.[24]

---

[21]Metzger, Textual Commentary, 459-460, has a full discussion.
[22]So Haenchen observes, Apostelgeschichte, 506 n. 3.
[23]The solution used in 1:14 was attempted for Damaris also. Chrysostom could simply presume that she was the wife of Damaris, On the Priesthood, 4.7.
[24]For a standard discussion see R. Soeder, Die Apokryphen Apostelgeschichten (WZAW 3; Stuttgart: Kohlhammer, 1932) 150-158.

Christianity, according to the "western reviser," is not aimed at enticing gullible women of prominence and means into its ranks, nor does it want women to serve as its ministers and missionaries. Jesus did not have women disciples, women who could appear braver than Peter and Co. by observing Jesus' death and burial, attempting to complete the latter, and being thereby rewarded through an angelic proclamation of the Easter kerygma.

There is no dearth of early Christian authorities who find such views highly virtuous. I point to one convenient example: the writer of the Pastorals. According to the Pastor, clergy are to be married. Women should stay home and have babies, for child-bearing has redemptive qualities. By no means are women to speak in Church. The Pastor wishes to dissociate the Christian religion from those cults which actively proselytize women to the damage of their reputations. Quite unlike Luke and the writer of the Apocryphal Acts, the Pastor specifically opposes such missionary tactics: "among them are those who make their way into households and capture weak women, who will listen to anybody and can never arrive at a knowledge of the truth" (2 Tim 3:6-7).[25]

It is quite likely that 1 Cor 14:33b-36 comes from the hand of an editor who held 1 Tim 2:8-15 in fond admiration.[26] Such an editor would have found the "western reviser" a fellow of kindred spirit. John 21 is another interesting text. Like the editor of the "western text," the composer of this appendix wished it to be made clear that only appearances to men "counted."[27] In the light of the present discussion it is worth noting that the same person who here wishes to disqualify Mary Magdalene as an official witness

---

[25]One of the most recent works, in a burgeoning series of articles and monographs devoted to the social world of the Pastorals, is D. R. MacDonald, The Legend and the Apostle (Philadelphia: Westminster, 1983).

[26]See H. Conzelmann, 1 Corinthians (Philadelphia: Fortress, 1975) 246, esp. n. 55.

[27]John 21:14 enumerates (following the counting of signs?) this as the "third" appearance. This is pedantically defensible if appeal is made to the word μαθηταῖς, but it is highly likely that the continuator wished to exclude the appearance to Mary.

PERVO

and bearer of the Easter message also spoke of the
leadership role of Peter in the normative episcopal
terminology of "shepherding." Such governance, which
becomes the catholic church order, was not in line
with the Johannine notion (in general) of Peter, who
is outshone by the Beloved Disciple; and it certainly
involves a shift in image from Jesus as the (single)
shepherd.[28]

IV
Historical and Methodological Implications

The "western reviser," the Pastor, and the Johannine
continuator are moving along converging lines. On
the other side stand the Acts of Paul and Thecla and
a large amount of ultimately heretical literature.
The "tendencies" of Condex Bezae and the western traditions from which it derives are part of a rather consistent and well-attested theological program. There
is more than a certain lack a gallantry towards the
female sex, a proclivity toward harmless (or harmful)
glorification of the apostles, as an occasional lack
of sensitivity about Judaism. The "western reviser"
sought to do for Luke what the Pastor did for Paul.
Through those editorial activities, Luke and Acts
were even more unambiguously suited for the needs
of emergent catholic Christianity. W. Ramsay was
thus essentially correct, although he did not give
adequate attention to internal Christian conflict.

Similarities to the Pastorals are not accidental;
for most modern editors date the beginnings of the
"western" text in the first half of the second century
C.E.,[29] and the wealth of geographic variations and
enrichments suggest that Asia Minor is the region
in which the revision was made.[30] Both the "western
reviser" and the Pastor are rather pedantic representatives of a kind of common-sense orthodoxy. Both are
aware of being very much overshadowed by their predecessors, whose heritage they wish to make secure by

[28]Of relevance here is the conflict between Peter and
Mary Magdalene in extra-canonical texts, including
the Gospel of Mary and the Pistis Sophia.
[29]So, for example, Ropes, Text, ccxxiii-ccxxiv; Hanson,
"Provenance," and Martini, "La Tradition," 34.
[30]Ramsay's list, Church, 162-165, is impressive. Hanson
argues for Rome.

tying up some loose ends. Such tying up included interpolation and deletion and the composition of new documents, all doubtless believed to be justified.

Comparison with Marcion is apt. He, too, produced a revised version of Luke, together with an edition of Paul's letters. Was the "western revision" a counterblast? The textual situation is very complicated with regard to the Epistles, but it seems quite possible that both Marcion and the "western reviser" had similar texts and sources, came from the same general region, and had resort to the same methods.

The "western revision" has many affinities to right-wing Deutero-Paulinism of second century C.E. Asia Minor. It demonstrates that one technique of that movement was the editing of earlier texts. If it can be established that an editor touched up Luke and Acts to make them appear more universal and less pro-Jewish, more authoritarian and catholic in ecclesiology, and less receptive to women in certain capacities, it is not unlikely that some similar improvements were made elsewhere, although the evidence may be lost. The "western" evidence reveals not only a Deutero-Pauline mind, it also profiles a Deutero-Pauline technique. That technique of editorial revision is thus part of the res ipsa of text criticism and therefore demands more serious consideration in the various editions, translations, and their apparatuses.

INDEX OF MODERN AUTHORS

INDEX OF PASSAGES FROM ANCIENT LITERATURE

74169

CATHOLIC THEOLOGICAL UNION
BS2361.2.L581985   C002
THE LIVING TEXT LANHAM, MD.

3 0311 00021 1594

WITHDRAWN

DEMCO